Talking with
SERIAL KILLERS
MURDEROUS MEDICS

Born in 1948 in Winchester, Hampshire, **Christopher Berry-Dee** is descended from Dr John Dee, Court Astrologer to Queen Elizabeth I. He is a highly respected writer on matters concerning all aspects of criminology from law enforcement to forensic psychology, and is the UK's bestselling true-crime author.

Christopher has interviewed and interrogated over 30 of the world's most notorious killers – serial, mass and one-off – including Peter Sutcliffe, Ted Bundy, Aileen Wuornos, Dennis Nilsen and Joanna Dennehy. He was co-producer/interviewer for the acclaimed 12-part TV documentary series *The Serial Killers*, and has appeared on television as a consultant on serial homicide, and, in the series *Born to Kill?*, on the cases of Fred and Rose West, the 'Moors Murderers' and Dr Harold Shipman. He has also assisted in criminal investigations as far afield as Russia and the United States.

Notable book successes include: *Monster* (the basis for the movie of the same title, about Aileen Wuornos); *Dad Help Me Please*, about the tragic Derek Bentley, hanged for a murder he did not commit (subsequently subject of the film *Let Him Have It*); and *Talking with Serial Killers*, his international bestseller, now, with its sequel, *Talking with Serial Killers: World's Most Evil*, required reading at the FBI Behavioral Analysis Unit Academy at Quantico, Virginia. His *Talking with Psychopaths and Savages: A Journey Into the Evil Mind*, was the UK's bestselling true-crime title of 2017; its successor volume, *Talking with Psychopaths and Savages: Beyond Evil*, was published in 2019. In 2020 a new edition of his *Talking with Serial Killers: Dead Men Talking* appeared, and he has since published *Talking with Serial Killers: Stalkers*, *Talking with Psychopaths and Savages: Mass Murderers and Spree Killers*, *Talking with Serial Killers: Sleeping with Psychopaths* and, in 2023, *Talking with Psychopaths and Savages: Letters from Serial Killers*. His most recent book is *Talking with Psychopaths: Guilty but Insane* (2024).

https://www.christopherberrydee.com//

CHRISTOPHER BERRY-DEE

Talking with
SERIAL KILLERS
MURDEROUS MEDICS

jb

First published in the UK by John Blake Publishing
An imprint of Bonnier Books UK
5th Floor, HYLO, 105 Bunhill Row,
London, EC1Y 8LZ

A CIP catalogue record for this book is available from the British Library.

Trade paperback ISBN: 978-1-78946-809-0
Paperback ISBN: 978-1-78946-812-0

Also available as an ebook and an audiobook

1 3 5 7 9 10 8 6 4 2

Designed and typeset by Envy Design Ltd
Printed and bound in Great Britain by CPI (UK) Ltd, Croydon CR0 4YY

The authorised representative in the EEA is
Bonnier Books UK (Ireland) Limited.
Registered office address:
Block B, The Crescent Building
Northwood, Santry
Dublin 9, D09 C6X8, Ireland
compliance@bonnierbooks.ie

www.bonnierbooks.co.uk

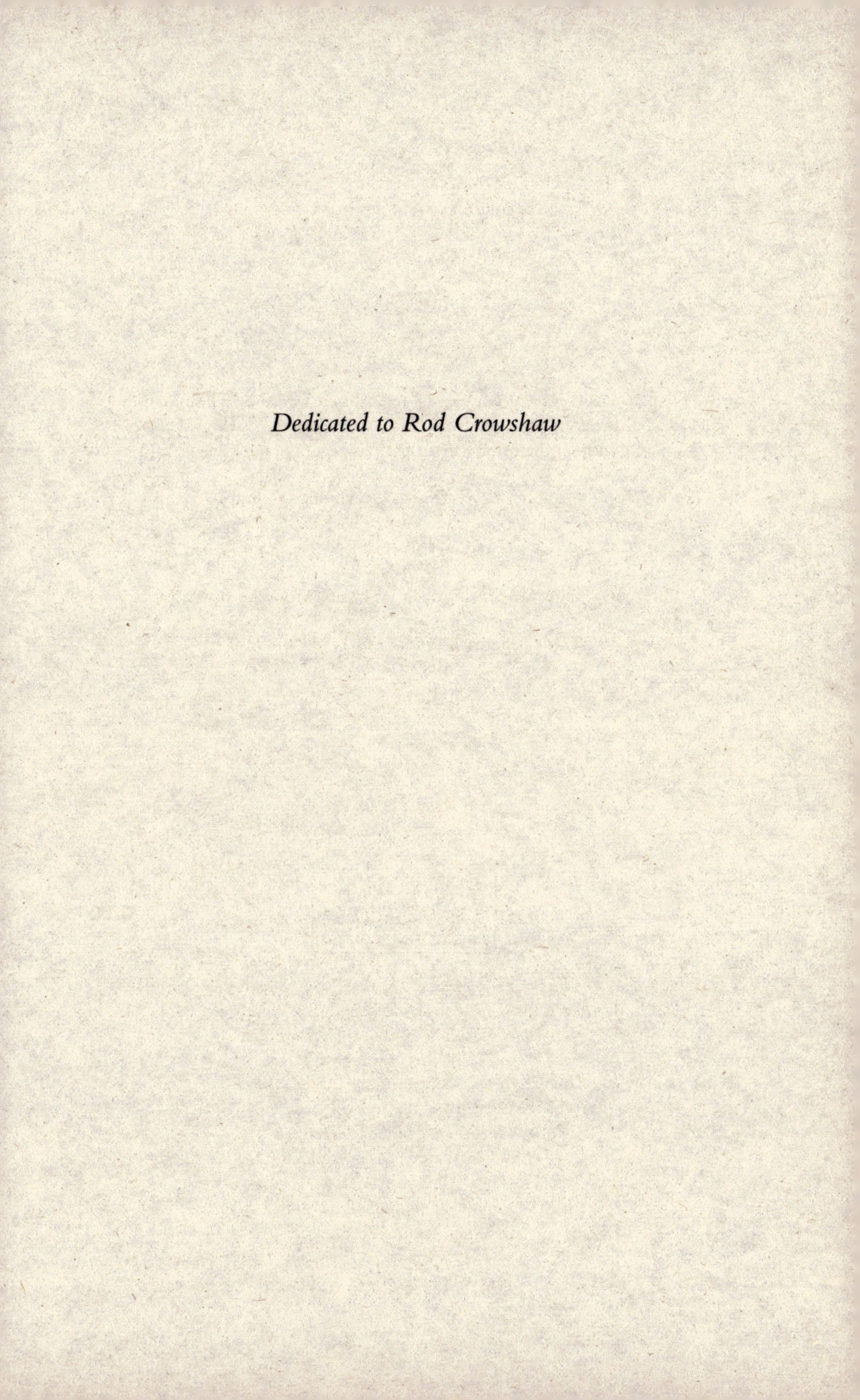

Dedicated to Rod Crowshaw

Contents

Health Warning

This book could damage your health!

Hallo, my name is Christopher. I am so pleased to have met you and I truly, sincerely hope that you are feeling tickety-boo, in good spirits, with all your parts running more-or-less up to speed. However, if the opposite should unfortunately be the case; that you're waiting for a doctor's appointment, about to go under a surgeon's knife or on the point of making a will, then maybe this book is *not* for you.

I must also add: if you give this book, along with a bunch of grapes, to a friend in hospital, it will *not* make for them a good night's read – that's a given!

Prologue:

In for a penny, in for a pound

Time and Tide wait for no man.
— GEOFFREY CHAUCER (C.1343–25 OCTOBER 1400)

A prologue is supposed to be short in heralding the main event, but as this book is now *your* book, bless you, it might be of value not to skip these first pages in your enthusiastic search of dastardly deeds most foul. The reason? I am about to set the scene for all that is to follow: in for a penny, in for a pound.

Taking Chaucer's proverb slightly out of original context we could, if we were morbidly inclined, apply it to the Grim Reaper. Moreover, even to begin to understand the more recent horrific murders and the psychopathologies of the *very few* killers employed in today's medical professions, I will invite you on the road again to travel back through the black annals of medical history to the splendid Victorian era, to cover some medical murderers in depth. There we find that the psychological motivators of past monsters in white coats, crisp bustling uniforms or scrubs were just the same in bygone times as they are today. Following this, we will bring ourselves more-or-less up to date and into the minds of the first people we most often see when we open our eyes, to frequently the last when our peepers close for ever: doctors, nurses and carers. 'Tis a grim subject indeed, but that is *precisely* what this book is all about, yet my reader is guaranteed a whole bunch of smiles along the way just to lighten the load.

> Poisons and medicines are often the same substance given with *different intents*. (author's italics)
> — English physician Peter Mere Latham,
> MD (1789–1875)

Intent is motive, is it not?

A notable thinker of his time, William Wills, author of *An Essay on the Principles of Circumstantial Evidence: Illustrated by Numerous Cases* (1838), remarked:

> A man's motives may be good but his intentions bad. For example a loaf is stolen; the intention was to steal, the act therefore criminal although the motive to save a starving child was good. Generally speaking however, intent and motive are so entwined that quite understandably we might find some difficulty in separating them.

In many of the following homicides committed by medically trained individuals we find the same paradoxes occurring time and again, with some murdering their patients not for financial gain but alleging that they are doing the sufferer a 'favour' by putting them out of their misery, as though the intention is good. 'Ah, this would be euthanasia,' I hear you mutter … to which 'No, that's not correct,' I say. So why do I bring to the table a few historical cases? In truth, they provide an absolute treasure trove of criminological information; with books, records, papers and trial transcripts about these events being as unique as they are illuminating. These tomes are beautifully crafted. They were written by people who truly knew their stuff and although some might say that these dusty papers were penned somewhat 'stiffly' by contemporary standards, there is a certain eloquence to be found throughout.

I have accumulated a mass of this golden-olden-day true-crime literature over the decades, which has brought me to the conclusion that yesteryear's evil doctors, nurses and other medical people harboured the same motives, displayed many of the same Seven Deadly Sins, *and used* very much the same methods to dispatch their vulnerable victims as do our medical killers today. By *methods, I largely mean, of course,* silently using toxic chemicals, for one cannot murder a trusting hospital patient or a visitor to a doctor's surgery using a firearm or an axe, that much is obvious. So I thought: 'Why not use these older case histories as benchmarks to compare the perpetrators with their more recent murderous kin, for in doing so we might learn much from the past that might, perhaps, allow us to red flag the likes of nurses Beverley Allitt and Stephan Letter, the ilk of parsimonious, obnoxious Dr Shipman, before they strike again. Wishful thinking? Maybe yes, maybe no!

Up the close an' doon the stair,
But an' ben wi' Burke and Hare.
Burke's the butcher, Hare's the thief,
Knox the boy that buys the beef.
– Popular song during the period of William
Burke's trial in 1829

It would be true to suggest that so socially camouflaged are serial murderers generally that one cannot spot them before they strike. It goes without saying that advertising their murderous intentions would defeat the object of the attack – another obvious observation, of course. Yet the killers in this book are flawlessly presentable, striking not in some damp, dingy alley at night such as predators Ted Bundy or Peter Sutcliffe, oh no! All but one of the medical monsters included within these pages sat by their patients' bedsides offering comfort and reassurance; while hiding a dark, hidden agenda: to kill by plying their victims with lethal doses of strychnine or injections of morphia or a pillow pressed down hard – or pinching the nose, forcing the mouth shut while kneeling on the patient's chest, the technique known as 'burking'. This was the favoured method of murdering used by William Burke and William Hare, who, in 1828, sold corpses to Dr Robert Knox for dissection at his anatomy lectures in Edinburgh. Nursing aides Gwendoline Graham and Cathy May Wood (both of whom I previously interviewed in 1984 in their respective prisons, and have written about before) also burked their elderly, frail prey while on night duty at the Alpine Manor nursing home in Walker, a suburb of Grand Rapids, Michigan, in 1987. So straight away we see parallels here with suffocation as a way to extinguish life.

An analogy of sorts

My other reason for including notable historical cases in this book is that the passage of time seemingly numbs the shock-horror of the loss of loved ones. The heartache and grief, the neatly clipped grass over deep graves with their sides falling in under cold headstones. The mournful processions and sad eulogies endured by families and friends back then were just as tragic as they are today. Therefore, we must not dismiss their sad histories just because they have been reduced to yellowing paper, the ink slowly fading away. Indeed, we can learn much from their deaths, for they still whisper to us from their tombs, as do those medical killers screaming in terror as they plunged through the hangman's trap, and afterwards stiffly thrown into a pit of slaked lime behind grim prison walls.

During our road trip in quest of murderous medics I follow the deaths of these earlier victims and the motives of their murderers as would a medical examiner at the autopsy of someone who will be far, far longer dead than they ever were alive. The forensic pathologist is the detective of death. The corpse on his laboratory table is telling him or her much: the subject's age; possible lifestyle; general health while alive; when and how the person died, and by what means. As Michael M. Baden, MD, Chief Forensic Pathologist, New York State Police, and former Chief Medical Examiner, New York City, rather eloquently put it: 'The deceased is communicating with me and I am a good watcher and listener.' Therefore, I think that we should dissect these historic cases in much the same forensic light and, although any individual's behaviour varies with mood and circumstance, if we take good and bad human behaviour collectively we find common themes and schemes throughout. That is our species' nature, which remains pretty much constant, as have the motives to commit crime throughout the generations.

An eye for an eye, tooth for a tooth

Woe to the wicked! Disaster is upon them! They will be paid back for what their hands have done.
– Isaiah 3:11 (NIV)

I'm no bible thumper by any length of chalk. I have never met Mr Isaiah who lived at 'Apt 3:11', yet he does have a point, don't you think? – inter alia: the punishment should fit the guilty act. And, I am obliged to say that the crimes in this book were not collected in accordance with the 'I wants to make your flesh creep' ambition of the fat boy in Charles Dickens's *The Pickwick Papers*, because some are not the most terrible of murders but in several cases the most extraordinary ones, while others will blow your mind. Neither is this book an annotated catalogue of the Chamber of Horrors, although some of the killers mentioned at some time or another might well have stood as wax effigies for all to see – and made one's flesh creep, too!

There are killings in this book that have stood the clinical test of time; the sombre annals of murder most foul brightened here and there with such interludes as the total lunacy of Dr Cream, the obnoxious greed of Dr John Bodkin Adams, the sinister punctiliousness of Dr Harold Shipman. We will meet death-dealing nurses Beverley Allitt, Lucy Letby, the God-awful 'Jolly Jane' Toppan, and Richard Angelo, among others, along our way. We will find Keystone Cop-type blunders. Dramatic sigh-of-relief acquittals. Exhumations aplenty, and some French serial killings that bore the dark shadow of 'Mme Guillotine', *and* the so-called hanging judges pointing the terrified condemned towards 'Master Gallows'. I hope that the point of interest will shift throughout the narrative from the machinations of our doctors and angels of death to the ingenuity of the clued-in-or-not-so-clued-in detectives; from the unusualness of motive to the singularity of execution; from scenes of domestic life to the last dramatic act of public prosecution. We will travel from place to place, and on the way will discover there are more than a few pretty in-for-a-penny, in-for-a-pound medical cover-ups too.

Honoré de Balzac called his huge series of novels *La comédie humaine*, and within the following pages is the tragic-comedy of real-life – stories varied by every conceivable change of scene and circumstance, in village and town, cottage, mansion and slum, from doctors' surgeries to the busy wards of hospitals, all ringing the changes on tragedy, farce, pathos, passion. Our medical characters are morbidly raised to epic proportions by intensity of emotions, walking under the arc-lamps of publicity surrounded, as the last act begins, by all the pomp and circumstance of the law, when they are metaphorically stripped naked to reveal themselves as the detestable little creatures that they truly are.

In the following cases of homicide by medically trained

people there is no virtue nor, as has sometimes been the fashion – Fyodor Dostoevsky's *Crime and Punishment* is an example – any attempt to exalt the criminal, to picture him or her as a person wronged by society, overcoming unjust obstructions by intelligence and daring. Had Fyodor not remembered 'eye for an eye, tooth for tooth'? Never mind the New Testament advice to to turn the other cheek. I'm a tad more old-fashioned on this score. The original 'let's not mess about' quote is derived from the Code of Hammurabi; a system of 282 laws organised by the Mesopotamian king, Hammurabi, who reigned until 1750 BCE. One of the punishments prescribed in the code was: 'If a man put out the eye of another man, his eye shall be put out.' This is called 'mirror punishment' – the rule being that retribution must *exactly* equal the crime. Exodus and Leviticus in the Old Testament, as well as Babylonian law, back this up, and why not, say I? Indeed, after reading this book you might have your own opinions about any judgment awarded. I will leave that up to you. These days, and this is only my irascible opinion – you will, rightly, have your own, which I will respect – many societies have strayed so far towards liberalism that any consideration of the condemnation of wanton takers of human life leans towards dripping wet, hand-wringing sympathetic leniency; overriding not only the suffering of the victim but but also of their heartbroken kith and kin for the alleged good of us all. For example: many readers will remember, and continue to associate, the late Lord Longford primarily with his unpopular campaign to parole the through-and-through, utterly evil 'Moors Murderer', Myra Hindley, but this was in reality just one part of a prisons crusade that lasted for 70 years based upon his naive belief that every offender, whatever their crime, could be rehabilitated. Gosh, I bet he would have loved the British serial killer Joanne Dennehy, nurses Allitt and Letby, and Dr Shipman. Even Peter Sutcliffe, aka 'the Yorkshire Ripper', come to that. It is all too easy to imagine His Lordship preaching: 'Yes, I can fix Pete's deeply ingrained homicidal, fake-psycho tendencies. He is a good watercolourist; we just need to direct his attention away from bludgeoning and stabbing women to death and give him a half decent box of paints.'

There is none of that upside-down, extreme liberal malarkey in this book because a review of the medical Rogue's Gallery that follows creates an entirely different impression. Studies of *all* evil criminals reveal masks beneath which lie depravity; vanity, secretiveness, meanness, snobbishness, mercilessness, arrogance. Yet in this book I have added many other egocentric people given to donning white coats, stethoscopes around their necks, black bags at hand, nurses bustling around with love in their eyes, murder in their hearts.

Soft justice … pink cells and pets … cushy jails she could serve time in.

>   – *Daily Mail*, Tuesday, 22 August 2023:
>   on Nurse Letby

It seems pitiful to me that some of our modern-day medical killer ilk are not prescribed any uncompromising eye-for-an eye retribution. Okay, I'll tell you why: it's because the likes of British nurses Beverley Allitt and Lucy Letby are presently living within the Home Office correctional estate, treated like guests who have just booked into a four-star hotel and being cosseted with first-rate medical support and a balanced, healthy diet around the fucking clock, that's why! I have visited several Russian prisons. Sablino, about 40km south of St Petersburg, springs to mind. I took a TV camera in there. I have previously written of my experiences of, and mixed emotions about, the harsh reality of the Russian Federation's windswept, isolated women's penal colony that *is* Sablino. That's precisely where Letby and Allitt should be, living in crammed dormitories, hot-bunking with the stench of hundreds of cats everywhere. Get them out shovelling snow all day in minus-30 degrees and below, and earning their keep making clear plastic audio-cassette cases in a workshop overseen by armed guards with vicious dogs snapping at their heels. Rehabilitation for murdering helpless babies be damned!

Correctional BS

I had considered writing to Allitt and Letby to ask them if they would like to comment on their serial murders for this book. I got as far as telephoning HMP Low Newton in Co. Durham, only to be informed: 'Just wait a moment, sir, let me enquire as to Miss Letby's busy schedule.' This was followed by a *very long* wait because initially staff couldn't find her in, or on, the Home Office prison estate, on account of the fact that half of the screws were off sick with the stress of being paid peanuts and obliged to frequent food banks, with the remainder in the canteen with their feet up. Until … wait for it: 'I'm sorry to have kept you waiting, sir. Miss Letby is having her hair done in the salon at the moment while she selects a soft pink rinse to match the new bedding and drapes that she's ordered from a magazine at the taxpayers' expense. Perhaps, sir, you could try phoning another day, and rack up another hefty phone bill at *your* expense while we check that she is not having her alternate weekly pedicure/manicure when you call … Thank you for contacting HMP Low Newton.'

Yes, I know that my editor is going to insist that the aforegoing rant is an exaggeration, and that it makes me seemingly a cold-hearted kind of guy. Hey, what's wrong with some keep-fit rock-breaking exercises being added to the correctional curriculum? Breaking sweat while smashing up granite in a quarry, just like the good old days down at Dartmoor Prison, might be healthily constructive. Er … of course not. These days matters arising from Health and Safety regulations have to be adhered to. God forbid that a con inconveniently drops a hammer on one's toes. And that also prevents making these inherently evil people do some painting and decorating around the place, because the outside contractors periodically seem more preoccupied in smuggling in dope and mobile phones to make life inside more con-comfortable for these losers.

Of course, I made some of that rant up, as you will have already guessed, but I am sure that you catch my drift. Nevertheless, my critics from the 'Lord Longford School of Soft Knocks' will demand that I be shot, or at the very least that someone confiscates my PC keyboard, or that I sign up for some forgive-all-and-everyone re-education. Point of fact: watch how any high-minded reformists do a disgruntled volte-face when someone very close to them has their life snuffed out by a person who should never have been conceived, let alone born, in the first instance. So with a lot gotten off of my chest:

'Tis true that Time and Tide wait for no man – nor does Doctor Death!

CHRISTOPHER BERRY–DEE
UK AND EL NIDO, PALAWAN, PHILIPPINES
christopherberrydee.com

Introduction: Perspectives

*So we fix our eyes not on what is seen but what is
unseen, since what is seen is temporary, but what
is unseen is eternal.*

– 2 Corinthians 4:18 (NIV)

Every book has to originate from somewhere deep in a pensmith's mind. More often than not my ideas hatch when I sleep, or at least when I try to sleep. I'm not entirely sure why this happens but it does, so the genesis for this book more or less started this way ... and a *long* way away it was, too. In the Philippines, to be precise – so off we go, and if you already have medical travel insurance, forget it, and soon you will know why.

Before I introduce you to the characters listed in the Contents, with longevity at the forefront of my mind, and starting out on a low note before we hit some high ones, then some *really* low ones, I recall Thomas Fuller, MD's quote in his *Gnomologia* of 1732: 'I know nobody that has a mind to die this year.' Then I enquired of myself, as I sat cross-legged on a rattan mat on a dismal rainy night in Palawan, with a glass of the finest Buffalo Trace Kentucky Straight Bourbon, a pack of rip-off Marlboro Red cigarettes at hand: 'What are my chances of being murdered by a medical doctor, nurse, midwife, health visitor, care worker or paramedic, should one of these be required to cure any or all ills?' You see, it had belatedly occurred to your author that my alleged semi-wonton lifestyle is bringing me much closer to my sell-by date and those fabled pearly gates than I'd initially planned. Facing a few hospital and doctors' appointments en route to the undertaker, a chapel of rest, and a hole in the ground, or a thoroughly efficient cremation followed by a wake attended by all my closest friends: two people anxious to hear what I *might* have bequeathed them in my will. Then I got to thinking – which I am inclined to do *very* occasionally – that medical people are pretty much the first of our species we see upon entering this world, and more-or-less the last people we see when we exit, give or take a few appointments during the interim. So there is every chance that we might get to know these professionals rather well.

Now ever the 'Mr Curious'; sipping some more high-octane tipple on this increasingly blustery night, I set out to find out what *were* my chances of being murdered by a medical person. For example, I learned from The King's Fund that, in 2022, there were circa 132,900 doctors, 350,900 nursing staff (including midwives and health visitors) and 36,600 managers out of a total workforce of 1.26 million in the British National

Health Service (NHS). It should be noted that The King's Fund adds a rider: 'All figures are full-time equivalent', which only proves par for any statistics, or anyone's perspective at any time on *any* subject known to humanity. No one really has a single clue as to how many volunteers there are/were who give up their free time to bail out the NHS when things get as sticky as shit, especially when so many of these wonderful people are paid significantly less than homeless church mice on social benefits. (A slight exaggeration, I'll admit.)

Medical health insurance

Accompanied by the orchestral sounds of a developing super typhoon – as backing, the base rumble of an earthquake from the constant movement of some of our planet's tectonic plates – I strove as hard as was possible but still couldn't figure out how many dedicated doctors and nurses are presently on strike, or leaving the NHS to scarper abroad in efforts to earn a decent salary. Or how many staff are being PC-ed out of their minds because some NHS hospitals seem to have gone gender crazy? Actually, I didn't find 'consultants' mentioned anywhere because at the time of writing in 2023-4, they were striking along with the doctors. So, to say it straight, there will not be as many doctors and nurses and consultants on duty, meaning my chances of being murdered by one are considerably reduced if, and when, I opt to fall ill back in the UK.

With that taken under advisement, if one is a tourist it's in one's best interests to come a cropper, terminally or otherwise, in one's home country, because I confirm that getting ill or injured in the Philippines is a NO–NO, period!

For example – and I like examples, and perhaps you do too: if you get knocked down by a jeepney or a pedicab, the crew of the ambulance – when it *eventually* crawls through the traffic – and *before* one is loaded up, ask how much money you have on your credit or debit card, or ready cash in your pocket. If you can't speak – in all likelihood you won't be able to utter a coherent word if you have been hit by a 5-ton bus carrying 100 people and many bananas – on arrival at some hospital your passport is confiscated and a security guard put on the door to your room, until you cough up enough dough to get some medication, bandages and so on at a hundred times the price of something sold in Boots, then sent on your way. Forget any health insurance you have. I mean FORGET IT! Filipino medical persons (note politically correct term) demand cash up front. You can trawl through countless websites that promise help if you get ill anywhere across the world. Some firms will even fly you home if you get very sick. But mention the Philippines – although I hate to say this – get sick there and it's a no-no. If a westerner dies in Phil, they will be parked in a non-airconditioned funeral parlour until they turn green or someone likes them enough to have their mortal remains FedExed home. And that, dear reader, *is entirely true!*

Oh, and if you are a deceased Brit, HM Embassy at 120 Upper McKinley Hill, Metro Manila, will not fork out a single peso towards postage and packing. I speak from experience because several years ago my very dear friend, Pete Aldred, suffered a heart attack in a Manila hotel at the age of 55. An ambulance was called. He died en route to hospital, and to be frank with you, no one had a clue as to what next to do with him. No family, only about 5 million social media followers, and *still* no one had any idea, let alone organised a whip-round to have his body flown back to the UK. So there he lay in some morgue, turning green, until the authorities dug a big hole, splashed petrol over dead Pete and whoosh, up he went to Heaven. Did I offer any financial assistance? Nope! – because Pete would have liked that, given that he knew and deeply respected the fact that I am pathologically meaner than Scrooge. That's the way your author is, you see.

Please bear with me here if I digress further. I did get very nearly death-door sick in Lapu Lapu, only to be advised by Filipina friends *not* to call a doctor. Not that a doctor would have murdered me, gosh no! They get rich by keeping you alive (as in fleecing you) for as long as possible. I think that they swear to a version of the Hippocratic Oath drawn up by the Philippine Health Insurance Corporation (PhilHealth) and the Philippine National Bank. No, my Filipina friends advised me to visit a Watsons pharmacy, where a lass rushed out to guide me to a chair and prop my walking stick up against a glittering display of hair products. Listening patiently to my woes, chiefly that I had lost about two stone in as many days, then … wait for it … she returned with a bottle of little white pills: two in the morning, two at night, total cost 250 pesos. The following day I was a pharmaceutical miracle to behold. I felt as right as rain even though it was monsoon-pissing-down outside. More to the point of this overlong preamble, with my confessing that I don't know how many doctors, nurses, midwives, and health visitors, freebie volunteers, consultants and overpaid competent/incompetent health managers exist across the world, my calculations of the chances of some medically trained person murdering anyone else are a damned sight less than the chances of winning the National Lottery. I am not a gambling man but you'd have a much better chance of seeing a three-legged elephant being punted as 2-to-1 odds-on favourite for the Derby, so, being too tight-fisted to squander even a penny on such a losing wicket, I rate my chances of being injected with a litre of morphine as *minus* zero – maybe.

To close, it would be correct to say that serial killers spring from all walks of life. It is because medical serial killers are almost so rare that when one of them *is* brought to justice, society goes into a frenzy.

Well, I must go now because it's my bedtime. I pray that when I wake on the morrow this typhoon or tsunami, or whatever it is, hasn't swept El Nido into the Andaman Sea; to wash me ashore on the beautiful sugar-sand palm-lined Lagen Island – dress code: Robinson Crusoe hat over a birthday suit. Because it is a long way to swim to Greece, where we will examine the Hippocratic Oath, all of which *should* have you glued to your chair for at least ten minutes at most, I promise (allegedly).

CHRISTOPHER BERRY-DEE
UK and Philippines

The Hippocratic Oath

God heals, and the doctor takes the fees.
– Benjamin Franklin, FRS, FRSA, FRSE (1706–90)

Our Father of Medicine

Over this bright sunny morning menu – oodles of noodles, dried fish and out-of-date rice on a banana tree frond – I did some more thinking, which enabled me to do something that medical students call 'research'. As most readers will already know, 'research is seeing what everybody else has seen and thinking what nobody else has thought of,' according to Albert Szent-Györgyi (1893–1986), the Hungarian biochemist known for his work on vitamins and oxidation.

So, during *my* research I learned that the Greek philosopher and physician Hippocrates lived between 460 BCE and 380 BCE. The writings collected in the *Corpus Hippocraticum*, some 60 pieces closely associated with him, provide a wealth of information on biomedical methodology, and also offer one of the first considered codes of 'professional ethics' (something in very short supply amongst politicians these days, as most readers would agree). Moreover, they promote the idea that prevention is better than cure. There is a popular English-language proverb first recorded in the nineteenth century, though with older origins: 'An apple a day keeps the doctor away'. This by extension means that if one eats healthy food, one should remain as fit as a fiddle and not need to see the doctor very often. By further extension, it also means that the fewer physicians and nurses one sees, the less chance of being murdered by one. Like almost all proverbs/maxims/dictums, another variant of the saying is recorded, from Pembrokeshire and dated to 1886: 'Eat an apple on going to bed and you'll keep the doctor from earning his bread'. Keeping that advice in mind, let's focus on the main man himself.

Apart from some rather fine marble busts in a number of museums, we have no other clues as to what Hippocrates really looked like – the Polaroid Land Camera had yet to be invented. However, among the few things we should know about him are that he was born at Kos, in the Dodecanese islands of Greece, and died in Larissa, in Thessaly, which, as you will probably know if you are one for all-inclusive holidays, is *also* in Greece, where they eat moussaka, drink retsina and ouzo, then sleep for the remainder of the day; the last is right up my street whichever country I am holidaying in or visiting.

Known as the 'Father of Medicine', Hippocrates kept himself very busy during his lifetime so he only managed to sire two sons: Thessalus and Draco/Dracon (the latter being the Greco-Latin word for dragon or serpent). For readers who like stargazing, the name Draco refers to a circumpolar constellation in the northern sky said to resemble a dragon. I bet you didn't know this until now, and to be honest with you, neither did I. However, more medically related research led me to learn that Thessalus became a physician like his dad. One of the founders of the Dogmatic school of medicine, he spent some time at the court of Archelaus, King of Macedonia. So young Thessalus was no medical slouch, either, and a devoted follower of his father's teachings. In essence, Hippocrates Sr believed that a body became ill when there was an imbalance in the four fluid humours: blood, black bile, yellow bile and phlegm. If the humours were in balance then one's physical and mental wellbeing were up to scratch. However, he and and a predecessor, the medical writer, scientist and philosopher Alcmaeon of Croton (born c.510 BCE), set forth that an extreme excess or deficiency of any of the four humours can be a sign of illness. In his studies, Hippocrates sought a remedy to restore this imbalance through diet, lifestyle and the environment.

To try and place this in greater perspective, back then there were no books/blogs/internet sites promoting stuff such as: *Eat Your Way to Health and Fitness*, or the indispensable must-read, *Examining Stools: The Turd-Watcher's Guide to Wellbeing*. Nope, none of that, and that's all I can say about Hippocrates & Sons, because fuller accounts of their remarkable achievements can be found elsewhere. Let it be said that while the *Hippocratic Corpus* is a collection by many hands, much of it not written by the great man himself, his thinking has for centuries provided guiding principles for all medical doctors who, at the least, *should* follow the same guidelines imposed by Hippocratic medicine. Unfortunately, some of them don't.

There are many variants of the Hippocratic Oath, which has been adapted over the centuries as medicine developed. A translation of the original Greek, which dates from between the fifth and the third centuries BCE, begins: 'I swear by Apollo Healer, by Asclepius, by Hygieia, by Panacea, and by all the gods and goddesses, making them my witnesses, that I will carry out, according to my ability and judgment, this oath and this indenture'. Since the relevance of this has faded since classical times, there have been many later attempts to encapsulate the oath's principles, of which probably the most significant is the Declaration of Geneva issued by the World Medical Association (WMA) in 1948. There have also been attempts at secular versions subsequently. Curiously, the famous phrase 'First do no harm' does not actually appear in the original oath and seems to have been largely adopted in UK and US medicine in the mid-nineteenth century; a similarly worded phrase does appear in another text of the *Hippocratic Corpus*, however.

At this point I would dearly like to expound on the Hippocratic Oath till numerous cows come home, but there have been many versions of it, so it is all but impossible to suggest a definitive text; any reader interested, though, can find the most recent adaptation of the WMA's Geneva Declaration online here: https://www.wma.net/policies-post/wma-declaration-of-geneva/ Besides, the ins and outs of it all would not only use too much ink, but might throw my publisher's vital humours out of kilter, with my editor saying: 'Christopher, simply say that the Hippocratic Oath is taken by trainee medical doctors who pledge to keep their patients alive and not fucking murder them!'

Of course, my publisher would never use such colourful language – Heaven forbid – but they might respond with something like: 'Enough already. So, what about the nurses? – because some of them commit homicide too.' And here's the thing: in the UK, NHS nurses take a sort of oath called the 'Nightingale Pledge', named after Florence Nightingale 1820–1910, regarded as the founder of modern nursing. During their graduation or pinning ceremonies, they may be invited to recite this, one version of which begins:

I solemnly pledge myself before God and in the presence of this assembly to pass my life in purity and to practice my profession faithfully. I will abstain from whatever is deleterious and mischievous and will not take or knowingly administer any harmful drug.

(Noting for the record, no evidence exists that Miss Nightingale murdered anyone, and this makes her a good nurse in my book.)

As for 'carers', they only have to have 'a good heart', although some have been shown to have black hearts indeed. Later in this book we will meet 'Jolly Jane' Toppan and a few more like her. Where paramedics are concerned, they only need a licence to drive an ambulance long enough to get you to hospital, where you might anyway be murdered by one of the aforementioned.

Whatever the ins and out and whys and wherefores, the abiding principles of 'First do no harm' remains, nearly two and a half millennia after they were set out in the *Hippocratic Corpus*. This in part explains public horror and disgust at medical killers, for they commit what is known in Scotland as 'murder under trust'. We trust our medical professionals to heal us, or at least to do their best to do so – deliberately to kill a patient is therefore a grievous betrayal.

So I shall leave this chapter on a high note with Benjamin Jowett's 1899 observation: 'Nowhere probably is there more true feeling, and nowhere worse taste, than in a churchyard.' And a grave subject this book might turn out to be.

Motives

I have the perfect cure for a sore throat — cut it!
— Sir Alfred Joseph Hitchcock,
KBE (1899–1980)

No book on murder most foul would be complete without mentioning 'motive', for what follows poses the question: 'What were the following medical killers' dastardly reasons for wantonly extinguishing lives, when Hippocrates, Florence Nightingale and so many others had bent over backwards in doing all they could to mend folk, giving them a chance of living another day?'

To assist us, I pulled down my well-thumbed copy of *Seven Murderers*[1] by Travers Christmas Humphreys, QC, of the Inner Temple, barrister-at-law (1901–83). He was also a judge; his history of seven murder trials in which he was involved being a must-read and, if anyone knows a thing or

---

1 London, William Heinemann, 1931.

two about motives, he was the legal eagle on whose chambers' door one would have knocked. The foreword to Judge Humphreys' book was penned by none other than Sir Archibald Bodkin, KCB, JP, Director of Public Prosecutions 1920–30, who begins: 'I can cordially recommend this book to all those who, for one reason or another, take an interest in criminal cases.' How gentlemanly that is, don't you think? And the way it should be, too. A very courteous man, and an erudite one, too, I suspect.

I also learned that among other riveting subjects and infamous case histories, Humphreys discusses motive, quoting from the work mentioned in the Prologue, *An Essay on the Principles of Circumstantial Evidence*. Written by William Wills and published in 1838, this work has been selected by scholars as being culturally important and forms part of the knowledge base of civilisation as we know it. So, if the distinguished, well-read Mr Wills and Christmas Humphreys knew a thing or two about motive, I cordially invite you to read the following, because it might help you to understand the wicked motives of the medical killers whom we will meet soon enough:

> Motive may be described as the mental mainspring of the crime, and it is not to be confused with the intention with which the crime was done.
>
> – Judge Travers Christmas Humphreys

Wills describes the commonest forms of motives as:
- the desire of avenging some real or fanciful wrong; of getting rid of a rival or obnoxious connection;

- of escaping from the pressure of pecuniary or other obligation;
- of obtaining plunder or other coveted objects;
- of preserving reputation, or of gratifying some other selfish or malignant passion.

Wills sums these up more concisely as 'Money, Hatred, and Women.'

It is also correct to say that proof of motive is never necessary in the proving of the crime. Absence of any discoverable motive is of little consequence in deciding whether or not the accused person committed the crime, for even the most astute jury is helpless in deciding the mental processes, which, according to Wills, 'actuate the criminal'. It would, however, be naive to forget that where a motive *is* proved, it is at least a factor of importance to be taken into account.

By now, readers may muttering, 'Okay, so we've dusted off Hippocrates And other ancient Greeks. We get the oath stuff, and the excellent odds given by bookies on a three-legged jumbo winning a flat race, so let's get on to the murdering doctors and nurses and anyone else who can prescribe pills or stick a needle in one's arm with homicidal intent, can we?' Yes, of course we will, starting right now by going back in time to Glasgow, Scotland.

Dr Edward William Pritchard

*Farewell, brother. I die in twenty hours from this –
Romans viii, 34–39. Mary Jane, darling mother, and you
I will meet, as you said the last time you spoke to me, under
happier circumstances. Bless you and yours prayed
the dying penitent.*

– DR WILLIAM PRITCHARD: LETTER PRIOR
TO HIS EXECUTION

Execution

Starting this chapter on a Shakespearean note by travelling the scene from place to place, the most momentous events of 1865 were the assassination of President Lincoln and the end of the four-year-long US Civil War. (No doubt the present incumbent of the White House could have stopped the war in five-and-20 minutes with the help of Russia. Or do I mean North Korea?)

In England – the less neurotic and more psychologically

balanced side of the Pond – the Salvation Army began on the streets of East London when tin-rattling Methodists Mr William and Mrs (Catherine) Booth, abandoned the traditional concept of a church pulpit to take God's word directly to the people. This really upset the traditionalists because it cut out the middleman; money that might have gone on to some offering plate, into a collection box or into a priest's cassock, started going into these upstarts' tins. while Sally Ann-uniformed musicians played 'Alas! And Did My Saviour Bleed' or 'How Great Thou Art' while standing before a Debenhams (founded 1778) shopfront in the pouring rain.

Of marginally less interest: 1865 was the year when 24 vessels were wrecked around the Dubh Artach reef off the west coast of Scotland in a storm, and not by coincidence 165 emigrants left the island of Raasay, between the Isle of Skye and the mainland for Australia. Medically speaking, the pioneering surgeon Joseph Lister didn't travel Down Under, but started to experiment with antiseptic surgery in Glasgow using carbolic acid. This was also the year that the fourth cholera pandemic reached Scotland. With all that said, something far more important for the public's entertainment caught everyone's fancy: the public execution of Dr Pritchard: '… the scene being enacted with all the pomp and circumstance of medieval justice, and throughout the interrogations and processions he bore himself with dignity and courage. It may be said of him as many another great criminal that he died better than he lived,' ran a lively report in the *Edinburgh Evening Courant*.

Some of us not necessarily diehard true-crime aficion-nados – especially those loyal visitors and contributors to

the annual CrimeCon UK events in London *and* Glasgow –
might welcome such a spectacle as follows simply because
Dr Pritchard surely qualified for the 'eye for an eye, tooth
for a tooth' rule in spades. And why? Because the 'short
drop' hanging scene was enacted near to the Salt Market end
of Glasgow Green; the event being witnessed by a crowd of
nearly 100,000, most of whom had assembled overnight,
with some heavy drinking in ale houses and taverns. It is also
correct to say that the 'long drop' had yet to be invented, so
the slow, primitive process suffered by Dr Pritchard would
not have been to his liking. Well, it wouldn't, would it? –
with the condemned strangling to death and the executioner
darting beneath the scaffold to pull down on the struggling
doctor's kicking legs until he had reached his murderous
sell-by date.

And this is where – as I promised earlier – historic reportage
comes eloquently to the fore. Here is the *Edinburgh Evening
Courant*'s ever-so-eager account of events as they unfolded
outside Glasgow's South Jail, verbatim:

> The scaffold is a large black-painted box, the interior
> of which is about 12 feet square, the sides rising 3 feet
> above the platform. The height of the beam is about 8
> or 9 feet and the rope was placed so as to let the culprit
> fall between 3 and 4 feet. The frame of the scaffold is
> on wheels and is put together for the most part with
> bolts. The platform is reached by a broad flight of steps.
> Underneath the scaffold, as usual, a coffin was placed.
> It was a plain black shell and scarcely long enough for
> the body it was to contain.

'Enough,' I hear you say, but I say please remember an eye for an eye, a tooth for a tooth as the *Edinburgh Evening Courant*'s account continues, before the reporter left the scene, pencil in hand, perhaps repairing to the nearest tavern to file their copy:

> As the procession came into view of the crowd there was some jeering, but this slowly died away and it was in complete silence that Callcroft the executioner drew the bolt. Doctor Pritchard appeared to suffer great agony, for he was seen to struggle his shoulders about a dozen times, and only when after Callcroft had gone beneath the scaffold and straightened his legs did all movement cease.

Gosh, we get none of this riveting press coverage today, do we? Back then, the populace needed something exciting to make their day, and I hope to do the same for my readers in relating one of the most fascinating cases of medical homicide in all of history.

This was to be the last public hanging in Glasgow, although not in Scotland. For the last moments in life Dr Pritchard wore his best coat and trousers, and his patent-leather boots. At 8.10 p.m., he was 'launched into eternity' on the gallows; his body was not cut down for more than 30 minutes after that. What might have pleased him was that some members of the Phrenological Society of Edinburgh had come to take a cast of his head. From their examination they concluded that the desire to please was his ruling passion, and that he exhibited low cunning and well-developed self-esteem. The history of phrenology goes way back and makes for fascinating study. However, the members of the society who came to measure the doctor's head might have easily determined all of that simply by reading the newspapers which, it is fair to say, more than comprehensively covered the three-day trial.

In truth …

When I began casting around for the first killer to start this book, I realised that not much that is good can be said about Dr Edward William Pritchard. He self-allegedly loved his children, but that love didn't extend to their mother and grandmother. He met his death with dignity, but he was a braggart, a hypocrite, and one of the cruellest medical murderers in the dark annals of crime.

Born in Southsea, Hampshire, into a naval family, with his father, John White Pritchard, holding the rank of captain, Pritchard's ambition had always been to become popular like his father, yet he left behind a record the infamy of which is, even today, not wholly forgotten, for different types of murder merit different degrees of censure. Murder by poison, which requires forethought and preparation, is the most infamous, yet even among poisoners there must be precedence. Someone who murders by administering a single fatal dose may well object to being ranked with one who destroys a victim by slow torture, for gradual poisoning is the most subtle, perhaps the most artistic, method of killing.

The Continent has produced many brilliant masters of this evil craft, but the acknowledged leader – one might say the founder – of the 'British School of Poisoning' was Dr Edward William Pritchard, he being a kind of Hippocratic Oath-keeper in reverse. Also of interest to us is the fact that Pritchard has other claims to immorality: he committed his long-drawn-out homicidal spree for absolutely *no* discoverable reason. Even the prosecution at trial could not allege an adequate motive. This fact alone makes his case somewhat unusual, but when we consider 'motive' in its purest sense – well, we all have different reasons for doing things to satisfy our needs – we should perhaps look a bit harder into Pritchard's narrative.

Early days

Physicians have a unique place in society, although I will not labour too long on Dr Pritchard – aka 'the Human Crocodile' – from the fake tears he shed at trial – because we have many other murdering doctors' and nurses' heads to delve into. It is enough to say that although his trial took place in Scotland, England must bear the responsibility for his birth. His parents were of sufficient means and social standing to ensure that Edward received a sound education. He claimed to have graduated at King's College Hospital in 1846, and then, no doubt with a copy of the Hippocratic Oath in his pocket, joined the Royal Navy and served as an assistant surgeon on HMS *Victory*;[2] according to him, he spent another four years on board various naval vessels, sailing extensively across the Pacific, to Egypt and through the Arctic.

Returning to Portsmouth aboard HMS *Hecate* (a wooden four-gun Hydra-class paddle sloop fitted out for survey work), he met Mary Jane Taylor, daughter of Michael Taylor, a retired silk and lace merchant who resided at the Grange,

---

2 Nelson's flagship at the Battle of Trafalgar more than 40 years earlier; she is still in service with the Royal Navy today.

22 Minto Street, Edinburgh (the house still stands). The couple married in 1851, having five children, of whom the oldest was 13 at the time of Pritchard's trial. We find him next having resigned from the Royal Navy and in general practice in Hunmanby, Yorkshire, in 1859. He published several books about his travels and on the 'water cure' (hydrotherapy or hydropathy), as well as articles in *The Lancet*.

Through his connection with the Taylors, Pritchard moved to Glasgow, where he lived at various addresses, and from Whit Sunday 1864, 15 May, in Clarence Place, then part of Sauchiehall Street. There he succeeded in getting together a respectable medical practice, although it would be fair to say that his financial position was never on a firm footing. He was usually in debt. Nonetheless, through his contributions to the newspapers on such topics as cancer, gout, a sprinkling of Hippocrates' thinking on the influence of vegetable medicines and an apple-a-day upon diseases, he achieved the street cred of a man of culture, a reputation that was enhanced by the active part he played in Glasgow's social life. From here onwards, however, things started sailing south.

Travel makes you a great storyteller.

– Fijian saying

Dr Pritchard was a prominent Mason, meaning that he was 'on the square', although his morals were anything but. He was a director of the Glasgow Athenaeum, an institution founded in 1847 'to provide courses in commerce, languages, music and the fine arts', and won considerable fame by giving lectures in the library there about his voyages. It would appear, however, that his tongue had travelled even farther than the rest of him. To cite one example: his descriptions of Fiji were never the same twice and possessed only one common feature: namely, a complete *lack* of resemblance to the real islands! One gem from those lectures has been preserved and must be quoted because it illustrates the boastful, figurative style of speech affected by Dr Pritchard: 'I have plucked the eaglets from their eyries in the deserts of Arabia and hunted the Nubian lion in the prairies of North America,' all of which remarkable account must have been seasoned heavily with bullshit. That said, however, many supposedly clever people bought into him hook, line and sinker, so he would have made for a typical politician today.

Another illuminating story about Pritchard deserves telling. At one time he professed a prodigious admiration for the Italian soldier, revolutionary and patriot Giuseppe Garibaldi, who was then at the height of his powers. Garibaldi was one of the great men of the nineteenth century, and also a remarkably successful general and naval commander, which, in Pritchard's mind, ripened in the course of a week or so into a self-alleged warm, personal friendship. In order to quicken his regard for his hero, Pritchard presented *himself* with a walking stick with the following legend: 'To Edward William Pritchard from his friend General Garibaldi'. Naturally, the latter would not have known the doctor had he thrown himself prostrate at his feet.

Incidentally, if you like something to nibble with your tea, the Garibaldi (or, less appealingly, 'squashed fly') biscuit was invented by Peek Frean & Co. of London in 1861, the Italian having visited Tyneside in 1854; he would return to Britain and a hero's welcome ten years later. Well, life would be much duller if one didn't learn something trivial but amusing every day, wouldn't it?

A medical charlatan in the making

Lying is an indispensable part of making life tolerable.
– Bergen Baldwin Evans (1904–78):
US academic and TV host

As we travel through more of this doctor's narrative we learn that he subsequently elaborated his spurious Garibaldi relationship and tried to restore his waning professional credibility by writing fake testimonials to himself from eminent London doctors who, like Garibaldi, had never heard of him either. Pritchard's chief ambition in life was to be admired by his peers; a harmless enough vanity, we might agree, had there been anything of worth to support it. But, as has already been shown, the means that he employed to achieve this end were as ludicrous as they were patently inadequate.

As all my readers will understand by now, Dr Pritchard flattered and bragged and lied to pretty much everyone with whom he fell into acquaintance. He even caused his photograph to be advertised by all the Glasgow stationers and sold at considerably less than cost price in order that the humblest might be able to secure a memento of the 'eminent doctor', 'explorer', and 'friend of Garibaldi'. In contemporary times we might call this a 'marketing loss-leader', so it's no wonder that Pritchard was mostly broke.

How many people did he murder? In the overall scheme

of things we might consider him a serial killer lightweight, for he sent to their graves only his wife and his mother-in-law by poisoning them with antimony. The Pritchard household at 131 Sauchiehall Street consisted of Dr and Mrs Pritchard, four of their children, a cook and a nurse/housemaid, 16-year-old Mary MacLeod. Mrs Pritchard became unwell in October 1864, but it was significant that her health improved when she went back to her parents' home at 1 Lauder Road, Edinburgh, for a month at the end of the year. Back in Glasgow, having now recuperated, her symptoms reappeared – at that time mainly sickness after meals. She was seldom able to eat with the family, and food was sent or taken to her room by Dr Pritchard, although on occasion, it was carried up by Mary MacLeod. Her first serious attack of illness came in February 1865, this time pain and cramp as well as sickness. She was seen by two doctors; one did not consider her case to be serious, while the other prescribed a simple diet, and recommended, without success, that she be removed to the care of her brother, a doctor in Penrith.

Never in this world

On 10 February 1865, Pritchard's mother-in-law, 70-year-old Jane Taylor, came to Glasgow to look after her daughter. She never returned alive to Edinburgh. Three days later, Jane fell sick after taking some tapioca, remarking – with far greater insight than she knew – that she must be suffering from the same complaint as her daughter. On 24 February she became ill. Her son-in-law called in a neighbour, Dr James Paterson, who had been in practice for more than 30 years and until recently had been Professor of Midwifery at Glasgow's Andersonian University. When Dr Paterson arrived, Pritchard remarked that his mother-in-law had fallen from a chair and added that 'she was in the habit of taking a drop'. They then went to the bedroom in which Jane was lying, fully dressed. Dr Paterson was later to tell the trial court that he had expressed the opinion that she was dying under the influence of a powerful narcotic. Pritchard clapped her on the shoulder, saying: 'You are getting better, darling,' to which the other doctor remarked: 'Never in this world.' Pritchard then told Paterson that his mother-in-law was in the habit of taking Battley's solution of opium (which could be bought over the counter in those days), and that it was highly probable that she had taken 'a good swig at it'. Poor Jane Taylor died on 28 February 1865, having survived just 18 days in her son-in-law's household.

Shortly thereafter, Mary Pritchard's condition declined further. Servants noticed the 'horrible taste' or 'burning sensation' produced by food that was intended for her – cheese on 13 March, egg flip two days later. On 17 March she took a severe turn for the worse and became light-headed after her husband was seen to have given her something to drink. Dr Paterson was called in during the evening and found that her condition had taken an alarming turn for the worse. After dictating a prescription he left. About 1 a.m., Mary Pritchard, aged only 38, died while the servants were preparing a mustard poultice. Two days later, Dr Pritchard certified the cause of death as 'gastric fever', its duration two months. That same day he accompanied the body of his wife to Edinburgh for its interment beside that of her mother in the Grange Cemetery. In a macabre twist, at his request the coffin was opened at the Taylors' house and he kissed his dead wife on the lips, exhibiting, we are told, 'a great deal of feeling'. As he stepped off the train at Queen Street Station in Glasgow on his return from the funeral, however, he was arrested. This followed the receipt by the Procurator Fiscal (the Scots term for a public prosecutor) of an anonymous letter pointing to the suspicious circumstances in which mother and daughter had died … a letter most likely sent by Dr Paterson.

The question of motive?

So, what were the issues at the trial? Where Mary Pritchard was concerned, it was not in dispute that she had died from chronic poisoning by antimony. Her body was impregnated with it: ten grams were recovered from her liver and intestines. The Crown's case was that Dr Pritchard had the means, the opportunity and the skillset to administer this toxic substance. He had made considerable purchases of antimony and other poisons, more than were required by an ordinary medical practitioner. And as we have seen in this narrative, he had also frequently indulged in gratuitous falsehoods, so that any motive he gave for the murders had to be taken with a pinch of salt, at best. The defence maintained that that it was too improbable that Dr Pritchard would have wanted to poison his wife, having regard to his position, his education and his so-called affection for her. It was no use suggesting that she had been poisoned by one of the cooks, because the poisoning started before one of them came, and continued after the other one left the household. Hence, the defence introduced the suggestion that the guilt lay with

Mary MacLeod, who had been the nurse/housemaid since Whit Sunday (24 May) 1863.

As regards the elderly Jane Taylor, there was a dispute over the cause of her death. The Crown maintained that she died as the result of the combined effect of antimony, aconite and opium (the latter being due to taking Battley's solution). Antimony and aconite were found in the last bottle of Battley's that she had used. The defence, realising that they were backing the losing horse, did not offer any medical evidence, merely suggesting that she had died from the effects of opium alone.

The plot thickens

We have firmly established whodunit, where Dr Pritchard dunit and how he dunit, but there seems to be no real motive to be found anywhere. Or is there?

Pre-dating the double murders of his mother-in-law and his wife, Pritchard had been suspected of murdering a 25-year-old servant girl named Elizabeth McGrain. On 5 May 1863, a fire started in her room in the Pritchards' house at 11 Berkeley Terrace, Glasgow, but it seems that she made no attempt to escape, suggesting that she was unconscious, drugged or already dead. Dr Pritchard was never tried for this crime.

I suggest that his wife had held grave suspicions over her husband's alleged fidelity following Elizabeth's death and that this was reinforced when the doctor personally hired the freckle-faced 16-year-old Mary MacLeod, who had come from Islay, the southernmost island of the Inner Hebrides. The young woman said in evidence that in 1863, Pritchard had given her a ring and seduced her. In May of the following year she found herself pregnant with his child. 'He said that he would put it right,' she told the jury – a euphemism, no doubt, for an abortion, which he carried out. Needless to say, their liaison continued thereafter, including during the time when Pritchard's wife became ill and was in Edinburgh.

Mary MacLeod also testified that before Mrs Pritchard had fallen ill, the 38-year-old doctor spoke to her about marrying her, but did not say more. When pressed, Mary said that Pritchard had told her that he would marry her if his wife died before him. In 1865 he had given Mary a brooch and a locket containing his photograph, and admitted that he and she had been seen by his wife kissing in a bedroom. Mary wanted to go away but Mrs Pritchard would not let her, saying that she would speak to the doctor, who was a 'nasty dirty man'. This had been in the summer of 1864. So now we have at least a motive for the 'wicked and felonious deaths' of two women.

A second possible motive for murder was financial gain. It was true that Pritchard was short of money and getting along by the seat of his pants. Mrs Taylor's will was to leave him a liferent[3] in two-thirds of £2,500 until the children came of age. Yet during his trial, no evidence was presented that Pritchard knew of the will. In any event, he was an idol in her eyes, at least this is what *he* claimed, and was probably more valuable to him alive than dead – as a source of future loans, it has to be said. For my part, although we will never know what exactly was in Pritchard's mind, I follow William Roughead's thinking. The chronicler of Pritchard's trial

---

3   In Scots law a liferent is a right to receive for life the benefits of a property or other asset without the right to dispose of or destroy it.

(and many others), Roughhead thought that the man in the dock had tired of his wife and 'found her continued existence incompatible with the free pursuit of a lawless pastime'.

The reader will remember this quote, cited above, by Bergen Baldwin Evans: 'Lying is an indispensable part of making life tolerable.' So it is interesting to consider that during his time in prison, Pritchard admitted his guilt, not just on one occasion but with three separate confessions, each conflicting with the other:

1. That he had murdered his wife by an overdose of chloroform when Mary MacLeod was present, and that Mary was aware that the food she took to his wife was poisoned.

2. That he had given his wife the chloroform at her own earnest request. He believed that his mother-in-law had died through an overdose of Battley's opium solution, and after her death he had put aconite in the bottle 'in order to prove death by misadventure in case any enquiry should take place'. (Although highly poisonous, aconite was used in some medical treatments.) He added that his wife had been aware of his misconduct with young Mary, 'and rather sought to cover my wickedness and folly'. During the fortnight when Mrs Taylor was nursing her daughter she had caught him with Mary in the consulting room.

3. Perhaps as a result of the labours of ministers of the Church who had wrestled with his reluctance to come to terms with the truth, Pritchard accepted that he had murdered both women and that Mrs Taylor's death

had been caused in the manner set out in the charge against him. As to his motive, he could not assign any beyond a species of 'terrible madness' and the use of 'ardent spirits' (strong drink).

Is there another doctor in the house?

Before I close this chapter on Pritchard, I must draw readers' attention to a remarkable lecture, 'Some Reflections on the Case of Dr Pritchard', given by the distinguished Scottish judge Lord (William) Cullen of Whitekirk at Parliament House, Edinburgh, in 1998. Here, attention is drawn back to Dr Paterson, to encounter '… a case within a case', as Lord Cullen relates. In short, during and after the trial Dr Paterson came in for a great deal of criticism for not having at least tried to intervene when he first realised that Jane Taylor was under the influence of opium and was dying. More so because lying next to her was her daughter, Mary Pritchard, '… in a state of pitiful agitation and distress'.

Giving his evidence, Paterson said that Mrs Pritchard: '… seemed to be exceedingly weak and exhausted; her features sharp and thin with a high, hectic flush; her voice very weak and peculiar as if she was verging on the collapsed state of cholera; her countenance conveying the idea of a semi-imbecile'. He said that he could not rid his mind of the idea, or rather the conviction, that she was under the depressing influence of antimony. In cross-examination he said that his impression was that she was being poisoned by its long-continued administration.

In re-examination, Paterson proved to be even more definite: he believed that somebody was administering antimony to her for the purpose of procuring her death. He went on to say that he saw her twice more before her death on 18 March. Lord Cullen writes: 'On 3 March Dr Paterson visited her as a result, he said, of a chance meeting with Pritchard. Her symptoms and his opinions were unchanged. It was more like a friend's call of condolence, because he understood that Dr Pritchard was attending Mary.' However, Paterson left 'a prescription for champagne, brandy and ice etc.' When he was called in by Pritchard on the 17th he was very much struck by her 'terribly altered appearance and particularly by her wild expression'. This time Paterson prescribed morphia, wine, chlorodyne and cinnamon water.

At this point we come to the crux of it all, for a number of searching questions were then asked of Paterson. Why had he not told Pritchard of his concern? Faced with that pointed question in cross-examination he weakly replied: 'It would not have been a very safe matter to do that.' Asked in re-examination to explain that answer, he said that: 'This would not have been very natural.' Asked whether his suspicions concerned Pritchard, he said that he would rather not answer the question, even though he knew that Mary Pritchard was literally dying in excruciating pain from toxic poisoning in front of his very eyes.

Trying to dodge more bullets, he replied when asked why he had not told Mrs Pritchard: 'Because the treatment I prescribed for her, provided she got nothing else, was quite sufficient, in my opinion.'

Why had he not gone back to see her? 'She was not my patient … it is the etiquette of our profession that the consultant has no right to go back to see the patient!'

Why had he not told the authorities? 'There was another doctor in the house. I did my best by apprising the Registrar ... by refusing to certify the death,' to which the Lord Justice Clerk himself delivered a scathing rebuke: 'I care not for professional etiquette or professional rule. There is a rule of life, and a consideration that is far higher than these, and that is, the duty that every right-minded man owes to his neighbour to prevent the destruction of human life in this world, and in that duty I cannot but say that Dr Paterson failed.' There is no doubt that Paterson deserved this censure. While he may have done no medical harm either to Jane Taylor or Mary Pritchard, his failure to act on his suspicions – on the evidence before his eyes – undoubtedly breached his duty under the Hippocratic Oath.

Lord Cullen adds a ghoulish postscript: '... in 1910, when the workmen were digging in the foundations of the old South Jail they came across a grave over which lay a slab with the letters W. W. P. The body was examined and once more the skull was the subject of scientific examination. The corpse still wore patent leather boots which – unlike Dr Pritchard's reputation – were in a perfect state of preservation.'

I could never have ended any chapter better than that!

Note: for further reading: *Report of the Trial of Dr. Pritchard for Murder. Trial at the High Court of Judiciary, Edinburgh, before the Lord Chief Justice-Clark, Lord Ardmillan, and Lord Jerviswoode, on 3d, 4th, 5th, 6th, and 7th July 1865*, Edinburgh, Oliver and Boyd, 1865.

Dr William Palmer

Everyone lies to their neighbour; they flatter with their lips but harbour deception in their hearts.

Psalm 12:2–4 (NIV)

Pre-dating Dr Pritchard by a few years was the case of Dr William Palmer, aka the 'Rugeley Poisoner' or the 'Prince of Poisoners' (1824–56). He too was hanged.

On this case perhaps we should devote more time because he was convicted purely on circumstantial evidence, fuelled by rumour. Born in Rugeley, Staffordshire, in 1824, he was the sixth of seven surviving children of what used to be termed 'bad stock' – or, as Americans say, 'from the wrong side of the tracks'. It was perhaps inevitable, therefore, that Palmer was committing petty crime before he'd entered his teens. His father, a sawyer whose modest job somehow brought him considerable wealth, died when William was 12, leaving his widow a considerable sum of money, and some £7,000 each to his children when they reached the age of 21, unmarried.

William, who soon acquired the reputation of a tearaway, especially when he began to collect girlfriends, started to rely on his indulgent mother for money.

When he was 17 he was apprenticed to a Liverpool chemist's, soon to be dismissed for stealing cash that had been sent in for prescriptions. (It is possible that at the bottom of this was an older and rather grasping girlfriend, Jane Widnall, who had got wind of his prospective inheritance but was thwarted by the terms of Palmer's father's will.)

Palmer was then taken on as an assistant to a Dr Tylecote in a nearby village, and soon Jane Widnall reappeared, still with an eye on his upcoming inheritance. (She also kept on eye on Peter Smirke, another of Tylecote's assistants, whom she eventually married.) To placate Jane, it is said, Palmer resorted to stealing money from Tylecote and the two of them fled together. They soon ran out of money and returned but, unsurprisingly, Dr Tylecote would not take Palmer back.

Palmer was next taken on by Stafford Infirmary as a 'walking pupil', having paid the sum of five guineas. The year was 1844, and he was 20 years old and soon to receive his inheritance. How good a pupil he was is questionable: he much preferred having fun with the ladies and the excitements of gambling. He did, however, become interested in poisons at about this time.

It is believed that around this time he fathered an illegitimate child, and that, furthermore, shortly after the baby was brought to him, it died. In an age of high infant mortality, this was unremarkable. But it is not impossible that he was experimenting with poisons and simultaneously disposing of a financial liability; or perhaps he had been handling poisons and traces were left on his hands. Some ten or 12 years later, this incident went through the village rumour mill and was blown up out of proportion: he was responsible, it was claimed, for at least 14 illegitimate births and, what's more, was running an abortion clinic from his employer's premises ... Realistically, neither would have even been likely, let alone possible.

That Palmer actually qualified as a doctor is almost beyond belief – and indeed, it was probably entirely due to his mother's financial intervention. He left Stafford for St Bartholomew's Hospital, London. 'St Bart's' or simply 'Bart's', was founded in 1123 by an Augustinian monk named Rahere, a favourite of King Henry I, and is today recognised as the oldest hospital still functioning from its original site in the UK, if not the oldest in the whole wide world. (Hôtel-Dieu in Paris, which also still functions as a hospital, was established nearly three centuries earlier, but it was moved in the nineteenth century.)

In August 1946, now a fully fledged physician, Palmer returned to his birthplace, Rugeley. During the interim before he received his diploma, he resumed his lifestyle of drinking, gambling and flirting (at the least), and this is where a shadow falls: one cold October evening he and a friend, a man called Timmis, met plumber and glazier George Abley at the Lamb and Flag public house in Little Haywood, a nearby village. (The Lamb and Flag still exists today, one of two pubs in the village; I'm told that it offers a great roast lunch.) Palmer and Timmis took bets on how much brandy they could persuade Abley to drink. He knocked back two tumblersful and had begun on a third when he suddenly staggered out, complaining of feeling ill. His companions continued to entertain themselves and an hour or two had passed before they remembered Abley and went to look for him. They found him lying on the cold stable floor, clutching his stomach and moaning in pain, and carried him home and put him to bed; there, during the night, he died.

Despite the circumstances of Abley's death, nothing was ever proved against Palmer, although local village gossip rumoured that he had an interest in the very pretty Mrs Abley. Given what we know of the doctor's philandering nature, we might surmise that the rumour-mongers were correct in that instance – but it is unlikely that he had been doing more than flirting with her. Palmer had nothing to gain by Abley's death, which was put down to natural causes – his health, it was noted, had not been good and it was reckoned that two large tumblers of brandy on an empty stomach, followed by over an hour slumped in the cold, had been too much for him. The coroner recorded his cause of death as 'Exhaustion the result of diseased blood vessels of the lung'.

The Thorntons

While still working for Dr Tylecote, Palmer had met a young lady of quite a different class from the young women he knew. Anne (or 'Ann', often called 'Annie') Thornton (or Brookes) was the illegitimate offspring of a Colonel William Brookes and his housekeeper, Anne (also known as Mary) Thornton. Described by the *Illustrated News* of 2 February 1856 as a 'low vulgar woman', Mary Thornton by all accounts came to be an alcoholic harridan, and when the colonel died, their daughter, then aged about seven, was made the ward of a Mr Charles Dawson, with whose family she went to live. Dawson was very much against Annie's association with Palmer, doubtless having heard of the young man's many dalliances and of his constant seeking after money – Brookes had left the Thorntons considerably well off and in possession of a number of properties, and Dawson understandably assumed it was Annie's fortune Palmer was after. But Palmer persisted in his courtship, writing to Annie while he was at St Bart's, 'I snatch a moment from my studies to write to your dear, dear, little self …'

William Palmer married Anne Thornton in St Nicholas Church, Abbots Bromley, on 7 October 1847; he was 23, Annie 20. He had recently set up his practice in Rugely in a house opposite the Talbot Arms public house. As a doctor, he seems to have been well-liked, one former patient many years later remembered him for his kindness; and it appears that he was successful – so much so that he bought himself several racehorses and hired an assistant. The future for him and his popular young wife was bright.

A leopard can't change its spots, however, and Palmer found it impossible to 'settle down to a life of domesticity and honest toil', as one source puts it.[4] We mustn't forget that Palmer was an inveterate gambler, and he was soon leaving his medical practice in the hands of his assistant while he was placing bets at the races, then drinking away his losses or celebrating his wins. His losses far outweighed his winnings, and, combined with the considerable cost of running a stable of racehorses, his earnings and his wife's inheritance were

---

4   Brian Lane and Wilfred Gregg, *The New Encyclopedia of Serial Killers*, London, Headline, 1996.

eaten up by his gambling and extravagances. He was addicted. Debts mounted up – bills went unpaid; loans, including from Palmer's mother and his drunken mother-in-law, all bore down upon him. Palmer's desperation if anything made his gambling more reckless. There were even rumours that he was 'nobbling' rivals' horses – administering drugs to slow them down to give his own a chance. He was also said to have resorted to fraud and forgery (of his mother's signature, for instance).

When, in early January 1949, Mary Thornton was found in a state of alcoholic delirium, Palmer had her brought to live with him and Annie so they could look after her. There she died two weeks later, on 18 January 1849. This was convenient as far as Palmer's debts to her were concerned, but to his disappointment the properties she owned were not passed down to her daughter. What killed her? Her cause of death was recorded as 'apoplexy', a loose term that was used for sudden death immediately following sudden loss of consciousness – a stroke, for instance, or heart attack. While her symptoms suggest alcohol poisoning as the root cause, could she have died from another sort of poisoning? It would have taken little to tip the balance – but bearing in mind Mrs Thornton's state of health, would it have been worth the bother?

Leonard Bladen, a brewery worker from London, had suffered internal injuries when a heavy cart had run into him and was told to rest. Instead he went to the races at Chester, where he met his good friend William Palmer – who owed him money. They caroused and placed bets on horses. Bladen was lucky, William less so. They agreed that, although Bladen was still weak and in pain from his accident, he should go to Rugeley and spend a few days with Palmer and collect his debts. While in Rugeley he began to feel very ill and he died in agony on 10 May 1850. His cause of death was recorded as 'Injury of the Hip Joint 5 or 6 months. Abscess in Pelvis 12 days. Certified' – this was quite plausible, so little was made of the coincidence. Bladen's widow was, however, puzzled that her husband had no money on him. No doubt it was now lining William Palmer's pockets.

Poisons

As mentioned earlier, William Palmer was reportedly especially interested in poisons. Poisons were indeed a subject of great interest in Victorian society – there was little or no regulation governing their acquisition and use, and they were to be found in numerous manufactured items – arsenic, of mineral derivation, was used in cosmetics, paints, wallpapers; cyanide, a widely found chemical compound, and produced by some plants as a form of pesticide, was used extensively in manufacturing industries; strychnine (see also pp.81–3, 89–101), derived from plants, was used medically and non-medically, in small quantities, as a stimulant, and to kill animals, notably rats. To readers of Agatha Christie's novels, both cyanide and strychnine are known to be frighteningly efficient murder weapons. While the effects of arsenic as a toxin are generally slow to develop (it is, among other things, carcinogenic), which can make it hard to detect as a murder weapon, cyanide and strychnine, on the other hand, can be quick-acting and brutal. A fatal dose of cyanide can kill within minutes, causing convulsions, coma and cardiac arrest. The effects of strychnine poisoning are especially dramatic and horrifying to behold, beginning with muscle spasms around the neck, head and jaw – tetanic convulsions, like those caused by tetanus – and before long the whole body is convulsing violently until the victim dies from asphyxiation brought on by paralysis of the respiratory system.

It is with strychnine that Palmer is especially associated – although only one piece of hard evidence seems to have existed. But he was medically trained and allegedly had a particular interest in poisons. He would, therefore, presumably have known how little to administer to present symptoms over time – before a final dose would prove fatal. Imprecise and risky as this would be, we must remember that he was a gambler.

The children

William Brookes Palmer – 'Little Willy' to his father – was born in either late December 1848 or early January 1849 (some sources say 1850 – but church records show him to have been christened in January 1849). He seems to have been a welcome addition to the household, though of course to the debt-ridden Palmer he must have represented an added expense. He outlived the rest of his immediate family, eventually moving to London, where he worked as a solicitor. He died in 1926.

Annie Palmer was to give birth to another four children. Sadly, all died in early infancy: Elizabeth died aged ten weeks and was buried on 8 January 1851; exactly one year later, one-month-old Henry was buried; he was followed by Frank, who lived for only a few hours and was buried on

21 December 1852, and John died aged three days, to be buried on 30 January 1854.

The cause of death for all four was given as 'convulsions', more a symptom than a cause. While convulsions can indicate ingestion of a toxic substance, they might indicate many other conditions, especially in a baby. We are unlikely ever to know whether poison was administered to one or all of the babies. Infant mortality was high before the twentieth century and the deaths were not questioned. Or at least not until after Palmer's conviction. It would have taken very little to kill a very young child, which would otherwise have grown into another mouth to feed. But would a gambler like Palmer have looked so far ahead? And wouldn't a medical man like him have had some idea how to ensure his wife did not fall pregnant?

A few years later, nine months after Annie Palmer's death, Palmer's housemaid gave birth to his son; five months later, the baby died, his cause of death recorded as erysipelas, a bacterial skin infection. That these infant deaths, and that of the child allegedly his, born to a girlfriend in 1844, were convenient cannot be denied. Equally, they prove nothing.

It is, however, remarkable that people seemed to make a habit of dropping down dead when they had spent time with William Palmer. In October 1852, his disreputable and very boozy uncle, Joseph Bentley, had been drinking with him when he fell off his chair, apparently in a drunken stupor. He died three days later of, according to his death certificate, 'Malignant Disease of the stomach', a diagnosis vague enough to cover multiple conditions.

Life insurance

In the course of the nineteenth century the practice of taking out life insurance grew, and in April 1854, Palmer reportedly insured his wife's life for £13,000 – a considerable amount of money at the time. This was to arouse suspicions later.

On 18 September that year, Annie went with her sister-in-law to a concert in Liverpool, where they spent the night. When she got home, she felt unwell and took to her bed. She was soon very ill and a doctor (not Palmer) was sent for, who diagnosed English cholera; there was a cholera epidemic at the time, and ports – such as Liverpool – were frequently an entry point for infectious diseases. Annie Palmer died on 29 September, and it seems most likely that her cause of death was indeed cholera, as stated on her death certificate, which was signed by the two doctors who had attended her.

Another convenient death?

According to Mrs Palmer's doctors, William Palmer dosed her with a small amount of diluted prussic acid (hydrogen cyanide) to reduce the violent vomiting, but nothing else. When, over a year later, her body was exhumed for autopsy, the only potential toxin to be found was a trace of antimony, an element that would be unlikely to kill a person unless they were exposed to it over a long period. It was in those days used in cosmetics and occasionally medicinally (today it is mostly used as a fire retardant).

Emboldened, perhaps, by receiving Annie's life insurance money, high as the cost was, Palmer soon set about persuading his brother Walter to let him insure his life. Walter Palmer had been comparatively well-off and successful in business, but had started to drink heavily; his business failed, his wife left him, and he drank ever more heavily. William saw how badly affected his health was … Insuring the life of someone not likely to live very long, with himself as benefactor, seemed a good money-making scheme. It was a struggle to keep his brother off drink for long enough, but eventually Palmer succeeded in insuring his life. The gamble did not work, however – Walter Palmer died too soon afterwards, in August 1855, and the insurance company became suspicious and refused to pay out. Later, rumours began to circulate that William had poisoned his brother. If he did, it was a serious misjudgement.

John Parsons Cook

As 1855 drew to a close, Palmer was not only up to his neck in debt but also in the claws of moneylenders, and worried that he might get done for having forged his mother's signature on some documents. (The following year, after Palmer's conviction, a strange story appeared in the *Illustrated Times* coverage of his trial: at some point in 1855, it was claimed, Palmer and a few of his companions – George Bates, an unsuccessful farmer and occasional employee at Palmer's stables; John Parsons Green, a former solicitor and fellow gambler; the village postmaster, Samuel Cheshire, and the Palmer family solicitor and friend, Jeremiah Smith – came up with the idea that they should insure Bates's life. The insurers were not taken in, especially as Bates did not understand what was at stake.)

In November that year Palmer visited Shrewsbury Handicap Races with a group of friends including the aforementioned John Parsons Cook, described as a sickly young man who had quit his job in favour of gambling and the high life when he inherited a large amount of money. At the races on the 13th, Cook won on pretty much every race, his winnings totalling £3,000, while, as seemed to be par for the course, Palmer lost his shirt.

That evening Cook threw a celebratory party at the Raven Hotel, in Barrow Street, Much Wenlock, where they were staying; Palmer did not attend as he had to return briefly to Rugeley. The following evening, however, they all dined together at the Raven, where Cook was suddenly taken ill. It is reported that he accused Palmer of drugging him – but this did not stop him from allowing Palmer to treat him – so could he have been joking? He retired to his room and a doctor was sent for. The following morning, the 15th, Cook felt a bit better and came down for breakfast, and travelled that evening with Palmer (who had that day suffered another heavy loss at the races) to Rugeley, where he took a room at the Talbot Arms, opposite Palmer's house. He went to bed early as he still felt ill, but was well enough to dine with Palmer the following day. By the next day, Saturday 17 November, Cook was feeling much worse and had started throwing up. On Sunday, Palmer called in his friend and family doctor, the elderly Dr Bamford, and on the following day went to London to collect Cook's horsey windfall with the intention of paying off his own debts. At some point around then, he wrote to Cook's old friend and family doctor, Dr Jones.

On his return to Rugeley, Palmer found Cook slightly better, but the young man relapsed once more, then to rally again. On the next day, Tuesday, Dr Jones arrived and arranged to share Cook's bedroom in the Talbot Arms. According to *The Illustrated Times Weekly Newspaper* of 2 February 1856, at around 11 p.m., Palmer gave Cook two morphine pills before retiring for the night. Twenty minutes later, Jones was woken up by Cook, begging him to summon Palmer, who hurried over and administered to the unfortunate Cook two 'ammonia pills'. The newspaper continued:

> A terrible scene now ensued. Wildly shrieking, the patient tossed about in fearful convulsions; his limbs were so rigid that it was impossible to raise him, though he entreated that they would do so, as he felt that he was suffocating. Every muscle was convulsed; his body bent upwards like a bow; they turned him over on his left side; the action of the heart gradually ceased; and he was dead.

John Parsons Cook died at 1 a.m. on Wednesday 23 November. My readers will note that the symptoms described by the paper's informant or informants match those of strychnine poisoning. Cook's previous symptoms were ignored. It was the alleged poisoning of Cook that finally led to Palmer's arrest, and the arrest may have come about only because William Stevens, Cook's stepfather, became suspicious of Palmer's claims about Cook's finances, and demanded a post-mortem.

On 25 November, Dr Bamford signed Cook's death certificate, citing 'apoplexy' as the cause of death – Dr Jones was later to swear under oath that it was 'tetanus'. The requested post-mortem took place – in the Talbot Arms itself – on the 26th. It was a shambles. Overseeing it was Dr Harland, the physician who had passed the drunkard Walter Palmer as fit to be insured; to carry it out was a medical student, Devonshire, and a pharmacist's assistant, Newton; neither had ever carried one out before. Newton was said to have downed two glasses of brandy to steady his nerves. As Devonshire was cutting open the stomach, it seems that Palmer contrived to bump into him and some of the stomach's contents spilled into the body; the rest was placed in a sealed jar, which was briefly removed by Palmer.

The sample was sent to Professor Taylor, Fellow of the College of Physicians at Guy's Hospital and sometimes called the 'father of British forensic medicine'. Not good enough, he said, try again. So, on 28 November, the second post-mortem examination was carried out and a selection of organs sent to Dr Taylor.

It is at this point that Palmer began to show signs of panic – bribing the postmaster to intercept letters between Taylor and the coroner, and trying to bribe the coroner when he had read Taylor's report to the coroner that 'We (Dr Rees and I) have this day finished our analysis, and find no traces of either strychnine, prussic acid, or opium.' Palmer was reassured that he would not be convicted of murder. At the same time, however, he had confined himself to bed on account of some illness (suspicious?) and was facing charges of forgery.

At the inquest, Dr Taylor pronounced that although he had not found any strychnine in Cook's body, the symptoms reported to him pointed to Cook having been murdered by Palmer. This was enough to have Palmer arrested.

The trial and the execution

The trial, held in more neutral London, began on 14 May 1856, and was a sensation. The press had a wonderful time during the weeks leading up to it and the public happily lapped up all the details. Palmer himself was quiet, polite and calm, only repeatedly asserting his innocence, and curiously insistent that Cook was not killed by *strychnine*. That it might have been some other poison or lethal substance that killed him does not, however, seem to have been considered worth pursuing. And there was one damning piece of evidence – it was known that Palmer had bought a few grains of strychnine a few days before Cook's death.

Both Prosecution and Defence called upon multiple expert witnesses, possibly some 20 in all, all highly qualified medical men from the most reputable universities and hospitals, who expounded upon strychnine's effects and symptoms, and its likelihood or not of having been the cause of Cook's death. This, if anything, might have caused further confusion in an already confusing case, with opinions flying to and fro as to the symptoms of strychnine poisoning. Especially as the press was not as firmly restricted in their reportage during the weeks prior to the trial. Everybody had an opinion. The simple trio of means, motive and opportunity was enough to condemn him – as a medical man, he had the means; as a friend, he had the opportunity, and the motive was self-evidently financial. With emotive language thrown in, like the summation in the *Glasgow Herald* of 16 June, which would have confirmed in the jurors' minds the validity of their verdict that Palmer was guilty: 'The strychniated victims of Palmer were no more in his estimation than loaded dice, prepared cards, or drugged animals.'

The *Bedfordshire Advertiser*, cited in the *Glasgow Herald* of 16 June 1856, took a more even stance:

> As a passing remark, we may observe that many of the accounts which have appeared in the daily and provincial papers during the week have been founded on rumour rather than on well-ascertained facts, and have, therefore, been calculated to mislead.

The jury were unanimous in their verdict of Guilty: the medical evidence against Palmer was convincing and press reports persuasive. The Revd Thomas Palmer, one of the defendant's brothers, wrote to no avail to the presiding judge, Lord Chief Justice Campbell:

> It is most probable that the accused would have been convicted, more from the strong medical opinions against him than from the medical facts of the case.

The contradictions

The case of Dr William Palmer, the Rugeley Poisoner, still attracts debate today. It was, for one thing, so full of contradictions:

Cook was deemed to have died as a result of strychnine poisoning – not a trace of strychnine was found in his body.

Palmer himself seemed to have been well liked: the *Illustrated News* of 19 January 1856 told us that 'William Palmer was popular with the poor and with the public generally;

for he had a pleasant manner,' but was soon raking up his past, embellishing the tales with claims from local people – the old man who insisted Palmer at a young age had managed to father 14 children, for example. And as for his friends: 'If one were now to believe all the stories of gentlemen who had drunk their liquor in Palmer's company of late years it would be demonstrated that he was hankering after murder day and night.'

From the little that may be gathered about Palmer's wife, it would seem that he was very fond of his 'poor dear Annie' – yet he seems at least to have nudged her towards death. Could he have seen that her health was weak and that she might not survive, for instance, a bout of cholera, when he took out insurance on her life? As for men such as Abley, Bladen or Cook – they were his friends and yet he was apparently prepared to kill them, in spite of having presumably taken the Hippocratic Oath. (It might be worth remarking that every one of his alleged victims was unwell to start with.) It cannot be denied that all these deaths were of some financial benefit to him.

No proof was ever found of Palmer's guilt – but circumstantial evidence pointed overwhelmingly to his being guilty, and not only this but it led to his receiving the death sentence.

'They have hanged my saintly Billy' (William Palmer's mother)

Throughout his trial and up to the very end, Palmer asserted his innocence. But he walked to the scaffold at Stafford Gaol calmly, careful, the press noted, not to walk in the puddles of rain. A crowd of 30,000 or more had gathered to view the hanging on 14 June 1856.

Now let us acquaint ourselves with 'Throttler Smith'. Described in press reports as a tall, heavy-built brute of a man, George Smith was originally a nailer by trade, and also worked as a higgler (an itinerant seller of small items; a pedlar). His activities were frequently on the wrong side of the law, however, and he was in and out of jail for poaching, petty larceny, and, it is said, running through the market town of Wednesbury almost fully naked. It was while in Stafford Gaol, this time for debt, that he became by chance a hangmans's assistant. The hangman William Calcraft's usual assistant failed to show up and the prison governor called for a volunteer among the inmates. In exchange for his debt being annulled, George Smith became an apprentice hangman. This was some 16 years earlier.

Palmer, as reported by the press, calmly climbed the steps to the drop, shook the executioner's hand and was heard to say to him, 'God bless you'. He was dead minutes later.

The ropemaker who made the rope with which Palmer was hanged was Daniel Coates, a porter at Stafford Railway Station, who recruited the other men employed at the station to work on it. Having an eye to the main chance, Coates made the rope far longer than necessary, cut up the surplus into short lengths of two to three inches and sold them as morbid souvenirs. In one instance, a half-crown[5] was obtained for about two inches.

A Canadian newspaper commented wryly:

------

5   A coin with value of 2 shillings and 6 pence (12½p).

The rope that hanged Dr Palmer is selling in Lockmaben, Dumfrieshire [*sic*], at 5s. per inch. The seller is a man from Dudley, where Smith the hangman resides. The 'interesting relic', it is said, meets with ready purchasers. The rope has also been selling extensively in England, it is said, and of course is being spun as the demand for it increases. (The *Morning Journal*, Halifax, Nova Scotia, 16 July 1856.)

So Palmer was given more than enough rope to hang himself, and in my view he truly deserved it.

Dr Thomas Neill Cream

Every man is guilty of all the good he did not do.
VOLTAIRE (FRANÇOIS-MARIE AROUET, 1694–1778)

And, this notable case is worth more than a bottle of ink because during the late 1880s, while Scotland Yard detectives were trying to track down the notorious Jack the Ripper, another serial killer began to terrorise London. (For the benefit of any North American readers, I am specifically referring to London in England, founded in 47 CE – not London, Ohio, or London, Ontario, which were founded in 1811 and 1826 respectively.) Although the victims were of similar type to Jack's, this other murderer's MO was entirely different and, while the East End killer's true identity has never been established, 'the Lambeth Poisoner' was identified as a person who had sworn to 'do no harm': Thomas Neill Cream had taken the Hippocratic Oath.

Born on 27 May 1850, in Scotland, Thomas and his entire family – mother, father and eight brothers and sisters – left their

Glasgow home in 1854 bound for Canada. Young Thomas and his siblings were raised in Quebec, where his father became the manager of a thriving lumber and shipbuilding business. It seemed that the lad would follow in his father's footsteps, but he felt that his future lay elsewhere, so, in 1872, aged 22, he registered at the prestigious McGill University in Montreal to study for a degree in medicine.

A peach of an idea

McGill University was founded on 31 March 1821 with a bequest from the Scottish merchant James McGill; although for quite justifiable reasons Cream's name is missing from the list of notable alumni, who include the singer-songwriter, poet and novelist Leonard Cohen, the songwriter and composer Burt Bacharach, and James Naismith, the inventor of basketball. The latter had been tasked to come up with an indoor team game to help athletes keep warm and presumably in shape in winter. While carrying out more medical research for this book I noted that Naismith utilised a soccer-style ball and a peach basket, although I seem to have lost my way here, wondering what a peach basket has to do with medical murder most foul.

Thomas was clearly a good student. He was also known as a flashy dresser, perhaps making the most of his father's new-found wealth (there is no mention of him writing or singing songs, or bouncing around a gym trying to chuck a ball into any types of basket). He graduated 'with merit' on 31 March 1876; his thesis being on the effects of chloroform, and he also gave an address to his fellow students entitled ... wait for it ... 'The Evils of Malpractice in the Medical Profession'.

At around the time Cream was passing his final exams he met Miss Flora Elizabeth Brooks, the daughter of a well-off hotelier from Waterloo, Ontario. Shortly thereafter Flora became pregnant, was aborted by Cream and nearly died as a result, to the fury of her father. Brooks Sr would settle for nothing less than wedlock so, on 11 September of that year, Thomas was frog-marched down the aisle in some church. He then did the not-so-decent thing. The following day, without even waking Flora from the marital bed, he packed his portmanteau and travelled to England, where he enrolled as a post-graduate student at St Thomas's Hospital, London. He rounded off his medical education with a qualification from the Royal College of Physicians and Surgeons in Edinburgh. The Brooks family never saw nor heard from him again. Flora mostly recovered from the botched abortion, but died from consumption the following year.

As Brian Lane and Wilfred Gregg write – possibly with tongue-in-cheek – in *The New Encyclopedia of Serial Killers*: 'Thus did Thomas Neill Cream become one of the few genuinely competent medics to turn murderer.' Well, if that accolade is not good enough for entry into McGill's alumni hall of fame, God only knows what is. By the time he had obtained qualifications as a physician-surgeon in 1878, Cream's wife had died from TB, although it has been claimed that she fell ill after taking medicine sent to her by her absent husband. Whatever the truth – or otherwise – of that, he did not allow any grass to grow on her grave. Far from it: following Flora's death, Cream returned to Canada and established a medical practice in London, Ontario, despite not having a licence to practice in the province, something that was to cause problems, although it did not prevent patients from visiting his surgery. It was, however, the death of his patient and alleged mistress, Catherine Hutchinson Gardener (some sources say Gardner), in 1879 that first brought him to the attention of the authorities.

Catherine 'Kate' Hutchinson Gardener

From the very first, Dr Cream was not a competent killer, to which he might have hesitantly agreed as the hangman's noose was slipped over his head. Since by now he was an abortionist and a peddler of quack medicines, one might have predicted that his career would have plunged downhill fast, but this would be wrong. At around this time a young chambermaid called Kate Gardener was found dead in the privy at the back of his newly opened surgery at 204 Dundas Street. By her side was a bottle of chloroform; she had been killed with a cloth soaked in the liquid

Now things began to go seriously awry, for in August 1880 Kate had let it be known to friends that she was visiting Dr Cream in the hope of procuring an abortion. In fear of being dismissed in disgrace by her employer as a 'fallen woman' – as in fallen from the grace of God – she wanted to arrange this illegal procedure to which, she said, the doctor had agreed. 'Loose morals' – sexual immorality – were often addressed with legal severity, 'sexual disorder' was regarded as a serious social problem, so 'fallen women' received little sympathy, and often faced outright hostility.

Hetty Sorrel, in George Eliot's *Adam Bede* (1859), is the quintessential Victoria 'fallen woman'; that is, a low-class maiden who is seduced by the idea of a life of 'lace, satin and jewels,' and is seduced by a man above her station who has neither desire nor intention to marry her. Dr Cream was a highly educated man from respectable Scottish stock, and ranked well above Kate's station. He was a doctor with a reputable practice who had attended one of the most famous universities in Canada, while the deceased, a lowly chambermaid, was found under suspicious circumstances. Little wonder, therefore, that despite the prevailing moral rectitude of the time and the overwhelming strength of the evidence offered against him, Cream avoided prosecution for murder. Besides, the post-mortem examination apparently showed that Kate had died from an overdose of 'self-inflicted chloroform'. This was highly unlikely because one cannot hold a cloth drenched in chloroform over one's face for long enough in an effort to commit suicide. With that established as a fact, we can safely assume that someone else held the cloth over her face, so the finger *has* to be pointed at Cream. His guilt is further compounded when we learn that Kate had penned him a letter in which she claimed that a local businessman had been the father of her child. The doctor also stated that Kate had been suicidal following his refusal to perform the abortion.

There was one *big* problem with all of this, however: Kate could not read or write, so it follows that her alleged handwriting and signature were forged. Yet despite the inconsistencies, the police didn't investigate the death any further. We shall soon see that Cream had a pathological habit of writing fake letters to other people in attempts to throw any blame for his murders on to others, so we might well assume that Kate had been carrying his child. Nevertheless, having dodged the bullet, so to speak, but with his reputation in tatters, he decided it was time to leave Canada and shift himself rapidly to the United States. But was he struck off the medical register? ... NO!

Quack

Those good old days of gaslight and horse-drawn carriages were also the era of patent or 'quack' medicine, one of the great frauds of Thomas Cream's time. Its success relied on the fact that for most people, doctors and dentists were too expensive, thereby creating a great demand for cheaper, alternative forms of medicine. It therefore followed that quack medicines earned their makers a fortune so that by the end of the nineteenth century, Americans were spending $75 million a year (around $2.3 billion at today's values) on patent remedies. Not much has changed since, either. According to the Statista website, our US cousins spend approximately $406 billion a year on prescription drugs, with the Centers for Medicare and Medicaid Services, a federal agency, telling us that this amount includes retail drug spending but excludes 'non-retail'. Nor does it include the sort of stuff one can cook up in one's kitchen or grow as a bumper crop in one's back yard. No wonder some American politicians today don't seem to know what day of the week it is, while peddling outrageous falsehoods about matters of public health.

Yet the promises made in the nineteenth-century practitioners' advertisements were often just as outrageous and impossible. For the poor and uneducated, however, a chance of being cured for next to nothing was too good to miss. If duping the sick and anxious was one thing, though, some of the remedies contained narcotics and opiates, such as opium and cocaine, which would create an addiction that would need to be fed. Let's look at just one of these quack medicines, so please pay attention now because you will *love* this ... I promise.

Holloway's Ointment and Pills

Pictured on the box is the prettiest young woman in all of Greek mythology: Hygeia, the Ancient Greek goddess of health and hygiene (the latter word derives from her name) – and nowadays a dead cert for the cover and centrefold of a top-shelf magazine. Dispensing with the myth that refined, if prudish, Victorians covered up their table legs for fear of offending visitors, there she is, showing a risqué amount of form that might almost have amounted to soft porn back then. Hygeia is doing some product placement for 'Holloway's Ointment and Pills', which promise remedies for gout, rheumatism, lumbago, sciatica, scrofula, erysipelas and 'other skin diseases'. If perchance you were a sailor this heal-all, cure-all and oil-on-troubled-waters quackery could cure scurvy; it being marketed as such as an afterthought because there were many sailors around at that time too. And I would be remiss if I did not mention the 'purifying of blood and invigoration of the nerves'. You can bet your bottom dollar that Professor Thomas Holloway – a colourful advertising genius and quack purveyor of pills and ointments in nineteenth-century Europe – made a pretty penny out of this wheeze; indeed, he ended up one of the richest men in Britain.[6] To promote

---

6   To be fair to Holloway, he was also a philanthropist and among other acts founded Royal Holloway College in Surrey, now part of the University of London.

his quackery he produced thousands of one-penny copper tokens with Joseph Moore's bust of Holloway on one side and our old friend Hygeia on the other. These even have some collectors' value today in case you are into tokens, but I am tempted not to leave matters there. Let's, for example, bring Holloway's medicinal wheeze up to date. Let's imagine any good-looking contemporary female celebrity – Taylor Swift, say, or perhaps Margot Robbie – posing almost starkers in an ad for pills promising 'invigoration of the nerves'. Sales would go ballistic.

Leaving such medical trivia aside, let's move ourselves to the 'Windy City' of Chicago, Illinois, where Dr Cream, who was not known to practise kindness in most things, set up a shady medical practice at 435 West Madison Street.

In case you are apartment hunting, this exact address is now called Maeve Apartments and is advertised as 'a boutique elevator building ... pet-friendly, central air/central heat, in-unit washer and dryer', and so forth. Nevertheless, back in Cream's day the street was swarming with prostitutes, so it is no surprise that this red-light district became a prime location for a doctor willing to perform illegal abortions. Yet despite his usual line of work, he had bizarre relationships with women whom he viewed as immoral. While it was said that he regularly carried pornographic photographs around with him, he was also often heard talking about loose women in terms that were far from agreeable. The police seemingly knew what went on inside his practice. Back then the Chicago PD was corrupt from top to bottom, so for the most part the cops turned a blind eye – most probably for a few dollars or more in wink-and-nod backhanders.

With that said, wherever Thomas Cream went, the Grim Reaper went with him.

Mary Ann Faulkner

On 23 August 1880, the doctor was taken into custody on a charge of causing the death of Mary Ann Faulkner – some sources call her 'Julia Falkner'. Her body was found in his assistant's apartment on Madison Street. Although it was suspected that she had died after Dr Cream had performed an abortion on her, the matter was allowed to drop due to lack of evidence.

Miss Stack

A few months later, in December 1880, Cream tried to place the blame for the death of a Miss Stack on a local pharmacist, sending a letter accusing the druggist of having mixed up her prescription. He used this false accusation to try and extort money from the man, but in this failed. Again there were no consequences for Cream until the death of a Mr Daniel Stott the following year, and here is where things get juicy – which should liven things up a bit for any reader with puritanical leanings.

Daniel Stott

Supplementary to his earnings from abortion, Cream also marketed a remedy for epilepsy. His claims of this miracle cure certainly attracted a large number of faithful patients, one of whom was a wealthy railroad agent named Daniel Stott. In more recent times, there are medical treatments to help most people with epilepsy, aimed at reducing the number of seizures a patient suffers or even preventing them completely. Treatments may include anti-epileptic drugs, surgery to remove a small part of the brain that causes the seizures, a procedure to place a small electrical device inside the body that can help control seizures, or a ketogenic diet. The latter was originally developed to treat drug-resistant epilepsy in children, but took off when its weight-loss properties were recognised; it is a low-carbohydrate diet typically rich in foods like butter, cheese, eggs, meat, fatty fish, nuts and seeds. (Hippocrates might have approved, for he wrote: 'Let food be thy medicine and medicine be thy food.') But wait a moment, perhaps Cream was on to something for just *maybe* he had stolen a march on one of the earliest modern medicines for epilepsy: potassium bromide, an anti-convulsant and sedative which was introduced by the English doctor Sir Charles Locock, Bt, in 1857.

Sir Charles (1799–1875) is worth a passing mention. An obstetrician to Queen Victoria, he was created first baronet for his services to the sovereign. He was a fine man and his history is well worth a read if one wants to learn more about him.[7] Sadly, however, there was a downside to Sir Charles's idea, for bromide extracts a heavy cost in terms of toxicity (though it is still used in veterinary medicine).

It is fair to say that Cream didn't use any electrical gizmos or cut into anyone's brain, nor did he invent the keto diet. He didn't use potassium bromide, either. What he *did*

---

7   His fifth son, Colonel Herbert Locock, Royal Engineers, co-authored *The Drainage Manual* – a book that another Scottish serial killer, Dennis Nilsen, would have benefited from reading, given that he flushed body parts down his loo only to be discovered when the drains got blocked up.

prescribe was strychnine, which can be drop-dead lethal even in tiny doses. Nevertheless, Stott's health did improve, at least for a *very* short period. So impressed was he with the medicine that, in an extremely bad move like a turkey voting for Thanksgiving, he sent his 33-year-old wife Julia to Chicago, to the aforementioned West Madison Street, for supplies of the pills that the libidinous Cream marketed as his cure for epilepsy.

It was initially thought that Daniel Stott had died of an epileptic fit at his home in Boone County. That wasn't the case. The devious 30-year-old doctor seduced Julia; soon they were having a racy affair and he convinced her to take out double-indemnity life insurance on her unsuspecting spouse before plying him with the poisonous pills he, Cream, would supply. Stott died within moments of taking what he thought was medication for his seizures, and the matter could, or should, have ended there, leaving Cream and Julia to share the insurance pay-out. In a repeat of what had gone before, however, Cream decided to blame a pharmacist for the death. He would sue the man on Julia's behalf to claim even more cash.

At this point I think we could call Dr Thomas Neill Cream by another name: 'Dr Fucking Idiot' springs to mind, because he then wrote to the coroner letting him know of his theory about the allegedly bungling chemist. The coroner initially ignored the accusation but after some thought, with suspicion now creeping into his mind, he decided to ask the district attorney (DA) to exhume Daniel's corpse. The latter agreed, and when the body was examined a quantity of strychnine sufficient to kill three people was found in his stomach. So the poison now joins us on our medical road trip.

Strychnine

Strychnine is a grand tonic... to take the flabbiness out of a man.

– H. G. Wells: The Invisible Man, 1897

In Arthur Conan Doyle's 1890 novel, *The Sign of Four*, Sherlock Holmes's stalwart companion Dr Watson deduces murder by strychnine from the unusual grimace on the victim's face.

On the silver screen, Alfred Hitchcock would also use strychnine as a poison in the 1960 shock-horror film *Psycho*, in which Norman Bates (Anthony Perkins) uses it to murder his mother before slashing to death the beautiful Marion Crane (Janet Leigh) while she was taking a shower. Well, no, actually. Apparently Miss Leigh felt that she didn't want to shower in her birthday suit because the lecherous, touchy-feely Hitchcock would have been ogling her behind the camera, so Marli Renfro became a body double. For $500, Marli, showgirl, model, actress and *Playboy* cover girl, stepped in and was graphically stabbed to death in one of cinema's most famous scenes, all of which allegedly ended her cover-girl career ... But I digress.

According to the *CrimeReads* website, Stephen King invoked strychnine in his 2014 novel, *Mr Mercedes*. Agatha Christie introduced strychnine as her favourite poison in her debut novel in 1920, *The Mysterious Affair at Styles*. But as J. H. H. Gaute and Robin Odell wrote in their 1982 study,

Murder 'Whatdunit', 'It is one of the paradoxes of poisoning by strychnine which may be benign or health-improving in small doses but lethal in larger doses.' It is a fact that in Thomas Cream's day, strychnine-based tonics were regularly prescribed for invalids recuperating after weakening illnesses, and one might suppose that Stott's health was fragile at the best of times. 'The effect is to sharpen the senses …' write Gaute and Odell, who finish off with a flourish: '… but once the minimal stimulation dose is exceeded the result can be violent and fatal.' Indeed, accidental deaths from strychnine poisoning were fairly common as a result of patients failing to shake the medicine bottle properly and overdosing themselves with the concentrated liquid that had accumulated at the bottom. Not that the labels meant very much to those who couldn't read. So now … *wait* for it … what follows is some botanical information. To say that strychnine is a particularly violent poison would be no understatement and, since this book is a sort of medical murderers' travelogue, off to India we must go to learn more.

Barking up the wrong tree

Strychnine was discovered by French chemists in 1818, although its toxic properties had been known in Asia and Europe for centuries before then. It is an alkaloid present in the poisonous disc-shaped seeds of the Asiatic strychnine or nux vomica tree (*Strychnos nux-vomica*), the bark of which contains another potentially less lethal but nonetheless dangerous substance brucine, which is a neurotoxin. In some parts of India people follow a religious ritual of drinking a herbal preparation made from the bark of the blackboard tree

(*Alstonia scholaris*) on the day of the new moon in July, but this too contains toxins, a cup that can or will kill you.

Although toxic, the seeds of the strychnine tree, also known as poison fruit, semen strychni (from Latin *semen*, seed) or Quaker buttons, can provide some medical benefit, and there are even claims that nux vomica helps with erectile dysfunction, although there is no real proof that it does and the exponentially increasing Indian subcontinent's population seems to indicate that they get on very well without it, no? In medicinal doses strychnine acts as a stimulant, and in Thomas Cream's day products like Tincture of Nux Vomica and Easton's Syrup were favoured proprietary medicines, given as a tonic to aid convalescence. Gaute and Odell: 'Sadly, it is in the nature of such medical discoveries that they find their way into criminal hands so in the latter half of the eighteenth century strychnine became a popular poison for murder.'

Exhumation

Up to this point in Cream's narrative he would have been best advised to have put away his pen and stationery and let sleeping coroners lie, because there had been nary a murmur or complaint, not even a whispered hint of murder most foul. But suspicion soon fell away from the chemist and on to the doctor, and it was his lover, Julia Stott, who cracked under pressure from the DA's questioning. In return for immunity from prosecution she turned State's evidence – in common criminal parlance she 'grassed' on the evil doctor before vanishing into obscurity.

With the authorities now aware of Cream's criminal

antecedents, for which previous district attorneys had dismally failed to lock him up, this time it was third time lucky for the law. Convicted of the murder of Daniel Stott, Prisoner 4374 Dr Thomas Neill Cream was *supposed* to spend the remainder of his days behind the grim walls of the Illinois State Penitentiary, at Joliet, some 40 miles south-west of Chicago. The place has some incredible history for those interested in prisons, especially with once-upon-a correctional-time, having escape in mind.

Joliet

If only … *if only* Prisoner 4374 Cream had served his full-life tariff then none of the later Lambeth poisonings could have occurred. Nevertheless, just under a decade later Illinois' Governor, Joseph W. Fifer, commuted his sentence after Cream's brother, Daniel, made a passionate plea for leniency. The doctor walked out of the Joliet's imposing gate and into the sunshine on 31 July 1891. Some claim that Governor Fifer was bribed, for while Cream was incarcerated his father had died, leaving an extremely valuable estate. It could be assumed, therefore, that there would soon be plenty of money washing around, and Fifer wasn't actually free of suspicions of corruption at around this time. If that was the case, then nothing much has changed today, with corrupt politicians found all over the place.

With that libel firmly established, Cream travelled to Canada to collect part of his inheritance of $16,000. Thereafter, he strolled up the gangplank of the RMS *Teutonic* – a two-funnelled, twin-screw ocean liner built in Belfast for the White Star Line, now bound for England. The US authorities had just exported a medical serial poisoner the likes of which our fair British Isles had never seen. God bless America!

The Lambeth Poisoner

Upon his arrival in Liverpool in October 1891, Cream made his way to London, where he stayed for a while at Anderton's Hotel, 164 Fleet Street. That was the year of the 'Great Blizzard' of 9–13 March, in which some 200 people and 6,000 animals perished. The Prime Minister of the day was the Conservative Robert Gascoyne-Cecil, third Marquess of Salisbury, the last prime minister to serve from the House of Lords. On 25 June, Arthur Conan Doyle's fictional detective Sherlock Holmes appeared in *The Strand Magazine* for the first time. The Salvation Army had upped the ante with soul-inspiring singalong songs such as 'I Know the Path of Pleasure Well' and 'In a Graveyard Lonely'.

Beyond these events, readers will recall that when Cream first arrived in Chicago he made a beeline for the red-light district, where he found a market for illegal abortion. It was, therefore, now in this doctor's criminal DNA to sniff out London, which had many red-light districts too.

On 7 October 1891, Cream took lodgings in Lambeth Palace Road, at the western end of which stands Lambeth Palace, the official London residence of the Archbishop of Canterbury.

A Golden Age

Back then, in the city's Victorian 'Golden Age', this thoroughfare was in the heart of South London's slum dwellings; a less than salubrious locality in which Cream was to commit a series of indiscriminate murders rivalling Jack the Ripper's reign of terror in the East End three years earlier. To try to place this into a seedier perspective – and I suspect that we all covet a degree of seediness – London or 'the Big Smoke' had poverty writ large over vast swathes of the city. Hundreds of thousands lived in overcrowded hovels with little or no sanitation, yet still maintaining ale houses aplenty – there were 19 along the 1.2-mile length of Oxford Street alone – although very few places of worship. (There were, however, some benefits afforded in a horse-drawn era that we do *not* enjoy today with our means of motorised conveyance: *no* double-yellow lines, *no* parking meters, *no* congestion charges, *no* ultra-low emission zones (ULEZs). Indeed, the only 'emissions' were likely to be swept up and used as manure for vegetable plots.

Although Charles Dickens had been dead for more than 20 years by 1891, his novels like *Oliver Twist* captured the life of London's poor. The city attracted prostitutes in droves, too, although this will come as no great surprise to anyone who is even remotely acquainted with the Seven Deadly Sins. Moreover, Thomas Cream was, it is fair to say, most certainly not shy – any more than was Dr Harold Shipman a century later – of dipping into his supply of illicit drugs and concoctions, which he had been addictively doing for years to self-medicate. The paintings of London street life in that period depict the Victorian era perfectly. I can highly recommend searching online for 'Victorian art depicting the poor', which will allow readers to get with the visual side of the programme, so to speak.

Matilda Clover

No sooner had Cream unpacked his portmanteau in London on 9 October 1891 than he made the acquaintance of a prostitute named Matilda Clover. She, like many of her kind, was on her uppers. Although sex was involved, readers should put any notion of the 1990 film *Pretty Woman* out of their minds. Our Dr Cream was *no* Richard Gere, and Matilda Clover *no* Julia Roberts. With Cream there was no swanky Beverly Wilshire hotel, no bubble bath, no private jet or anything remotely like that, for very good reasons: his activities took place within the confines of small rooms that we might call 'bedsits' today. As an aside, in Victorian times even wealthy people did not take a full bath daily. Poor people maybe once a week when they probably shared the same water with others, or they didn't bathe at all, period. This is important contextually because London's poor in the late nineteenth century lived grindingly hard lives; they did not need any more hardships in their lives. But it was at around this time that Cream purchased from a Mr Priest's chemist's shop some Quaker buttons and a box of empty gelatine capsules. One can guess at his intentions, even if there *were* claims that nux vomica was the Victorian equivalent of Viagra.

Ellen 'Nellie' Donworth

Mr James Styles was out and about during the evening of 13 October 1891. He was standing, or leaning against the wall of The Wellington public house at 81–3 Waterloo Road – now a Fullers pub, if anyone is interested – when by the light of the gas street lamps in Morpeth Terrace he saw a young, apparently drunk prostitute named Ellen Donworth, who staggered and then collapsed on to the pavement.

Perhaps there is nothing unusual about this, for these sorts of nocturnal happenings seem to have been passed down to modern times, as borne out in just about every British town and city when young people go out on the lash. Back in Victorian times, however, things were very different: knock off a copper's tall helmet and one was in deep trouble. Nevertheless, although not entirely sober himself, after speaking to a constable Styles managed to get Ellen to her home. Once there she had gasped out something like 'Aargh', after which her condition worsened. She began convulsing, so a doctor was summoned, who quickly diagnosed 'system poisoning', possibly from over-indulgence in alcohol.

En route to St Thomas's Hospital, Ellen confided that she had met a man in the York Hotel, 85 Waterloo Road (now the site of a Premier Inn). She described the 'gent' as having 'cross eyes, wearing a silk hat, with bushy whiskers'. He had plied her with a couple of draughts from a bottle of 'white stuff'.

So here we have an unfortunate young woman trying to eke out the most destitute existence in London – where all manner of vermin, insect, rodent and occasionally human outnumber the citizens by millions to one. And then she meets a well-dressed, well-heeled, well-travelled Scottish doctor, no less, with his black silk topper indicating to all and sundry that he is a person of substance and thus above her station. You can picture him, can't you? Ellen, God rest her soul, probably saw him as a profitable 'mark'. The upshot, however, was that she died on her way to the hospital, and this would have been the most hideous way to expire, as I shall show, although please close your eyes for a moment if you are of a delicate disposition.

Once strychnine enters the bloodstream – symptoms of its poisoning can even arise from external application – you might say that, medically speaking, the victim is on a one-way street with a grave at the far end. Ingesting nux vomica is *not* the way to go. Even a few crystals can prove fatal, and why? Well, it goes something like this:

Within minutes the body absorbs the drug, affecting the central nervous system; breathing difficulties result and the victim will also suffer convulsions. As the motor areas of the spinal column react to the poison they go on strike, causing the spine to arch and the muscles to dramatically become stiff and rigid. Enough, surely? Umm, not just yet because with much screaming and gasping, with only the victim's head and feet touching whatever they are lying on – a condition known as 'opisthotonus', which is a spasm lasting up to two or three minutes, during which the victim is conscious and in extreme pain – the contraction subsides as the muscles relax with the sufferer, who will now have bitten their bloodied lip while breathing a sigh of misguided relief. The convulsion is repeated, sometimes several times, producing a tetanic spasm and a grinning effect known as 'risus sardonicus' or rictus grin, which is accompanied by a wild-eyed, staring expression – and wouldn't you just? If the victim is *very* lucky, death may intervene within the hour, either from respiratory paralysis or sheer exhaustion. For anyone interested in toxic doses, an amount of 15mg has proved fatal, and 100mg will certainly get the murderous deed done. That was how Ellen Donworth, a young woman trying to scrape a pitiful living in a hostile world, met her grisly end.

You cannot teach an old dog new tricks

With post-mortem examination proving that Ellen, like his previous victims, had died from strychnine poisoning, and despite being in ample funds from his inheritance, Cream returned to his old tricks. Writing to the coroner using the pseudonym 'A. O'Brien', he said that in return for £3,000, he would name the killer of Ellen. He also dropped a line to William Frederick Smith, owner of WH Smith, accusing him of Ellen's murder. Sensing that you may well have bought this book from one of WH Smith's bookstores (and thank you, if you have), it falls upon me to explain that William Danvers Frederick Smith, second Viscount Hambleden (1868–1928), who studied at Eton and New College, Oxford, went on to become 'the head of the greatest publishing house in Christendom', according to the caption to a caricature that appeared in *Vanity Fair* magazine in 1904. So it must have come as no small shock to William Frederick to have been accused of murder most foul, don't you think? Come to think of it, if perchance you are in a WH Smith bookstore, you could approach the manager and say: 'Did you know that the Victorian serial killer, Dr Thomas Neill Cream, once accused your company's owner, and grandson of the founder, of murder?' Then wait for the response, which might be something like: 'Our books on mental self-help are up the stairs, third floor to the left. Have a good day.'

Back to Matilda Clover

A week after Ellen's death, on 20 October, our not-so-waltzing Matilda met again the man called 'Fred' – aka Doctor Cream – and whom she'd been with on the 9th of that month. Having been deserted by her husband, who left her to raise their only child alone, and having turned to drink, she lived at No. 27 Lambeth Street, sharing lodgings with her son and landlords Mr and Mrs Vowles. Their maid was a Miss Lucy Rose.

At 9 p.m., Matilda returned to Lambeth Street after a night out with 'Fred' in tow. They repaired to her room and began drinking. Before he left, he gave her four pills, telling her to take them before bed. Early the next morning, screams of pain ripped through the house. The Vowleses and Lucy Rose burst into Matilda's room to find their tenant convulsing in pain, wracked from head-to-toe with the previously mentioned symptoms of strychnine poisoning. Dying before a doctor could arrive, it was initially believed that Matilda's death was caused by alcohol consumption together with sedatives prescribed by a physician.

Instead of keeping his head down, once again Cream attempted to use the murder to extort money; this time contacting Sir William Broadbent, Bt,[8] a leading cardiologist and neurologist of the day and Physician-Extraordinary to Queen Victoria, claiming that he held evidence against him. Even a cursory glance at the life and career of Sir William would have scotched any ideas about the likelihood of this

---

8   Sir William Henry Broadbent, first Baronet, KCVO, FRS, FRCP (1835–1907)

gentleman killing prostitutes, but the seemingly unhinged mind of Cream led him to imagine that the eminent physician would be gullible enough to pay up. In fact, Broadbent contacted the police and a trap was set for the blackmailer. Cream didn't turn up.

Laura Sabbatini

Changing pace, Cream now took a short break from murdering people to fall in love; becoming engaged to be married. The object of his affections was Laura Sabbatini, a highly respectable young woman living with her equally respectable mother in equally respectable Berkhamsted, Hertfordshire. On 7 January 1892, leaving Laura – whom he later claimed was his one true love – in the lurch, Cream sailed for Canada for the final disbursement of his late father's funds; returning to England aboard the RMS *Britannica* on 2 April without, it seems, having committed any murders anywhere along the way.

Louise Alice Harvey

Now back in his digs at 103 Lambeth Palace Road, Cream met Louise Harvey, née Harris, outside St James's Hall, a concert hall situated between the Quadrant, Regent Street and Vine Street, close to Piccadilly. He introduced himself as Dr Neill. After procuring her 'services', he pressed for more information about herself. Wary of her new companion, the streetwise Louise told him a pack of lies but agreed to meet him later for a drink, with him telling her that he would bring some pills for her complexion. Meeting as arranged, Cream urged her to take the pills, but she only pretended to;

believing that she had, however, he made his excuses and left. Naturally, readers will now ask me what sort of pills Cream gave Louise. Well, here goes …

The Queen of Poisons

Odourless and colourless, arsenic was used as part of food colouring. It was also widely used in beauty products, such as arsenic complexion wafers that promised women pure white skin. Until as late as the 1920s, it was found in the fabric of baby carriages, fly papers, plant fertilisers and medicines. It is also said that some men used it as a tonic and aphrodisiac, though obviously only in tiny doses. Arsenic which, like antimony, is a metallic element, had also been used to murder many, *many* people, and was a favoured means of committing homicide, especially by women, in Victorian times.

For example, beautiful socialite Madeleine Hamilton Smith (1835–1928) poisoned her handsome French lover. Florence Elizabeth Chandler Maybrick (1862–1946) murdered her husband. Mary Ann Cotton (1832–73) laced her stepson's cup of tea with arsenic. So as not to let the men out of this, early in 1921 Katharine Armstrong, wife of a respectable British county solicitor, clerk in the magistrates' court and church warden, was found dead following an 'illness'. Her doctor at the time of her death gave the cause to be natural, but when her body was exhumed over a year later, traces of arsenic were identified in the remains.

Herbert Armstrong was arrested and tried in what was described by one American newspaper as 'the greatest poison drama of the century'. Armstrong, described by the same paper as 'a modern Borgia', was hanged at Gloucester Prison on 31 May 1922. Highly recommended is Stephen Bates's gripping tale *The Poisonous Solicitor* (2022), a real whodunit, as I can testify. But if one can't trust a solicitor, who can you trust – a doctor, perhaps?

Alice Marsh and Emma Shrivell

Alice and Emma, aged 21 and 18 respectively, were visiting London from Brighton and presently lodging at Stamford Street, Lambeth, which consisted (and still mainly consists) of four-storey terraced houses with basements. At about 1:45 in the morning of 12 April 1892, PC George Cumley was on his beat when he saw a man being shown out of the door of No. 118 by a young woman. This image would remain forever in his memory, for not two hours later, behind that very same door, both young women died in great suffering from strychnine poisoning. Cream had encountered the girls and returned with them to their place, where they spent some time drinking heavily and apparently having sex. Afterwards he gave them each three pills, kindly explaining that he was a doctor and the pills would prevent sexually transmitted diseases. He then made his excuses and left.

Close Encounters of the Third Time

To educate myself in my research, I looked up 'encountered' to learn that it means something different from 'met', which is the past tense and past participle of 'meet'. I learned that 'encounter' is both a noun and a transitive verb, and this distinction is important, because one might meet a serial killer – say by visiting him in prison – or one might encounter, for instance, Ted Bundy with his arm in a sling in a dark alley at night.

One encounters opposition. One encounters a thief, a typo, a dog on the road home, or one might encounter a streetwalker. 'Chance characterises an encounter, regardless of whether it leads to an exchange of phone numbers,' writes Patricia Evangelista in her internationally acclaimed book, *Some People Need Killing* (2023); adding: 'Encounters are casual, undesigned. You can plan for an encounter, but you do not plan for the timing of its occurrence, or else it would be marked in a Google calendar.'

Alice and Emma *encountered* Dr Cream on a gaslit Victorian street. At autopsy strychnine was found in their systems. Police, along with the newspapers, now knew that a serial killer was stalking the streets of nocturnal London, prostitutes his preferred prey, but the doctor himself proved to be the architect of his own downfall.

At the beginning of May, Deputy Coroner George Percival Wyatt – who was overseeing the inquests of the recent lethal poisonings – received a mysterious letter, addressed to the foreman of the coroner's jury, claiming that a medical student named Walter Harper, of St Thomas's Hospital, was behind the murders. What follows will come as no surprise to the reader now au fait with this physician's murderous antecedents.

Mad as a hatter

Cream now lapsed into a series of quite unaccountable and slanderous attacks upon the reputation of Walter Joseph Harper. The latter also lodged at No. 103 Lambeth Palace

Road and studied at St Thomas's Hospital, where Cream had once briefly worked. Walter was the son of the highly respectable Dr Joseph Harper of Barnstaple in North Devon. Quite how or why he aroused Cream's ire will forever remain a mystery. Needless to say, the garrulous Cream took to complaining to their mutual landlady, a Mrs Sleaper, accusing Walter of being the author of the No. 118 Stamford Street double poisonings. The landlady thought that Cream must be 'a lunatic', as she later described him at trial. With that, she let the matter drop, but then on 26 April 1892, something else dropped: it was an envelope through the letterbox of Dr Harper Sr's Barnstaple home, and it did for Dr Thomas Cream.

The reader will recall how Cream had gone to great pains in demanding the exhumation of Daniel Stott way back in Boone County, Illinois, which ensured that he served a lengthy term in prison. With Dr Harper & Son, we see the same monotonous psychology once again. Upon opening the letter – which was accompanied by a newspaper cutting relating to Ellen Donworth's death – Dr Harper read with utter bewilderment that the correspondent 'William H. Murray' held incontestable proof that his son had poisoned both Miss Marsh and Miss Shrivell and, for the small consideration of £1,500, the writer was generously prepared to supress the matter. (Note the similarity between 'W. H. Murray' and WH Smith). Indeed, the letter made it plain that if Dr Harper was unwilling to find the money, the 'evidence will be offered to the police on similar terms'. Precisely what was going through Dr Cream's head at this time is unfathomable. Here we have him demanding money in return for drawing the attention of detectives to his front door. Some accounts suggest that Dr Harper and his son ignored this ludicrous threat, that apparently Cream lost interest in his extortion bid, but that is incorrect. The Harpers immediately contacted the police and showed them the two letters they'd received. Detectives soon linked the letters sent to the Harpers to other accusatory correspondence. Among those from 'A. O'Brien' and 'William H. Murray' were letters from a 'M. Malone' seeking money to keep quiet about the death of Matilda Clover. This initially perplexed detectives, who still believed Matilda's death to have been caused by her heavy drinking and nothing more. Nevertheless, a handwriting expert consulted by the police would state that *all* of the correspondence was likely to have been penned by the same person. The question was, who?

John Haynes

Whether driven by clinical insanity brought about by syphilis, which according to some sources he may have contracted in the 1870s while studying at St Thomas's Hospital, or by a desperate, illogical desire to be associated with his own crimes, Cream now started to boast about his familiarity with the killings.

To an acquaintance named John Haynes, he not only revealed far more than he should reasonably have known about the events, but also actually took the other man on a guided tour of the murder houses. But Haynes was a former New York detective and both men discussed the murders with Cream apparently gleeful throughout – yet completely unaware that Louise Harvey, to whom he had given arsenic pills to 'improve her complexion', was still very much alive. When asked by Haynes how he knew so much about the murders, Cream claimed that he had read the post-mortem reports in the newspapers and in the *British Medical Journal*. The savvy American ex-cop didn't buy into any of Cream's explanations, but without letting on, he contacted an old friend who worked at Scotland Yard and informed him of the strange doctor that he'd met. With a bit of solid police work, detectives soon learned that Cream had a criminal record in Canada and the United States going back many years. Shortly thereafter, Haynes spoke to another acquaintance named Patrick McIntyre, and Cream's uncommon knowledge of the murders proved of even greater interest. McIntyre was a police inspector who promptly set a watch on the doctor's movements. On 12 May 1892, and quite by chance, Constable Cumley spotted Cream and recognised him as the man he had seen leaving the scene of the Stamford Street murders. He too put a tail on this by now highly probable suspect.

Arrest and trial

Cream was like the dog that kept chasing buses until one day a bus ran it over — again and again and again. Thus it was inevitable that, at 5.25 p.m. on 3 June 1892, Inspector John Tunbridge confronted the doctor in Lambeth Palace Road. Placed in cuffs, Cream's response was typical of the irritating arrogance that was to tell against him so heavily at trial: 'You have got the wrong man,' he said, 'but fire away!'

By the time the police were ready to charge Cream with attempted blackmail, Matilda Clover's body had been exhumed and analysed. At the inquest into her death, the jury brought in the following verdict: 'We are unanimously agreed that Matilda Clover died of strychnine poisoning and that the poison was administered by Dr Thomas Neill Cream with intent to destroy life.'

A most wicked judge

Charged with the murder of Matilda Clover and three others, Cream stood trial at the Old Bailey on 17 October 1892, Mr Justice Henry Hawkins (later first Baron Brampton) presiding. Although many people revered Judge Hawkins for his long and distinguished career and tough, no–nonsense stance, others described him as 'a most wicked judge', a hanging judge, although of course it is a jury that decides guilt or otherwise. It was the judge who merely donned the black cap to pass down the dread sentence of the law. (Of minor note, the black cap was not an actual cap in real form, but a piece of black cloth, for no cap would have looked anything other than ridiculous when placed over a judge's horsehair wig.) And it was Mr Justice Hawkins, all wrapped up in ermine and cold as a wintry day, who presided over notable cases such as those of George Henry Lamson, Mary Fitzpatrick and Albert Milsom with Henry Fowler, the two latter for the February 1896 Muswell Hill murder. Nevertheless, the evidence against Cream was overwhelming. The 'Lambeth Poisoner', as the press had nicknamed him, must have been shocked to the core when his intended victim, Louise Harvey, took the stand and gave evidence against him. Pointing an accusatory finger from the witness box, she told the court: 'That's the man who gave me some pills. I'd recognise him anywhere,' and that was all she needed to say. Three days later, Judge

Hawkins passed down another capital sentence to add to his record on the bench.

Still unable to believe that he could have been 'so badly used', as he complained, Thomas Cream *encountered* the hangman when he stepped on to the scaffold at London's Newgate Prison on 15 November 1892, to plunge into eternal infamy. The executioner was James Billington. While it was claimed that Cream went easily to the trap, in the split second before the lever was pulled the doomed man uttered the words: 'I am Jack …' Billington claimed that he meant 'Jack the Ripper', although many have since cast doubt on whether he said these words at all.

Theories range from Billington having made up this story to win the distinction of being the man who hanged the 'Ripper', to that from one of Cream's biographers, who claimed that the condemned man actually meant 'I'm ejaculating' – a most unlikely personal revelation considering the circumstances. And, of course, any conspiracy theories surrounding Cream's execution come to naught because at the time of the Whitechapel Murders in 1888 he was serving a long sentence in the Illinois State Penitentiary at Joliet. He would not be released for another three years.

Why?

Missing from *most* accounts of Thomas Cream's life of crime is his motive for the dreadful killings of prostitutes, and so I strongly recommend the meticulously researched book *Prisoner 4374* by A. J. Griffiths-Jones. I hit upon this remarkable account of Cream's life, from cradle to a grave filled with slaked lime behind prison walls, after listening to a podcast; after which I immediately ordered a copy online. Told from the standpoint of Cream himself, the narrative explains the twisted logic behind his actions and his reasons for committing murder most foul, after which a reader might well view the murderous doctor in a rather different light.

Prisoner 4374 won the award for Jack the Ripper Book of the Year 2016, deservedly so. I believe Ms Griffith-Jones has discovered Cream's motive, although I do not intend to give away any story-spoilers here. So before we move on, readers will be delighted to learn that arsenic and strychnine are pretty much impossible to obtain these days, for time and a tide of regulation wait for no medical murderer. Methods of committing medically induced homicide have likewise moved on from crude poisons to the administering of drugs that can be easily obtained by any licensed physician through any pharmacist or, from a hospital's or nursing home's drugs trolley, as we shall see soon enough.

Dr John Bodkin Adams

The doctor is often more to be feared than the disease.
— FRENCH PROVERB

Rich pickings

Now for some lighter entertainment.

As I research and write this chapter I'm listening to a compilation of the most popular music of the 1950s: 'Only You', 'Unchained Melody', 'Put Your Head on My Shoulder', 'In the Still of the Night' – all good soothing stuff. So having got into the swing of things, allow me to introduce our chief protagonist: the bespectacled, beady-eyed, rotund Dr John Bodkin Adams, who might have been considered a shoo-in for a part in one of Agatha Christie's Hercule Poirot stories.

We might call our imaginary production *Rich Pickings*, with the setting not dissimilar to Christie's Art Deco palace, the Majestic Hotel[9] in St Loo, Cornwall, but with a miserly TV production budget in place, now adapted to the resort town of Eastbourne, on England's sunny south-east coast ... the year being 1956, a mere 64 years after Dr Thomas Cream came to his end.

Maybe William Shakespeare would be proud of me here. Maybe he could have used this production for one of his move-the plot-around shows at 'The Globe Theatre'? Nevertheless, placed in more recent context, 1956 was the year dominated by the Suez Crisis. Possession of heroin, aka 'China white', 'dope', 'smack' and 'snow', became fully criminalised. The first AEC Routemaster bus in London started service, on Route 2. (If you're into/onto omnibuses and all matters concerning what was once called London Transport, the No. 2 runs between Norwood bus garage and Marylebone station.) Tourists from abroad love taking photos of our red buses on account of the fact that they don't have any of their own. Eastbourne doesn't have any red buses either, but any visitor might like the place very much, for it still smacks a little of 'old money' and the classier Victorian and Edwardian seaside resorts. Although the site has been occupied since the Bronze Age, and contains important remains from the Roman Occupation, it was as a seaside resort from the late eighteenth century that the town made its reputation.

It is fair to say that in 1956, Eastbourne — also known as 'the Empress of Watering Places' — was an Edwardian relic. To offer a faintly medical link, in 1752 a dissertation by the

---

9   Said to have been based on the Imperial Hotel in Torquay, Devon, which the novelist knew well.

eighteenth-century British physician Dr Richard Russell extolled the medicinal benefits of seaside bathing, although given the pollution of Britain's coastal waters with sewage nowadays, he probably wouldn't be doing quite so much extolling. Nevertheless, over time Eastbourne would become a deckchair resort for those who had reached an age when life was a question of fading memories; for genteel women gasping past their best-before dates, and retired, ungracious, walrus-moustached military officers dribbling away in bath chairs while listening to the string quartet in the opulent lounge of the Grand Hotel.

One doesn't spy many bath chairs in Eastbourne these days; it is more the case of electric scooters with bulb horns on the handlebars, Zimmer frames strapped on the back. Back in the 1950s, though, the well-heeled but elderly or infirm insisted on being wheeled around. Walking was frowned upon, any old person seen on their feet being greeted with the most unparliamentary language.

So the setting, and the all-star cast of our imaginary whodunit/whydunit/howdunit, even whereaboutsdunit, are as rich as are the complexities of Dr Bodkin Adams's lethal machinations. His elderly patients, who tended to be awash with cash, had a habit of dying under the influence of prescription drugs a-plenty, bequeathing fat legacies to him. So was he playing at God in helping them through the pearly gates, was he in it for the money, or was he, by some remarkable twist in this plot, innocent? That will be for the reader to decide.

Enter the Yard

Murder?... Murder? Can you prove it was murder?... I did not think you could prove murder... She was dying in any event!

– Dr John Bodkin Adams to Detective Superintendent Herbert Hannam, aka 'Hannam of Scotland Yard'

Playing the role of Christie's Chief Inspector James Japp – who was initially inspired by Detective Inspector Lestrade from Conan Doyle's Sherlock Holmes stories – Japp *and* Lestrade might almost come from Hannam's playbook. Nicknamed 'The Count' because of his sartorial elegance, expensive taste in cigars and imperious bearing, Hannam had such an upright carriage that when he strolled into the courts he seemed to be leaning backwards.

So here we have a portly, pious, Rolls-Royce-driving doctor swimming in ill-gotten legacies, soon to be arrested for poisoning wealthy old women for their money while living and practising in Kent Lodge, a dull grey villa on Trinity Trees (now Seaside Road) behind Eastbourne's Grand Parade. It should be noted that Browne's the Chemist – supplier of many of Adams's prescriptions – and Marsh's sweetshop – purveyor of the doctor's favourite brand of Swiss chocolate – were nearby and would soon gain a degree of notoriety by association with the utter cad, Dr John Bodkin Adams.

Soon we will have all the elements of a classic courtroom drama combined in Adams's trial: lurid newspaper headlines and famous bylines; the threat of the gallows; malicious witnesses; arguing experts; a top detective; a blundering prosecution, a dazzling defence. All that seem to have been missing were a Miss Marple or a Hercule Poirot. Nonetheless, although the doctor was acquitted, even today many still believe him to have been guilty of medically induced serial homicide.

Gertrude Hullett

The first victim to raise the coroner's suspicion was glamorous Gertrude 'Bobbie' Hullett. Widow of a schoolteacher named Tomlinson, she then married rich businessman and social lion 'Jack' Hullett, more than 20 years her senior, who himself was soon to expire. The vivacious Bobbie Hullett became known as the grande dame of Holywell Mount – a handsome mansion at 2 Dukes Drive, overlooking the English Channel. Bobbie was a member of a glittering set that included the English comedian, actor and stage and film producer Leslie Henson and his wife Harriet Dell; the singers Anne Ziegler and her husband Webster Booth, noted for singing 'So Deep is the Night' (set to Chopin's Étude Op. 10, No. 3) in *Demobbed*, a 1944 British musical comedy film, and the Australian-born actress Marie Lohr – all confirming that Bobbie Hullett was not only well heeled, but also well connected.

The plot thickens

Jack Hullett died in March 1956, and the grieving though now exceedingly rich Bobbie came under Adams's care, for he had treated her husband for some years. On 20 July 1956 she was found unconscious and was thought to have taken an overdose of barbiturates the previous day.

On the morning of Sunday, 22 July 1956, Eastbourne's coroner was surprised by a curious phone call. Dr Adams sought a favour. Would the coroner be prepared to arrange a private post-mortem on one of his patients? The coroner curtly declined to deviate from normal procedure, but asked: 'When did your patient die?' This was a reasonable enough question, but one to which Adams replied: 'Well ... she's not quite yet dead, but going downhill fast.' At this the coroner sat bolt upright, the phrase 'somewhat indecent haste' no doubt entering his mind.

On the following day, Bobbie Hullett *did* expire. At this point a junior partner in Adams's practice, who had realised that Bobbie Hullett was on her deathbed if not pretty much dead anyway, had insisted against his boss's wishes on a private post-mortem. He felt that an official autopsy must be conducted because he wanted to be sure that his senior partner's diagnosis of the patient's illness was correct. Moreover, the younger doctor suspected that there was more to the sudden demise of Mrs Hullett than Adams had said, believing that the patient was dying or had died from a drugs overdose.

This is no make-believe plot, for now we learn that Adams's partner was not the only one whose suspicions were aroused. Leslie Henson, who was performing in Dublin, telephoned Eastbourne's chief constable to express concerns. Being a household name, Henson was fast-tracked and asked to give a statement to the Garda Síochána, and explained that he had been distressed by the manner in which Dr Adams had kept Bobbie Hullett heavily sedated for the four months since the death of her second husband.

'My wife and I saw her turning into a drug addict,' the famous comedian told detectives. 'We saw her disintegrating mentally ... I am certain the pills sent her nearly mad, and through them she died.'

Edith Alice Morrell

To understand more about Adams's methodology, we have to go back six years and gently lift the body of Edith Morrell onto the autopsy table. Until her death in November 1950 she had lived in a ten-bedroom mansion on Eastbourne's Beachy Head Road, where today one doesn't get much change out of the half-million-pounds-and-rising-price of houses along that piece of upscale real estate. Edith's greatest ambition was to win the prestigious Samuel Arno Silver Cup for dahlias presented annually by the Eastbourne Horticultural Society. Bless her, for her gardener, James Carter, achieved this for her in 1948, and again in 1949. In her will she left Carter £500 and all her dahlia plants. So, if any reader is into dahlias and happens to be in a garden centre, enquire about their stocks of 'Edith Morrell' and 'Marden Ash'. They have large blooms, and, for what it's worth, I'm told they are popular with nurserymen.

Arrest

Edith had suffered a stroke in 1948, and before her death, had been bedridden; half paralysed, an irritable invalid with four nurses attending her around the clock and with Dr Adams on constant call. To ease her into the afterlife, he began to supply her with morphine and heroin and, after a while, he summoned her solicitor to come and execute a new will, in which the bombed-out-of-her-disintegrating-mind Edith bequeathed the doctor a chest of Georgian silver. A few months later, Adams contacted the solicitor again with instructions that Edith also wished to leave him her Rolls-Royce and jewellery, of which he would soon graciously take possession. But when the 1950 grouse season beckoned in August that year and he took a holiday in Scotland, the over-dependent Edith became peevish, resentful and jealous of his absence, to such a degree that he feared that she would rescind her will and he would get nothing. Faced with this dilemma, and with his mind set on a coming windfall, on his return to Eastbourne he pumped drugs into the ailing old woman until she died. He then gratefully took possession of the Rolls-Royce and the silver, while not forgetting to submit a hefty treatment bill for more than £1,700, which Edith's estate willingly settled after her death.

So let's return to 'Hannam of the Yard', who became involved in the Adams case after the local Eastbourne police called in Scotland Yard following Bobbie Hullett's death. Our super-sleuth believed he could now establish a murderous pattern: Adams made his victims dependent on drugs; he then coerced them to change their wills in his favour before easing them out of life with an overdose. 'It was as simple a series of murders as it was difficult to prove,' as Holmes might have said to Dr Watson at some time or another. Nevertheless, Hannam and his officers diligently sifted through a mass of material and selected a shortlist of about a dozen cases, then set about 'cracking the suspect' through a series of interviews. The approach was both polite and subtle – all standard Agatha Christie stuff – because the first meeting was contrived as though by accident when the detectives nonchalantly strolled past the doctor's garage just as he was putting his Rolls-Royce away. Feigning coincidental surprise, Hannam said: 'Good evening, doctor. Did you have a good grouse-shooting holiday in Scotland?'

More trivia coming up

There's nothing nicer than a plump roasted grouse with a rich wine gravy, lashings of bread sauce and a nice bottle of burgundy.

– Sir Terence Conran (1931–2020)

For those who are not au fait with grouse – the shooting of – they are a group of birds from the order Galliformes in the family Phasianidae. More interesting is that they have become genetically well-adapted over eons of breeding to stick their heads up at the smallest – I mean teensy-weensy bit smallest – sound of impending trouble, to give a double kick of one leg and zip from cover at speeds the designers of Concorde could never have imagined. So it was that the conversation between Hannam and Adams drifted from an account of the doctor's Scottish holiday home, where men with large guns reduce grouse to puffs of drifting feathers, to his staunchly Christian upbringing and the death of his overbearing mother, whom he now claimed was a 'sweet Christian soul' when in fact she had been the polar opposite. And it was left to Bodkin Adams to broach, nervously, the subject of: '… all these rumours, circulating the town and blackening my good name.' He put this down to jealousy, adding, somewhat oddly, 'I think it is all God's plan to teach me a new lesson.'

The presumption of regularity is borrowed from American legal practice. Its roots lie in the Latin phrase *omnia praesumuntur rite et solemniter esse acta donec probetur in contararium* (all things are presumed to have been rightly and duly performed until it is proved to the contrary). Now sensing that the doctor was onside, when Hannam expressed mild concern over some of the legacies, Adams spoke of them as having come from 'a very dear patient' or 'a lifelong friend', adding that 'a lot were instead of fees'. When Hannam mentioned the regularity of faulty cremation certificates, of which there had been numerous examples, the doctor exclaimed, 'Oh, that wasn't done wickedly. God only knows it wasn't. We always want cremations to go off smoothly for the dear relatives. If I said I knew I was getting money under a will, they might get suspicious so I like cremations and burials to go smoothly.' (Echoes here of Dr Harold Shipman's MO, with which we will acquaint ourselves later.)

The doctor was left to stew in his own juices through almost eight weeks of whispers, stares and sensational speculation, which became outright allegations wherever Britain's libel and slander laws didn't reach. Across the Channel in France and throughout the Continent, citizens read with gruesome relish about '*Le Barbe-Bleu d'Eastbourne*' (the Bluebeard of Eastbourne), although Adams had no beard.

At 8.30 p.m., on a Saturday in November, Hannam and his men returned to Kent Lodge with a search warrant under the Dangerous Drugs Act. The doctor was dressed in a dinner jacket and on the point of leaving to chair a YMCA prize-giving dinner, and it will come as no surprise to learn that the press had been tipped off – the house and surgery were besieged by journalists and photographers. Hannam ordered that the blinds be drawn before asking Adams if he could inspect the medical register that all doctors who handle dangerous restricted drugs are required to keep. 'I don't know what you mean,' the other man blustered. 'I keep no register,' adding, 'I very, very seldom used such drugs' – a comment indicative of consciousness of guilt or intent, as I am sure readers will already be aware.

Thereupon Hamman produced a formidable list of restricted drugs prescribed for *only* Edith Morrell – the rich Liverpool businessman's widow and the source of the doctor's first Rolls-Royce. Mrs Morrell had been dead for six years, but Hannam had been able to compile the list from chemists' ledgers. These indicated that massive doses of morphine *and* heroin had been given to Edith by Dr Adams.

> Hannam: Who prescribed the drugs?
> Adams: I did, nearly all. Perhaps the nurses gave some,
>   but mostly me.
> Hannam: Were any left over when she [Morrell] died?
> Adams: No, none. All was given to the patient.
> Hannam: Doctor, *you* prescribed for her 75 tablets of
>   heroin the day before she died.
> Adams: Poor soul, she was in terrible agony. It was all
>   used. I gave her the injections. Do you think it was
>   too much?

At that the doctor flopped on to his desk chair and sat sobbing with his head in his hands. His home and surgery searched from top to bottom, he was then spotted trying to slip something into his pockets: two bottles of morphine solution, one, he said, left over from treating a Mr Soden, who died in the Grand Hotel, the other for a Mrs Sharpe, who died before he could administer it.

At this point, it might be of interest, and in Dr John Bodkin Adams's favour, to highlight Mrs Morrell's last prescriptions, for they were at least six times greater than a healthy person could tolerate. On the other hand, it is fair to say that she could have built up a resistance to the drugs with the doses eventually killing her anyway. Are we to believe they were *all* believed by her doctor to be necessary to ease her pain? I think not, for we must take the following guilt indicators into consideration:

1. forged will to ensure a trouble-free cremation;
2. failure to keep a dangerous drugs register;
3. legacies in the doctor's favour to the exclusion of anyone else;
4. behaviour indicative of guilty conscience;
5. enjoying the fruits of suspicious deaths;
6. refusal to account for suspicious circumstances and his unsatisfactory explanations aligned with his indirect admissions of guilt and the attempt at concealing evidence ...

... although in themselves circumstantial evidence, upon them may hang the life of a fellow human being.

The law, as manipulated by clever and highly respectable rascals, still remains the best avenue for a career of honourable and leisurely plunder.
  – French novelist Gabriel Chevallier (1895–1969):
Clochemerle (1936)

On the chilly Saturday morning of 24 November 1956, the doctor was arrested and brought before the Eastbourne magistrates on 13 comparatively minor charges; four of them being misrepresentations under the 1902 Cremations Act '... with a view to procuring the burning of remains of Alice Morrell', a rich eccentric who still dressed in the styles of her Edwardian heyday. Did I not say earlier that the cast of characters alive or deceased in our apocryphal whodunit, whatdunit, howdunit, whereaboutsdunit could match anything that Agatha Christie could invent?

Where there's a will ...

... there's a way and, as my regular readers are aware, I am intrigued by the etymology of names, so what is a bodkin? The noun usually refers to a short narrow blade, such as a dagger or stiletto, or to a large blunt needle used to draw a tape or cord through the hem of something – for instance a drawstring bag. The surname, however, has a different origin. I am led to believe that the name is Irish (Galway) and English (Kent), from an unrecorded Middle English personal name 'Bodekin', an Anglo–Norman borrowing of a pet form of the personal name 'Baldwin'. You should also know that the name was described by the great Irish genealogist Edward MacLysaght as the name of one of 'Tribes of Galway', which is, of course, in Ireland. The name was also given to those who made and sold knives, swords and other such implements, perhaps indicating a link to the meaning of 'bodkin' given above.

So, given a link between his name and a lethal weapon, one might also say that this doctor's favourite proverb could have been 'Where there's a will, there's a way'. Originating in the seventeenth century, that proverb is mostly attributed to the English poet and priest George Herbert, who used a similar saying in his collection of proverbs, *Jacula Prudentum*, first published in 1640. Be that as it may, the medical establishment – obviously blithely dismissive of the facts that their colleague had forged wills, faked causes of death, signed false cremation certificates, attempted to suborn a Crown coroner, milked his patients to the tune of over a million pounds plus paintings, valuable jewellery, silverware, a brace of Rolls-Royce motor cars and just about anything else that wasn't nailed down – was up in arms over the 'Dr Bodkin Affair' and did all it could to promote the doctor's innocence.

Hell is other people.

– Jean-Paul Sartre (1905–80)

Founded on 9 July 1832, the British Medical Association (BMA) was and remains the leading voice advocating for outstanding healthcare and a healthy population. Its stated aim: 'To promote the medical and allied sciences and to maintain the honour and interests of the medical profession'. That's all very worthy of Hippocrates, is it not? Furthermore, it is an association providing its doctors and other members with 'excellent individual services and support throughout their lives' and, at that time of course, supporting the Hippocratic Oath-breaking Adams was a priority, coming under the remit of 'support'. Likewise was the duty of the General Medical Council (GMC), which was formed under the Medical Act 1858. So both associations, and another 17 medical overseeing bodies, regulated the UK's medical profession and all these organisations used different tests for competence/incompetence and out-and-out medical clusterfucks, as well as for digging their honourable members out of deep shit when the occasion arose. It comes as no surprise, therefore, that they had more than a passing interest in Dr John Bodkin Adams, and there were many reasons for this.

To bring this into the modern day: try suing a medical professional for cutting off the wrong leg or prescribing pills never intended for the proposed use. Attempt to have a hospital's top management sanctioned. You will end up penniless while the lawyers get rich during a three decade-long inquiry, with the buck being passed to and fro and to again, ad infinitum. It's almost always a no-win, period. So the very notion that Britain harboured a medical serial killer – a man who for more than three decades had been killing the most trusting of his patients for any cash or trinkets or cars they might leave him – was horrific. God in Heaven's sake, public trust was at stake. To have a doctor accused of murder was bad enough, but to see his own nurses and a junior partner testifying against him was unthinkable, and carried profoundly disturbing implications. But there were also fears of the case setting a precedent that could severely limit the prescription of drugs for the terminally ill, and which might put a doctor who failed to prolong the life of a dying patient in peril of a murder charge. The *Medical Press* summed up these fears in a long and heated – pull-the-wool-over-everyone's-eyes – leading article early in 1957:

This is the first time, as far as we know, that a doctor has been accused of murdering a patient by pursuing a line of treatment beyond all reasonable bounds. And indeed, the [forthcoming] trial would appear to be without precedent not only in this country, but in the Western World.

One consequence will be that in the future a great many of them will suffer considerably more than they have done in the past. Any doctor with *normal humanitarian impulses* has always felt in honour bound to reduce his patient's suffering to the minimum, and in cases where the prognosis was hopeless has seldom stopped to count the cost as measured in the day-to-day duration of the patient's life. [Author's italics.]

Many and many a patient has been 'kept under' at all costs to save him agony. This will, we imagine, scarcely be the case now, for every one of us will be looking for the smiler with the knife – somebody making notes to use against us later on.

Whatdunit, howdunit

At that time doctors subscribed to the Medical Defence Union (MDU), which had directed a firm of heavyweight solicitors, Hempsons,[10] to act for Adams. They in turn, selected Geoffrey Lawrence, QC, to head the legal team and provided him with the medical records of Mrs Morrell. Hempsons also hired Professor Keith Simpson – for many years a famous Home Office pathologist and a former pupil of Dr Arthur Douthwaite, the prosecution witness who, it was soon revealed, was a heavy morphine user himself, even though he condemned Adams for over-administering the same drug. Can the reader really believe this: a star medical prosecution witness who was on morphine for most of his working day? So, far from the medical profession protecting *all* of their own, the knives were out, for it was found to be convenient merely to protect *some* of their own when expedient. Even if he was not made out to be a hypocrite, Dr Douthwaite was made to pay the price for his dogged stand. The Presidency of the Royal College of Physicians, of which he was vice-president, expected to be his in the following year, was permanently denied him – quietly, as befitted the situation.

Agatha Christie herself could not have bettered these medico-legal shenanigans.

Mercy or murder?

For the reader who wishes to study the life and crimes of Dr John Bodkin Adams further, there is an overdose of fatal literary prescriptions to swallow because, alas, we must move on, with my editor-in-chief screaming 'Word count' into my ear. Although let it be said that even though Eastbourne's

---

10 Hempsons would later act for Dr Harold Shipman at trial.

most fashionable doctor was as guilty of murder as is possible, through a bungled case in a court of law he was judged otherwise. And here is the rub: this sordid affair raised fundamental issues about the value of life. Enter the medical lexicon the noun 'euthanasia', not in its original meaning of 'good death', but of 'physician-assisted suicide' – although in Adams's case the suicide apect is questionable.

Pre-dating Adams was the case of American doctor Herman N. Saunder, who was acquitted of murdering a cancer patient in 1950, so the former's acquittal averted a possibly ugly showdown over mercy killing. Adams had spoken of 'easing the passing' of Mrs Morrell, with his remarks going unclarified, but this raises the spectre of 'mercy murder' tainted by 'legacy hunting', does it not? More to the point of this book, we will meet others who have claimed the euthanasia defence, although this seemingly easy and humanitarian means of extinguishing life is not all that it's made up to be, so grip the sides of your chair and take a stiff drink, for all will be revealed later.

Mercy killing notwithstanding, in 1957 English law regarded euthanasia as murder. It is still illegal and can be prosecuted as murder or manslaughter. 'Assisting or encouraging' another person's suicide is prohibited by Section 2 of the Suicide Act 1961, as amended by the Coroners and Justice Act 2009. But the debate presently moves on. Courts of criminal law are now adopting a more lenient view, taking stock of the fact that because modern medicine can prolong life – and consequently prolong the process of dying – so too the number of mercy killings has increased. It is not for me to debate this issue further, with this proviso: if I was flattened by a Philippines jeepney, as described at the outset of this book, and then run over by the attending ambulance when it finally arrived, and with no reliable confirmation as to how my mortal remains *might*, if *ever* be posted home, I would be more than eternally grateful for any doctor to end it all painlessly for me. Yet this is *precisely* why the Bodkin Adams case holds such importance, because we must ask ourselves: do we recognise in him a good man who 'eased the passing' of his victims from humanitarian principles, or was he a charlatan sniffing out loopholes in the law to enrich himself in the process?

Cash injections

Adams deserved to hang twenty times over... the law made an ass of itself.

– Chief Superintendent Charles Hewitt, quoted in the 1980s; as a sergeant, he had been one of Hannam's officers on the Adams case.

Acquitted of murder in April 1957, in July that year Dr Adams pleaded guilty at Lewes Assizes to 14 charges of professional misconduct – all these misdemeanours wreathed during the murder investigation – and he was fined a total of £2,400 – equivalent to about £74,000 today. Five months after the trial, his right to possess or supply dangerous drugs was revoked by the Home Secretary. In November that same year, he was hauled before the General Medical Council's disciplinary panel, and his name was struck off the register of general practitioners. He would not be humbled, however, nor would he be driven from Kent Lodge. Though stripped of his right to practice medicine, he continued to treat loyal patients and to receive large legacies. In Marsh's sweetshop, where trade improved, he still bought his hand-made Swiss chocolates; moreover, no one in the town of Eastbourne would hear a word against him.

As sentiments cooled, Adams gradually eased himself back into public life, to the point where Eastbourne's carnival queen was able to parade through town in alleged victim Bobbie Hullett's Rolls-Royce without exciting too much ghoulish comment. Perhaps – and this can only be speculation – the lovely star of the show in the back of the Roller was far more interesting to the crowd than the portly, beady-eyed driver sitting in front of her.

After several unsuccessful applications, in 1961 Adams was restored to the GMC's register of general practitioners, yet he wasn't quite finished. Emboldened, he felt confident enough to turn on his previous accusers. A libel suit was filed. A settlement was hammered out. Thirteen newspapers agreed to pay an undisclosed but substantial sum for their excessive zeal of 'investigative reporting' in the pre-trial phase. The now-litigious doctor, at once bathing in his notoriety, kept a sharp eye open for transgressors. As late as 1969, he was able to collect £500 (equivalent to about £10,000 today), along with an abject apology from a weekly magazine that had thought it witty to invoke 'the shade of John Bodkin Adams' when commenting on his 'failure of cash injections to revive the pound sterling'. One might say that the doctor had brass balls – but I won't!

Obituary

In his later years Doctor John Bodkin Adams devoted more and more time to shooting, eventually becoming President and Honorary Medical Officer of the Clay Pigeon Shooting Association. He won his last cup at the age of 83. It was while shooting in Sussex a few months later, however, that he broke a leg. Complications set in. Within three days he was dead. Like his trial for murder, his funeral in July 1983, attended by 150 friends and patients, was yet another media event. Millions of television viewers tuned in. Then came the reading of the will. The great legacy hunter – for that was what he'd once been – left estate valued at £402,907 net (about £1.7 million today), to be neatly divided 47 ways, with no one to get more than £5,000. The beneficiaries included the doctor's one-time fiancée Nora O'Hara and 19 other women friends who had stood by him during his time of trouble. Everyone was remembered – the housekeeper, the chauffeur, the grocer, even the man from Marsh's sweetshop and someone who came once a week to wind up Adams's clock collection. He left his own doctor something, too.

Doctor who?

It was in planning this book that I settled on Dr Bodkin Adams as an example of a medical person killing for financial gain. Many who have studied this man believe him to have been a sort of kindly rogue, always with a cheeky eye and smile. I have visited Eastbourne several times, where the Adams case struck even more accord, and if the truth be known, not much has really changed in the town as I write, even nearly 70 years later. Of course American tourists still visit. There is still a salty, sea-breeze genteelness, an air of the British stiff upper lip, a Zimmer-frame refinement to the place. And if you stray from 'Charity Shop Street' and take a stroll along Cliff Road to gaze out for a moment over the English Channel and watch the wheeling gulls, the gentle and not-so-gentle tides, the anglers beach-casting hook, line and sinker, the glorious sunsets with not a single red bus in sight, one might imagine bumping into the ghost of the portly doctor, who greets you with a condescending, beneficent smile, as taught at undertaker's school. Then with polite, Earl Grey-and-Victoria sponge cake taste and Palm Court music pleasing one's ears, he discreetly enquires as to *your* state of health and *your* wealth, before vanishing once again into a swirling mist.

You see, there is something remarkable about places like Eastbourne such as is not to be found outside England. The murderous likes of Bodkin Adams with his bespoke Purdey shotguns, a taste for the finest chocolate, patterned antique silver and other fine things, along with favouring a bit of dishy Eastbourne womanhood with his twinkling eye when he was of a mind to. And all this brought me back to considering Agatha Christie's Hercule Poirot … but I fear I am waxing lyrical, for that was an era long gone.

As I ambled back to my car, I found myself thinking a lot about Adams's deceased patients, bless them. About those rich, blue-rinsed, drugged-up-to-the-eyeballs souls; Edith Morrell's dahlias; the Rolls-Royce with a young carnival beauty in the back; mahogany chests stuffed with Georgian silverware; and all the long hours that the doctor spent by his fading patients' bedsides, smiling at them, comforting them as they moaned, groaned, bickered and complained, while he calculated how much more morphine they could take and whether they were worth more to him dead than alive. I do recall thinking about the elegantly dressed, stiff-backed 'Hannam of the Yard'. A number of cremations carried out with doubtful paperwork. The entire clusterfuck of a trial, the Crown's star medical witness being a morphia addict himself. And all this in the outwardly respectable surroundings of a once fashionable but fading seaside resort. It made me feel positively emotional.

Eventually I found a café. I ordered a meal guaranteed to blow my cholesterol levels into outer space and fell to reflecting on this extraordinary case. And here's the thing: I sort-of like Dr John Bodkin Adams. No doubt for *all* the wrong reasons, but he did have class, didn't he just?

I hope the reader may visit Eastbourne some day, although Dr John Bodkin Adams (1899–1983) rests in peace in Coleraine Cemetery, County Londonderry, Northern Ireland. That, however, is in the opposite direction to where we journey next, because after travelling some 70 miles north-east of Eastbourne, we arrive in Dover to take a cross-Channel ferry – if they are not on strike.

Bienvenue en France!

Dr Marcel André Henri Félix Petiot

Messieurs, je vous demande de ne pas regarder.
Ce ne sera pas joli. (Gentlemen, I ask you not to look. This
will not be pretty.)

– Dr Marcel Petiot to the witnesses at his execution
by guillotine at the Prison Pénitentiaire de Paris-la
Santé, 25 May 1946

Off with his head

The last place in the universe in which a tadpole could wish
to be born is France. Why? Well, you see, these tiny, slippery
swimming things grow into *grenouilles* (that's frogs to you and
me) and, what do the French eat lots of? Yes, indeed, frog's
legs. Chicken or duck legs I understand, even a leg of lamb,
but frog's legs?

And I will tell you who else would have wished that he
had never been born in France … the slippery little doctor

with whom we now make our acquaintance: Dr Marcel André Henri Félix Petiot.

For any readers with a fascination for Madame la Guillotine, aka 'the Lady', aka '*la Veuve*' (the Widow), aka '*le Rasoir National*' (the National Razor), aka 'Louisette' – or 'Louison' – after its inventor, surgeon and physiologist Antoine Louis, who designed it to bring about a painless execution, the guillotine is synonymous with the terrors of the French Revolution. And Henri Desfourneaux certainly knew more than a thing or two more than your author does about this lethal contraption – he being the *gentilhomme* who chopped off Petiot's head. It would be correct to say that Desfourneaux had guillotining in his blood. And a lot of other citizens' blood on him, too. What is certainly of interest is that the post of executioner in France was hereditary, being handed down from generation to generation along with the portable guillotine, which they probably kept in their garden sheds. There, I think that sets this chapter off on a high note. But before we sail off for Dr Petiot and his godforsaken crimes, I would be failing in my duty to readers if I did not mention that the most famous family name among all French executioners was Sanson.

The Sansons

In the 1780s, seven brothers from the Sanson family each held the post of executioner for a particular town. To distinguish themselves from one another they took the town's name for their own: 'Monsieur Sanson de Blois', 'Monsieur Sanson de Rennes', and so on. You should know that the English didn't have much inclination for the guillotine, although an early version had been knocked up out of bits and pieces and used in the town of Halifax during the sixteenth century as an alternative to beheading by axe or sword. It is not easy to imagine a guillotine being operated by a 'Monsieur Somebody de Budleigh Salterton' or a 'Monsieur Somebody de Basingstoke'. It doesn't bear thinking about, really, but that's the French for you. Okay, they did invent the pencil sharpener, stapler, hairdryer, medical bandages, the hot-air balloon, the bra, Brigitte Bardot and the cinema, so I must not be too hard on them, but to cut things short, when Dr Petiot went to his death there was only *one* executioner at work in the whole of France.

Social charm, professional prestige

Alfred Hitchcock once said that 'People are like wines. There are good vintages and bad vintages,' and Dr Marcel Petiot was certainly one of the latter. He had started out in life at 3 a.m. on 17 January 1897, in the provincial town of Auxerre, about a hundred miles south-east of Paris and the capital of the Yonne *département*, and developed a pathological aversion to keeping his hands off other people's property, which began with pilfering trifling objects from his schoolfellows.

Pilfering was something for which he became noted throughout his life, but little of import to us is known of his very early years, so we jump to the age of five, by which time he was already showing considerable intelligence and could read perfectly. At the same time, he also exhibited certain rather disturbing sadistic tendencies. Once he was found dipping the hind legs of his cat into a pot of boiling water. A few weeks later, the poor creature was found suffocated in his bed. On another occasion, a relative caught him poking out the eyes of trapped birds with a needle and watching them with amusement as they hurled themselves against the sides of their cage. As all animal lovers – bird, cat, dog, indeed any living creature, no matter how big or small, will say: 'That teenaged French shithead should have been guillotined aged 15 with no bones about it.' *Mais non*, because Marcel eventually ended up as a student doctor in a mental hospital, of all places.

So how did Petiot get from A to B because his school record was similarly punctuated with misdemeanours? On at least one occasion he went before the courts, only for the judge to rule that he was mentally unfit to stand trial. By the time he gained his baccalauréat (the equivalent of today's British A-levels), he had already been expelled twice. The following winter, two years into the First World War, aged 19, he joined the French Army and was sent to the Western Front. In 1917, he was gassed and wounded by shrapnel, and displayed further signs of mental instability. Yet, despite making a swift recovery, Petiot's only notable activity in an otherwise singly undistinguished military career was the stealing of much-needed drugs to sell on the black market, for which he was jailed. After being sent to a psychiatric hospital he was sent back to the Front in June 1918.

Le jeune docteur

After spending the remainder of the war in a mental hospital, Petiot was discharged from the army in 1919 as medically unfit. He was awarded a military pension despite having been court-martialled for stealing drugs – the charges later dismissed because he was considered to be insane. The following year, while still under observation by army psychiatrists, he somehow – and God only knows how – managed to gain a place as a medical student at a mental hospital in Évreux, about 60 miles west of Paris, and it was to his secret delight that he gained his doctorate while still certified mentally unstable by the authorities. *Mon Dieu!* Readers will surely agree that one could not make this up if one tried!

Évreux

A commune in the Eure *département*, Évreux dates back to Roman times. These days its many attractions include a splendid cathedral, and I must be honest with readers now ... I'm a foodie. True to gastronomic inclination, at no expense to those same readers I wanted to sample what was on offer in Évreux before I tried to track down some descendants of the moronic fools who awarded Petiot a medical degree from the Faculté de Médecine de Paris. With that said, perhaps all of them were long dead, but at the least I wanted to try the menus on offer, only to be thwarted when I learned that there was yet another ferry plus rail-in-the-Chunnel plus doctors'-plus-nurses' strike. I cancelled my trip to find myself in a British fish-and-chips place between two charity shops in Dover, and paying thrice the price of my entire planned trip to Évreux.

Setting himself up

Now armed with the necessary medical qualifications, Dr Petiot returned to his native *département* of the Yonne and set himself up in general practice in the sleepy town of Villeneuve-sur-Yonne. By most accounts he was an excellent doctor, displaying both charm and professional expertise, although it was not long before rumours about his private life began to circulate. Nevertheless, very much from the playbook of the late Dr Bodkin Adams and the more recently late Dr Harold Shipman, he soon built up a thriving practice.

In 1926 colourful Petiot announced his intention to run for Mayor of Villeneuve. After campaigning tirelessly as a Socialist, he was elected with a huge majority by voters reasoning along the lines of: 'If one cannot trust a doctor who in Heavens name can one trust?', a truism – misguided or otherwise – that sometimes resonates elsewhere in this book, and in many of us today as we seek or undergo medical treatment. The following year he cemented all outward appearances of respectability by marrying the beautiful Georgette Lablais, whose father was a rich *charcutier* and successful restaurateur, owner of the swanky Chez Marius in the rue de Bourgogne, Paris, a favourite haunt of politicians and other well-heeled, well-attired movers and shakers. Mayor Dr Petiot quickly gained some upper-class credentials. He also acquired a street reputation for unorthodoxy, for being his own man, and for getting things done, all of which made him a popular figure among the majority of the townsfolk.

Can the reader see Petiot now? Because I can: handsome; a self-declared war hero who had allegedly fought tooth and nail to be pulled from the carnage of rat-infested trench warfare with some gassing and shrapnel wounds here and there, to emerge shell-shocked as a doctor selflessly dedicated to the saving and not the taking of lives. He has become the elected Mayor of Villeneuve with an established medical practice in the town. Aged 30, he has married petite 23-year-old Georgette, with their only child, a son, born a year later. He's a mover and shaker, is our handsome Marcel. He's our ass-kicking, upper-class-mimicking Socialist who knows it's not appropriate to order *Escargots sur purée de pommes de terre avec sauce à la menthe en accompagnement* – the eloquent, if over-the-top French way of saying 'Snails on mashed potato with mint sauce on the side'. But ... oh dear ... this uppityness also made him many enemies. In 1930, they seized upon a chance for revenge when Petiot was given a suspended prison sentence for misappropriation of funds. In his position of trust he was ideally situated for dipping his sticky fingers at regular intervals into the community chest to supplement his now slowly disintegrating medical practice.

Le Téflon docteur

It is now 1931. Marcel Petiot is forced to resign his post as mayor over mounting allegations of negligence, but although the municipal accounts were subsequently found to contain severe irregularities no further action was taken against him. Undaunted, this irrepressible charlatan used his spare time to get himself elected as a Socialist general councillor. At the end of that year, in a gesture of supreme defiance towards his critics, he narrowly missed re-election as Mayor of Villeneuve.

We now move to January 1933 (some accounts say 1935), when Petiot decided to relocate himself and his family to Paris. After his sudden departure from Villeneuve it was discovered that he had arranged for the local mains electricity to be directed straight to his house, thereby allowing him the use of free current at the taxpayers' expense; the details of how he achieved this being redacted from all documents relating to the case because of the high probability that 99 per cent of customers might, and possibly would, follow suit. But here is where 'Teflon' comes into the picture, because nothing of any substance ever seemed to stick until, eventually – and it was a *long* eventually – Petiot was stripped of his general councillor's office in his absence. Was he stripped of his licence to practise medicine? Of course not; indeed, for many years afterwards, and again just like Drs Adams and, much later, Shipman, his former patients in Villeneuve-sur-Yonne remembered Petiot with affection and gratitude, for he wore his white medical coat as though it were a suit of gossip-deflecting armour.

Sticks and stones may break my bones but words will never hurt me

In addition to the aforementioned public misdemeanours, ugly rumours abounded about Petiot's private life. For instance, soon after he took up residence in Villeneuve he was accused of stealing property from the house he rented. Citing his military service during the First World War, he defended himself on the grounds that he was a 'certified lunatic' – a defence he would use on several other occasions. Once again, one really could not make this up if one tried, but Dr Petiot did, and succeeded.

In 1926, his housekeeper and mistress – a pregnant Louisette Delaveau – disappeared in mysterious circumstances. She was never seen again. Well, that's not quite correct. While most of her remained missing, her head was found floating in the Seine. After being brought to court on a charge of murdering Louisette, Petiot was asked about his relationship with her. He gave a flippant reply that was to mark his contemptuous attitude to the court: 'She told everyone she was having sexual intercourse with me. In fact, I declined the honour, your Honour.' This retort brought howls of laughter from the public gallery, to which he bowed graciously, waving to the attending public and press, with the only person not laughing being the judge, who kept a judicially tight lip as the accused walked free.

In 1930, Petiot was again questioned by local police investigating a particularly bloody case of arson and murder involving one of his patients, a Madame Debauve. Several witnesses swore they had seen him leaving the crime scene but nothing further came of the case. He was also linked to the death of the chief witness in the case – also a patient of his – but Petiot, blessed with the gift of the gab, slipped out of these charges too.

Dr Petiot treats, but does not exploit, his patients.
                        – Dr Marcel Petiot's prospectus

After he had moved to 'Gay Paree', the mother of a dead child patient complained to the coroner that her daughter had been given a drug overdose. Other rumours flourished that Petiot was carrying out abortions and supplying drugs to addicts in return for cash, but now ensconced in Paris, he set about building up a new medical practice with characteristic energy, efficiency and dogged ruthlessness. Taking an apartment at 66 rue de Caumartin in the busy Gare Saint-Lazare district, Petiot placed a brass plaque outside the building and began circulating a glitzy, cure-all prospectus. Despite his unprofessional, not to say criminal, conduct, he was never struck off the medical register; indeed, in 1936, he was appointed *médecin d'état-civil*, with the authority to issue death certificates.

Petiot's kind of medical quackery and out-and-out medical fraud were not illegal in France at that time – such things were a matter of conscience. The President of the Court at his later trial scathingly referred to 'these prospectuses of a quack', to which Petiot cockily replied, 'Thank you for the advertisement.' Nevertheless, his medical flimflammery was such a success that Petiot soon had around 3,000 patients – many of whom would later attest to his skill and conscientiousness as a doctor. Moreover, he managed to amass a considerable fortune, although this sociopathic doctor still found it impossible to stay out of trouble for very long.

Petiot now plunged even deeper into all manner of profiteering. The year 1935 saw him arrested on suspicion of prescribing heroin to the aforementioned drug addicts. He was released due to lack of evidence. In 1936 he was arrested for shoplifting in a bookshop, having assaulted the store detective who had apprehended him. At the subsequent court hearing he pleaded insanity, quoting his war-service disability and subsequent regular psychiatric examinations – which in truth were few and far between, if indeed they happened at all. At one point he was treated for kleptomania, yet in the shoplifting case a sympathetic 'See no evil, hear no evil' bunch of proverbial juror monkeys found him '*non coupable*'. They literally patted him on the back when he told them that the entire matter had shaken him *so* badly that he would admit himself to a private sanatorium near Paris for seven months, at his own expense.

Moving on

Upon his discharge from the sanatorium, Petiot was approached by a wealthy Jew named Monsieur Gubisnow in his capacity as a medical consultant and enquired if there was any way he could help him and his family escape the excesses of the German Occupation that had followed the fall of France in June 1940. This the doctor agreed to arrange for an enormous price. 'But what is wealth compared with freedom of fear?' as Brian Lane and Wilfred Gregg write in *The New Encyclopedia of Serial Killers*: 'The most that could be said for the arrangement that followed, if the Gubisnow family found the occupying Nazis would hold no more terror; they had found an enemy infinitely worse – the greedy little doctor who had spiked their typhoid injections with strychnine.'

Over the following three years, Petiot murdered at least 27 people desperate to escape from the Nazis, including Jews and Resistance members. No doubt he would have continued to do so to line his own pockets if it hadn't been for some greasy black smoke coming from the furnace in which he disposed of the unwanted by-products of his thriving enterprise – more of which later.

In 1938, the final blot on Petiot's copybook prior to the Occupation of France by the Nazis came about when he found himself in trouble with a tax inspector for declaring less than one-tenth of his estimated annual income. Subsequent very complicated and lengthy investigations into his business affairs showed him to be the owner of 'several properties in Paris', and the bewildered taxman wrote in his report that he had 'found it hard to understand how an ordinary general practitioner could have amassed such a fortune *and* own a 15-bedroomed house at 21 rue le Sueur'. By the end of the Second World War, the taxman would have his answer.

Chamber of Horrors

The trial of Dr Marcel Petiot, which began on 18 March 1946, was, next to the Liberation in August and September 1944, the greatest event in post-war France. People had been starved of organically homegrown excitement during the German Occupation. Yes, Adolf Hitler had played a fleeting visit in June 1940, just after the French surrender, to look at the Eiffel Tower and a few other landmarks before returning to Germany. True, half the German Army had rolled up to conquer much of Europe, with sundry Allied battles aplenty too, but now the citizens' *bon appetit* was whetted by lurid press stories of Dr Petiot's activities. All the newspapers carried horrific details of the discoveries at 21 rue le Sueur, which helped create a sensational atmosphere, such as this headline:

Le Dr Marcel Petiot était une GRANDE nouvelle!

The indictment against Dr Petiot was not, I think we can agree, of a delicate nature. Far from it, for it contained the names of 27 persons whose bodies had been found at Petiot's 'death house': No. 21 rue le Sueur. The discovery had actually come about two years before the trial, in March 1944, when a badly smoking chimney directed attention to the property. But this smoke reeked of death, of which Europe had seen plenty by then. By now the war against Germany had turned in the Allies' favour, with the Normandy Landings only three months in the future, so there was more to preoccupy people than smoke belching all day from the chimney of No. 21 rue le Sueur – a side street in the fashionable Étoile district of Paris and close to the Arc de Triomphe. So, with all that taken into consideration, one might have thought that a Madame Marcaise – the occupier of No. 22 – would have had far more interesting things on her mind than complaining about greasy smuts that settled on her furniture even when the windows were closed. But the smoke did not dissipate, and nor did the lady's annoyance. By early evening on Saturday, 11 March, her husband, fearing that their neighbour's chimney might catch fire, rang the bell at No. 21. There was no reply. He telephoned the police.

Gendarmes

I never fail to be astounded, in recounting these terrible crimes, by the stupidity of the offenders, great or small, and Dr Marcel Petiot – a medical serial murderer on the grand scale – takes the proverbial biscuit. Police soon arrived at No. 21 to learn that the owner was living nearby. The doctor was contacted and said that he would come at once with the keys, but after kicking their heels for thirty minutes, the law could wait no longer. The cops called the fire brigade, who quickly forced entry to le premises. Guided by an appalling smell, the firefighters reached the basement, where they found the source of the offensive smoke – an iron stove fuelled with

... wait for it ... human bits and pieces. The floor around the stove was littered with parts of bodies: arms and legs, some with flesh flayed off, and corpses in every conceivable state of dismemberment. I mean, can readers imagine that scene? – because I can't. Nevertheless, while the police stood open-mouthed, Petiot arrived on a green bicycle. Without revealing his identity to the first officers he met, he rapidly assessed the situation and then positively swelled with pride as he proclaimed: 'What you will see in there are executed Germans and traitors and they are entrusted to me by *la Résistance*,' of which he maintained he was a member, and was in fear of the Gestapo.

The mere mention of the dreaded Gestapo made the police flinch, so, in a manner reminiscent of Inspector Jacques Clouseau in Blake Edwards' farcical *Pink Panther* films, the gendarmes allowed the patriotic man to cycle off before conducting a thorough search of the premises. In an outhouse they discovered a heap of quick lime-covered corpses. Inside the house was a medical consulting room joined by a passage to a mysterious, triangular-shaped room with thick, soundproof walls, a false door and a spyhole. Its purpose could only be imagined, but this was definitely not what one would expect to find at a normal doctor's surgery, was it? Meanwhile, where was Dr Petiot? He had got on his bike and pedalled away, and thus was not on hand to provide any explanations at all, *merci beaucoup*.

Grim jigsaw puzzle

At the mortuary the gruesome finds were examined by doctors. They had 34 recognisable limbs to work with.

Where each limb went, fitted to who and to what other bit, was initially anyone's guess. Bone fragments found everywhere totalled 33 pounds (15kg) of charred remains. There were a number of scalps, some with hair attached, others without, leaving the doctors scratching their own heads in concert and pretty much clueless about either the time or manner of death. But *maybe* there was something the experts *could* work on: the technique for dismemberment had been the same in every case – the collarbone, shoulder bones and arms had been removed in one piece, indisputably the work of a skilled dissector. I recognise that these details might somewhat spoil a reader's evening meal, but some good news is about to come our way. Petiot was eventually found in November 1944. It had not been difficult to lie low during the turmoil of the last days of the Occupation and the Liberation of France, for the last German forcres had left the country by the end of September. Indeed, Petiot graciously helped the detectives by revealing himself. Like an imbecile, he wrote a letter to the newspaper *Résistance*, refuting a claim that he had been a pro-Nazi collaborator. In this way his blatantly false patriotic motives led to his being arrested and charged with 27 counts of murder. This claim was a ruse invented by the police to flush him out. It worked.

The list of victims – which included names like 'Jo the Boxer', 'François the Corsican' and 'Paulette the Chinese' – had a ring of fantasy about it. The evidence which followed, coupled with Petiot's conduct, was equally bizarre. Clutching a large dossier, cocksure of manner, the doctor admitted responsibility for killing 19 of those named. They were, he alleged, all traitors and collaborators. He denied murdering the other eight despite the fact that their corpses had been found in his house. For good measure the garrulous dissembler confessed to killing another 44 people — also traitors, he said — making him the self-confessed serial killer of sixty-three victims.

Trial

My trial will be wonderful and will make everyone laugh.

— Dr Marcel Petiot: to his guards at La Santé Prison prior to his trial

Petiot's long trial inside the imposing, packed, tense and often in an uproar courtroom in the Palais de Justice (the Parisian equivalent of the Old Bailey) was one of the most extraordinary in French history, and at times was conducted in an atmosphere of a low *comédie judiciaire*. With his life's history made public, Petiot now faced his accusers. Avocat Général Pierre Dupin was the state's prosecuting attorney, but additionally, each of the victims' families was entitled to its own lawyer — in the event there were 12 present who were permitted to intervene at any time their particular case came up. This confusing state of affairs was not helped by the weight of the evidence, which amounted to several tons of material that had to be brought to the courtroom by a convoy of lorries. Yet Petiot and his lawyer — the able and charismatic Maître René Floriot — were so imperturbable that at times they dozed peacefully through the proceedings amidst a bustling flock of black-gowned assistants and courtroom staff.

The greatest criminal lawyer in France

The Petiot trial was the latest in a long line of celebrated cases for the 44-year-old Maître Floriot who, at the time, was highly regarded as *le plus grand avocat criminaliste en France*. A powerful, imposing figure, he rejected the speechifying style of defences favoured by his contemporaries, adopting instead a direct, logical approach based on a thorough mastery of the facts. (The name Floriot derives from Italian and Portuguese, originally from Latin *florius,* a variant of *florus*, 'blooming, flowering', which is also the root of the word 'florist' for a flower-seller.) Floriot specialised in defending near-impossible cases. Previously he had represented the treasonous Henri Lafont, a collaborator who headed the Carlingue, the collaborationist Vichy government's force of auxiliaries to the German security services, including the Gestapo, in Occupied France. Pre-war, Lafont had been a shadowy underworld figure, and during the Occupation he helped establish the Carlingue, which operated under his leadership from 1941 to 1944.

Although the defence would prove unsuccessful, Floriot had argued with some misguided precision that since Lafont had accepted German citizenship during the war it was, therefore, incorrect to try him in France. This was a losing wicket from the start, and the 42-year-old Lafont was executed by firing squad at Fort de Montrouge in Arcueil, in the southern suburbs of Paris, on 26 December 1944, alongside corrupt policeman Pierre Bonny and former football international-turned-criminal Alexandre Villaplane.

Je vais te casser les dents (I'm going to knock your teeth
out).

— Maître Véron: to Marcel Petiot at trial

I should explain that I will do just about *anything* to get my
books read in France and to curry some favour I even try
hard to do the translation thing. I even turn up, when asked,
for French TV, radio and podcasts, all of which can be a bit
of a bind because not a single Euro ever finds its way into
my wallet. Readers may know, too, that all too frequently I
take (well-deserved, I feel) potshots at our American cousins
across the Pond, but the French … well, take stock of what
happened next with Dr Petiot.

Mon Dieu avec des cloches et des sifflets (and if that doesn't
promote this book in France nothing will), because if it
hadn't been such a farce it would make for … well … farce.
On the first day of the trial, the prosecution made references
to Petiot's misdemeanours before the war, which Petiot
confidently dismissed, managing to make everyone look
stupid in the process. The clever, dynamic Maître Véron, who
represented the relatives of Marthe Khait and Yvan Drefus,
was able to catch the accused out on his supposed early career
in the Résistance because Véron had been a member himself,
saying: 'Docteur Petiot, I know more about *la Résistance* than
you ever will,' but the court's attention was soon diverted
and his opportunity to press the point slipped by.

On the second day Véron renewed his attack, only to be
denounced by Petiot as a 'defender of traitors and Jews'. A
furious Véron threatened to knock Petiot's teeth out there
and then.

The end of day three saw the trial descend into an even lower *comédie judiciaire* when the presiding magistrate, Président de la Tribunal Michel Leser, told an American reporter that Petiot was 'a monster' in front of two jurors. Nor did things get any better on day four when Petiot was questioned about a seven-year-old boy from the Kneller family. This important point should have given the prosecution a chance to blast Petiot's defence wide apart: 'How could a child so young be a traitor?' But this issue degenerated into total confusion as Dupin and Leser got their facts mixed up and began bickering among themselves as only the French can.

On day five the court was taken to inspect No. 21 rue le Sueur, and where there was much excitement as Petiot appeared to collapse on being confronted with the lime pit that had previously been overflowing with corpses. As it turned out, he had eaten almost nothing for three whole days and was merely faint with hunger, and so the case dragged on from being bargain-basement *comédie judiciaire* to the serious business of convicting a serial killer. As much as I would love to add more, Dr Marcel Petiot ended up having his head chopped off by our old friend Monsieur Desfourneaux de Paris.

> For the first time in my life I saw a man leaving death row, if not dancing, at least showing perfect calm.
> – Dr Albert Paul, Chief Coroner

Marcel Petiot killed for financial gain, as evidenced by his amassing a fortune in cash: 47 suitcases jam-packed with his victims' personal belongings, jewellery, 29 suits, 79 dresses and five fur coats, and that did not include the fees he charged for supposedly helping desperate people to escape Nazi-occupied France. His end came on the morning of 25 May 1946, at la Santé prison. As was then customary in France, the condemned man was informed only half an hour or so before execution, although some 36 hours beforehand, Floriot had managed to pass on a message warning his client of his impending fate. When the *juge d'instruction* who had handled the case looked as though he was going to faint as Petiot was led from his cell, the prisoner jokingly said that since he was a doctor, he could give the judge an injection to revive him. Still protesting his innocence and his easy conscience, Petiot allowed the priest to say a prayer over him for the sake of his wife.

At just after five in the morning, a relaxed and perfectly calm Petiot was led to the portable guillotine, where a small basket had been placed to catch his head. Those present reported that the blade fell at 5.05 a.m. As his head rolled into the basket, the doctor's eyes flickered open. He was still smiling.

Mad or evil?

Even to try to cover Petiot's life from cradle to bloody wicker basket in one chapter would be a hopeless task. For the reader interested in this man without scruples, devoid of all moral sensibility *and* a serial murdering doctor, a great deal of information about him can be found online. Nevertheless, in 1963, Ronald Seth – who had been a British agent in Paris in 1944 (although his service in SOE was at best highly equivocal) – published a book entitled *Petiot: Victim of Chance*. Seth believed that Petiot: '... contrary to the most widely held views, was a member of the Resistance group. I believe that this group was a Communist Resistance Group. I believe that the reason why Petiot steadfastly refused to name the members of the group was because Communists had threatened to harm his wife and his son if he did, and he loved his wife and son.' It is, however, a theory that has now been firmly debunked, as well as being tempered by the fact that Seth was a rabid anti-Communist.

For my part, I am inclined to look at Dr Petiot's life as a whole, as disgustingly fascinating a character as he was. We learn that in the months preceding his trial he was examined by three psychiatrists, all of whom attested that he was perfectly sane, merely wearing the persona of an insane person, as he had done many times previously to suit his own ends when it was convenient to him – a psychopathic doctor, indeed. So how did he come to be guilty of murder most foul? At face value, Petiot was a highly intelligent man who had made *something* of a sucess in the medical profession and in local politics. As doctor or mayor he presented with a considerable degree of charm and, on more than one occasion, was seen to put his avowed Socialist principles into practice. One of his impoverished patients in Paris, giving evidence at Petiot's trial, told the court how the doctor had treated him without charge, and had visited his sick family on a Sunday, which was almost unheard of for a wealthy city physician.

Petiot also appeared to have been a devoted husband and father. His wife swore that although he would become angry when she tried to meddle in his private affairs, he never once treated her with anything other than the 'utmost gentleness', and the family was 'always well provided for'. In this regard, Petiot was, and *is*, like so many serial killers who murder for *whatever* type of gain. Outwardly they present as 'normal', even as loving, caring husbands – Dennis Rader, aka 'BTK', being just one example.[11] It's their camouflage – an outward facade of normalcy. Behind this mask, however, Marcel Petiot showed clear signs of a fully emerged psychopath, which the medical examining board who issued him with a licence to treat the sick didn't spot – something that almost beggars belief.

From a relatively early age Petiot was known to sleepwalk and to wet the bed. These two traits, together with cruelty to animals and a love of fire and arson, we know today are all red flags hoisted to signal perhaps a more dangerous person to emerge later in life. During adolesence, delinquency gave way to *apparent* mental disorder, and at the time of his discharge from the military Petiot was reported to be suffering from fits of depression, amnesia and melancholia. As a doctor in Villeneuve-sur-Yonne he was exposed as a kleptomaniac, and of course at the time of his trial he had accumulated masses of stuff for much of which he had no use. His run-ins with council officials, the French tax authorities and the Paris police showed him to be a complusive liar, yet *still* he maintained his place on the medical register. We might attempt to excuse this, given the Occupation of France by Germany for five long years, with the nation well under the Nazi jackboot, but there was more. Later, the discovery in his consulting rooms

---

11 The initials stand for 'bind, torture, kill', Rader's modus operandi. He was convicted of at least ten murders committed in Kansas between 1974 and 1991. He remains in prison in the USA, aged 80.

of a collection of genitalia in specimen bottles, together with a carved wooden beast sporting an oversized phallus, undeniably hinted at strange sexual obsessions.

Le menteur expert (The expert liar)

Maybe the most revealing insight into the workings of Petiot's mind comes from his dealings with the police, who arrested him and those present at his trial. In all those instances he treated figures with apparent power over him with utter contempt and derision, as though he found it impossible to recognise any greater authority than himself. If such was the case, Petiot's psychiatrists would have been regarded as authority figures to be duped and deceived at will.

Given his undoubted intelligence, his proven capacity for lies and deception, and his year learning psychiatric-speak in a mental institution, is it not reasonable to suppose that Petiot faked his early so-called 'madness' simply to demonstrate to himself, and perhaps to the medical profession at large, how clever he was – as well as to get his own way? In similar vein Peter Sutcliffe, the Yorkshire Ripper, feigned insanity for many decades, conning the psychiatrists at the high-security hospital Broadmoor into believing that he was mentally ill when nothing could have been further from the truth. My final question, however, is this: had it not been for the Second World War, would Petiot have killed as many as he did? Yes, it is correct to say that pre-war, he had already committed murder, so by any account he had already established himself as a killer, and being the arch-opportunist that he was, the war would provide him with very rich pickings indeed.

Gâteau à la crème, ça vous tente?

Dr Harold Frederick Shipman, aka 'Dr Death'

The police complain I'm boring. No mistresses,
no home abroad, no money in Swiss banks, I'm normal.
If that is boring, I am.

– HAROLD SHIPMAN: UNDATED LETTER

Earlier in this book I cited William Wills' description of the commonest forms of motive:

- the desire of avenging some real or fanciful wrong;
- of getting rid of a rival or obnoxious connection;
- of escaping from the pressure of pecuniary or other obligation;
- of obtaining plunder or other coveted objects;
- of preserving reputation, or of gratifying some other selfish or malignant passion.

Thus far in this grim catalogue of murder most foul some, if not all, those points have come into play, so motive has to be worth considering as we examine the terrible crimes committed by others employed in the hallowed medical professions.

Our American cousins have invented almost everything – or so they often claim – but they did (probably) invent the hamburger, so let's give them credit for that. As for the world's most prolific medical serial killer ... this dubious accolade belongs to the UK.

He [Shipman] was a pathological liar with access to death-dealing drugs ... the perfect predator ... the perfect killing machine.

> – Christopher Berry-Dee: in *The Biggest Serial Killer of All Time* (episode of *Born to Kill?,* television documentary series) (video online)

I will not spend long going over Dr Shipman's case for these reasons:

- it has been gossiped about, written about, televised, filmed, red-top newspaper headlined about repeatedly, ad infinitum ad nauseam, since he was arrested in September 1998 and convicted in January 2000;
- doing so would suck so much literary oxygen out of this book that the remaining word count would be reduced to a 'Conclusion' covering a mere line of text at best;

- when I appeared as a consultant for the Channel
  4 documentary series *Born to Kill?*, I more or less
  said what I wanted to say back then. Therefore,
  it would be superfluous for me to recite yet again
  the narrative of the so-called 'Angel of Death', aka
  'Doctor Death', from cradle to suicide by hanging
  at HMP Wakefield on 13 January 2004.

Dr Shipman had sworn the aforementioned Hippocratic Oath, yet he went on to murder up to 250 of his patients in and around Todmorden in West Yorkshire and Hyde in Greater Manchester. Yes, you read that correctly – *250*, give or take. Published in January 2005, the final report of the Shipman Inquiry – chaired by Dame Janet Smith – concluded: '[This issue] raises troubling questions about the powers and responsibilities of the medical community in Britain and about the adequacy of procedures for certifying sudden death.' You betcha it did, for Shipman's crimes put the murders committed by Dr John Bodkin Adams into the shade. If truth be told, Shipman's murders were guided by Dr Adams' pseudo euthanasia medical playbook ... a sort of GP's guide to murdering patients and getting off scot-free, although without 'Fred' or 'Freddie' (as Shipman was also called) getting his hands on a Rolls-Royce, or very much else except some of his victims' jewellery, so far as can be told.

We can also discount anything Agatha Christie/Hercule Poirot-ish about the murderous bearded Shipman, who was as dull as the frontage of Bodkin Adams' grey-fronted Kent Lodge. Many who knew Fred Shipman – those who are still alive, that is – recall that he wore a tweed jacket, a Clydella or Viyella check shirt, cavalry-twill trousers, and brown, down-at-heel brogues. Some said he 'smelt crusty', too, but his elderly female patients seem to have looked forward to Dr Shipman paying them a call. 'He is such a nice man, is Doctor Harold,' many of them would say, almost in unison, with some adding, 'He loves a cup of tea, you know.'

What maketh this monster?

Over three decades, Dr Shipman murdered countless times before he was arrested on 7 September 1998. The case is truly unusual yet quintessentially British: as True Brit as unpredictable weather, red postboxes, holes in socks, quaint market towns and civil parishes like Todmorden and Hyde, and so on.

Born on 14 January 1946 into a working-class family on the Bestwood Council Estate in Nottingham, Harold Jr was the second of three children of lorry driver Harold Shipman Sr and Vera, both devout Methodists. Fred was a slightly aloof child; bright yet sullen, given to maintaining a distance between himself and his contemporaries. When growing up, he was an accomplished rugby player in youth leagues; and passed his 11 Plus in 1957 with the encouragement of his Bible-thumping mother, who wanted to lead him along the path of righteousness and thus into the light. Vera wanted Fred Jr to be special; moreover, she thought he was *very special* when, through his success in the 11 Plus exam, he gained entrance to Nottingham's prestigious High Pavement Grammar School that year.

His [Shipman's parents], like my parents, like lots and lots of other working-class parents, would have been so proud that 'our boy is going to the grammar school'.
– Bob Studholme: schoolboy friend of Shipman

While a young person may academically excel in junior years, the same may not be true upon entrance to higher education, where the pressures among peers from perhaps the more competitive pupils raised from better socioeconomic backgrounds can take a toll, so Fred's career at High Pavement was largely unspectacular. He went from being one of the brightest children at his previous school to a run-of-the-mill student among so many other brighter lads. It is here – although there is not much of value to be gained in considering the development of a child later metamorphosing into a serial killer – that I look at a young boy who'd had it drummed into him by his mother that he was special, *very* special, and that he could excel in everything he turned his mind to. Vera wanted her boy to escape the drudgery of working-class life. I envisage her not wanting her precious son to become a lorry driver like his dad or to spend the rest of his life on a council estate, where he would achieve next to nothing. What parent doesn't want their child to succeed? So we can't fault Vera Shipman for that, and I can sort of see into her head at this point because she loved her son, who was the brightest of her three children.

'Being the middle child with [older sister] Pauline who had left school at 15 and was no great academic, and Clive [younger brother] wasn't as bright as his brother either,' says Brian Whittle, journalist and co-author, with Jean Ritchie, of *Prescription for Murder* (2000).

As schoolboy friend Mike Heath said in the 2005 TV documentary series *Born to Kill?*: 'Fred was very serious. He had to work harder than most others and, I think… umm… I think that he had a real respect for his family, his parents. He thought that they had made a real effort, a sacrifice in paying for his grammar-school education.' Yet there can be a flip-side to this issue. At this point in the doctor's narrative I do not think that Harold Shipman was born to kill, and there is no suggestion that he underwent anything other than a standard working-class upbringing, if indeed there is such a thing. His prescribing of deadly amounts of morphine came much later, but from where did the genesis for committing murder most foul spring?

Undoubtedly, Vera Shipman was a controlling mother. The devout Methodist side to her character dictated strict adherence to the doctrine of nonconformity to the world, reflected by the Methodist's traditional standards of a commitment to teetotalism, proscription of gambling, regular attendance at class meetings and weekly observance of the Friday fast which, when taken in small doses, might work well for some, but not for those whose Friday nights are spent out on the lash followed by the inevitable hungover Saturdays. There can be no doubt that while his mother wanted her son to focus exclusively on his studies, Fred was not fully integrated into the real world.

In the Shipman episode of *Born to Kill?*, Dr David Holmes opines: 'He was allowed to build up fantasies of power, or fantasies that might have had a sexual connotation because Fred was never really allowed to grow socially, or sexually, or normally. For instance, Vera decided who Fred played with and when. She wanted to distinguish him from other boys and she was more ambitious for Harold than her other children.' On Shipman's part, it has been said by several of his former school pals that he simply 'slotted in; almost a broody non-person who was there and he followed the rules, never causing a problem'.

Tragedy in the family

On Friday, 21 June 1960, when Fred was just 17, Vera died of lung cancer, an illness he'd kept strangely quiet from his classmates. The family GP had visited the house regularly in the weeks before her death, giving welcome painkilling injections of morphine in ever-increasing doses. The following Monday, Fred met classmate Michael Heath on his way to school and told him his tragic news as though it were nothing of great significance. When asked how he felt about it, Fred said: 'I just put on my running shoes and went for a run.' 'It had been pouring with rain that day so he must have been saturated,' recalled Heath.

'Young Shipman grieved in a *very strange* way,' emphasises author Brian Whittle. 'It was an amazing thing but he must have been going through hell for months before.'

'It was Fred who sat with his mother and waited for the doctor to come. It was Fred who was at his mother's bedside when she died, which came as a traumatic shock to him,' the local GP recalled. One very interesting aspect is that Fred had not shown even the smallest interest in medicine, or mentioned that he had wanted to become a doctor, until *after* his mother's death. There can be little doubt, however, that a parallel connection between watching his mother being injected with morphia to ease her pain and his use of it to *execute* so many elderly people existed in his developing psychopathology.

'Execute?' Well, let's say it as it is: as in giving someone a lethal injection. Shipman became a medical executioner and not, as others might say tongue-in-cheek, 'a caring general practitioner putting his victims to sleep to ease their pain and suffering'. My point of reference here will be Texas or Florida, where the authorities also inject lethal substances into criminals found guilty of murder in the first degree – some of them patently innocent, it is also correct to say. As distasteful as it is to say so, Dr Harold Shipman was a real-life 'Doctor Death', yet his patients were in awe of him. They trusted their crusty family physician and, for the life of these dear souls, they never tolerated a word being said against him.

Sense of relief

I'm not going into 'shrink mode' here. I'm no trick-cyclist and I wouldn't know the difference between a Freudian slip and a banana split, so there is no intention to mislead with some suppositional Jung-cognisant psychobabble with a seasoning of Gestalt thrown in, but to my mind it is not difficult to understand young Fred Shipman's determination to succeed at all he set his mind to. This much has been established, but at what cost? As I often do in my books, I ask the reader to imagine being a young kid of Fred's age: working-class, raised by devout Methodists; dad a lorry driver; mum a controlling matriarch who demands that you *must* excel over your less gifted siblings. Parents not allowing you to mix with your peers in a healthy, social way; in effect isolating you from your peer group to focus 100 per cent on your studies and not much else. In a way I can identify with Mr and Mrs Shipman. They wanted Fred to stay out of trouble because at around this time many of the kids on this council estate were energetically following in their parents' footsteps; that is,inter alia, being frequent attendees at the local magistrates' court and fiddling the dole.

At that age the mind is still developing, it is being formatted and programmed to do your best, to *be* the best, with failure not an option because your parents have made what you perceive as a great sacrifice to raise you as the Methodist faith dictates. In other words, you owe your parents BIG TIME! Yes, congratulations because you won a place at a prestigious grammar school, well done you, but at what cost? Of course Mum and Dad are thrilled to bits. They are *so* proud of you. They tell all their Bestwood council-estate neighbours what a special son they have: 'Our Freddie will not be like the Joneses' brat who's just chucked a brick through the police station's window. Fred will go far, you know. He'll never just be working class like us, we will see to that, bless him.'

So, being a bright kid in a public junior school is one thing. Being thrust into a prestigious grammar school is something else entirely, because these seats of learning up the educational ante at a financial cost to parents – some of them by no means wealthy – but there is also emotional stress to the pupil who has an even more competitive peer group to contend with. In this regard, Fred now dropped from being considered a bright kid at junior school to a mediocre pupil at High Pavement Grammar School. This educational slippage is reflected in his school reports of the time, with which Vera was none too pleased, demanding even more effort from him.

I am not going weepy-soft over Freddie Shipman. Honest to God, I'm not, because what a murdering son of a bitch this doc-monster turned out to be. However, it is the fact that because Shipman metamorphosed into one of the most sickeningly evil physicians in world history – and he was organically home-grown on English soil, after all – and hailed from a profession that trained him from medical school onwards, that requires me to come to a conclusion that many will probably not like one bit. It is that I feel that Fred Shipman was well-pleased when his mother died, for what died with her was a restrictive regime and all the pressures upon him to succeed at any cost. Yes, I understand that this conclusion will truly upset some Methodists, or anyone else with God's compassion imprinted in their hearts, but here's the thing: Fred had only mentioned in passing to his school peers that his mother was 'sick'. There is a coldness to that, as if he saw the weight of parental pressure being lifted, although it took a while for the realisation to dawn on him.

The family's GP noted that at the moment of Vera's death Fred 'became very emotional'. Well, seeing one's mother – love her or not – exhale a death rattle and expire, with a cloth then tied under her chin, is not most people's idea of having a happy time. Beyond that, however, there is something else to consider, which I know may seem cruel. Fred's weeks of running at all hours of the day and night in all weathers as his mind grappled with this tragic loss (as many commentators have it), peer pressures at school, the mental strain of trying to please his demanding mother and her death, *may* have come as a great shock to him, yet his grief was fleeting. In other ways her demise brought him a refreshing sense of freedom and relief. Fred was now entering a new world. The running allowed him to get his head together, to get what upset existed out of his system.

Nevertheless, there had to be more than a causal link between dying and later becoming a physician. Dr Holmes believes that Fred might have had 'inexplicable feelings that were associated with the death event of his mother and suddenly felt that he was in that role, that of controller of life and death'. But perhaps we can sense something else here. It may be that he believed that he owed much to his mother, who then died before he could achieve the success that she had always wanted for him. Maybe, and I'm pushing my luck here, he had grown to despise his mother and enjoyed watching her slip off this mortal coil. This is all supposition, of course, but tucked away somewhere in Fred Shipman's mind was a growing disposition to kill – as in killing other elderly and sick people in his mother's image.

I might add that this is not such a crazy thing to suggest, because several of the nurses we will examine later murdered elderly patients because they despised them for being weak and complaining, Nurse Colin Norris among them. Indeed, there have been countless less famous or notorious serial killers who have killed old people, whom they viewed as being in the image of their strict, domineering mothers or grandmothers.

To kill or not to kill?

Fred Shipman failed to get the grades at A-level needed to study medicine at Leeds Medical School, yet he persisted.

After resitting his exams, he was accepted a year later in 1965, so did he decide to become a doctor to honour the Hippocratic Oath to help his patients – or with the intention of killing them?

After qualifying, Shipman went on to Pontefract Infirmary to train as a junior doctor. In the interim, the good-looking Fred fell in with an art student named Primrose Oxtoby. They met on a bus, of all places – no Agatha Christie glamour and sophistication to be found on the No. 9 – and very soon Primrose became pregnant. This was the first time in his life that Fred had been reckless, having been freed of his mother's shackles. The couple were married in a register office on 5 November 1966. There isn't even a single photograph in existence of their wedding, and this wedlock was born out of strict Methodist propriety – not love – so we see his late mother's influence controlling Fred yet again. Twelve months later, he was duly licensed to practice medicine.

Disturbingly, from his training as a doctor onwards, countless medical people, including psychiatrists and psychologists, never showed the faintest suspicion that they had a multiple-murdering doctor in their midst for more than 30 years.

According to the findings of the Shipman Inquiry, the doctor first committed murder at Pontefract Infirmary, when he killed a four-year-old girl, Susie Garfitt, who was dying. Her mother left the room to visit the hospital café, saying to him: 'Be kind to her.' He *may* have pretended to himself that this was a kind of euthanasia, that by killing Susie he was being kind to her and the mother. Later in this book we will look into the cases of Beverley Allitt and Lucy Letby, to see whether any parallels between these cases are to be found, but sadly, Susie did not die in her mother's arms, as the latter had wished, so even back then Shipman displayed a signal lack of human compassion in wanting to end a life, come what may.

An answer to a prayer

By 1974, Shipman was the father of two, and he joined the Ormerod Medical Centre in the market town of Todmorden in the West Riding of Yorkshire; a place popular as a filming location for programmes like *Happy Valley, My Summer of Love* and *Juliet Bravo*. Houses here are still affordable and you can walk for a pint of milk as easily as a pint of real ale. In this idyllic Upper Calder Valley setting he seemed to change character from a somewhat withdrawn, asocial, former mummy's boy to an outgoing, respected member of the community in the eyes of his colleagues and patients. There was no stress, no competitiveness in Todmorden. Fred felt comfortable.

Sweet Sarah Bell's story

Todmorden was not a complete stranger to murder most foul, so with passing interest we learn that a double murder took place at Christ Church, on 2 March 1868. The victims are buried in the churchyard, or at least they should be. Sarah Bell's tale unfolds as follows:

Miles Weatherhill (or Weatherill – sources differ), a 23-year-old weaver from the town, was forbidden from seeing his sweetheart Sarah Bell by her employer, the pinch-faced parson, Anthony John Plow, for whom she worked as a cook. Sarah was described in a contemporary broadsheet poem as 'fair and virtuous, young blooming, aged seventeen', but having disobeyed Plow by secretly meeting Miles, she was dismissed from her post. Having attracted local gossip-mongering displeasure she left Todmorden under a cloud: 'to her mother at York did go', leaving Miles and herself heartbroken. Miles Weatherhill went ballistic in every sense. Acquiring four pistols and an axe, he invaded the vicarage and exacted his revenge first on the parson and then bedchamber maid Jane Smith, who had spilled the beans to the vicar about the couple's ungodly trysts (possibly because she somewhat fancied strapping Miles for herself). He also attacked and wounded Mrs Plow.

'Bent on destruction, with intent to kill her, he did ill-treat, with a poker, and her crimson blood on the floor did spill': *The Times*, 5 March 1868. So that's what I call a bloody Lizzy Borden-type murder if ever there was one. Not surprisingly, Miss Smith died instantly. The sanctimonious parson, severely wounded by Miles's axe, met his maker a week later. Adding to the carnage, the bible-thumper's seriously wounded wife died a year later; her sickly five-week-old son also died, although not from the attack. On Saturday, 4 April 1868, Weatherhill became the last person to be hanged in front of an overexcited populace in Manchester, at the New Bailey Prison.

Local legend has it that the face of a young woman is sometimes seen in the window of the vicarage now in private ownership, but here is the bit I really like: *The Times* reportage ends with:

Young men and maidens, you constant lovers,
If true and honourable you make a vow,
Be just and upright, and oh, remember,

Todmorden Vicarage, and Parson Plow;
And all good people, oh, pray consider,
Where true love is planted, there let it dwell,
And recollect the Todmorden murders,
Young Miles the weaver, and Sarah Bell.
Miles and the true-love by death is parted,
In health and bloom, he the world did leave,
And his true love, quite broken-hearted,
For Miles the weaver, in pain do grieve;
At the early age of three and twenty,
In the shades below, with the worms do dwell,
On the fatal drop, he cried, broken-hearted,
May we meet in heaven, my sweet Sarah Bell.

Now, that's a tear-jerker and then I learned – and this will fascinate any reader who is a trainspotter – in December 1984, a goods train consisting of a locomotive and 13 petrol tanker trucks derailed in the Summit Tunnel between Todmorden and Littleborough, causing what is still considered one of the biggest underground fires in British transport history. Obviously 1 million litres (220,000) gallons of highly flammable gasoline doesn't improve when ignited by the heat from an overheated axle bearing. The train crew managed to extricate the locomotive and the following three tankers, and fire crews fought the intense blaze for four days. Remarkably, the tunnel, built between 1838–41, suffered minimal damage and is still in use today – a tribute to Victorian engineering at its best.

So back to the Ormerod medical practice in Todmorden which, at that time, had illness among the partners. 'A junior doctor joining us was a huge relief,' senior GP Dr Michael Grieve would later recall in *Born to Kill?*:

> We welcomed him [Shipman] with open arms. He was extremely good, almost manic in the way he carried out his duties. He brought us all the latest techniques available at the time and very much kept us up to the mark and well-informed. Fred was an answer to a prayer. He was just what we needed … and he had quite a devoted following who felt that he was the bee's knees and would do the best for them in all circumstances. In those days the doctors did not choose their patients, indeed it was a vice-versa arrangement with them choosing the GP that they liked.

Shipman had a different agenda, however, and staff in the medical offices where he worked soon began to see a different side to him. Dr Grieve remembered that '... he wouldn't let the nurses give injections for him. He wouldn't let the pathology technicians when they came out once a week to take blood samples from his patients. Fred would insist on doing all these things himself.' Yet no one had an inkling that he was involved in any kind of medical malpractice, which would emerge later when *three* of his patients died in *one* day.

Not as clever

If you tell the truth, you don't have to remember anything.

– Mark Twain

It was soon discovered that Shipman suffered from a drug addiction, so he was not as perfect as everyone imagined him to be. One of the other doctors happened to be in the local pharmacy when he was shown the drugs register and was startled to see that Shipman had amassed large amounts of pethidine (Demerol) not for his patients, but for himself. When confronted, Shipman admitted to being an addict, then weakly said, 'I was always taught not to give my patients anything that I had not tried myself.' It was this addiction, this dependency on pethidine, that sustained his manic behaviour, enabling him to take on the enormous medical workloads and get through them. Now, with his overblown ego shattered, the narcissistic Shipman came unstitched at the seams. He was sacked from the medical practice after throwing his medical bag across the room in a rage. Calling Dr Grieve the 'Devil incarnate', he stormed off, leaving a trail of expletives in his wake.

> It is at this point, when a serial killer is confronted by the obvious, they retreat, either with the excuse that 'Society has fitted me up... it's not my fault', or they explode, and that's what Shipman was basically doing with: 'How dare these little doctors, these little people much lower than me... how dare they question *me*? My mother always taught me this way. How dare they question and interrogate me. Who the hell are they?'
> – Christopher Berry-Dee: in *Born to Kill?*

One might have hoped or prayed that had the medical profession had its wits about it, Shipman should have had his licence to practise smartly withdrawn. He freely admitted to being a drug addict, something compounded by his forging of prescriptions to obtain pethidine for his own use. This amounted to criminal deception. But, oh no. The medical profession closed ranks, and when he went before Halifax Magistrates' Court in February 1976 for forging prescriptions, he was fined a paltry £600 and ordered to attend a drug-rehab clinic in York. Three years later, having convinced the GMC that he was cured of his addiction, he was allowed to return to practising medicine.

Having read *The Shipman Inquiry*, the final report of Dame Janet Smith's inquiry, from front to back and inside out, I would have been inclined to call it: *The Shipman Clusterfuck, with Bells and Whistles.*

Hyde

Hyde was such a lovely town. It was a proper, old-fashioned, traditional community, where sons and daughters still lived on their parents' doorsteps; they all lived near each other. They all understood each other. It was a very close community with a warm heart. So for Shipman to be able to kill so many people in such a small safe community was doubly devastating.

– Mikaela Sitford: *Manchester Evening News*
journalist, co–author, with Steve Panter, of *Addicted to
Murder: The True Story of Dr Harold Shipman* (2000)

It has been said elsewhere that Fred Shipman first became interested in medicine as he watched his mother receive morphine injections to ease the pain she suffered while dying of cancer; that later, as a doctor, he played at being God with power over life and death. I don't buy into the 'God' part, for there is nothing of godliness about doctors murdering trusting patients, period. I would consider his later addiction to death almost a paraphilia; its roots forming in an unhealthy juvenile voyeurism because Fred, aged 17 in 1963, was of the age when most teenagers were, or should have been, more interested in the television shows of the day: *Doctor Who*, *General Hospital*, *The Outer Limits* and the adorable *Patty Duke Show*, instead of watching his mother as she was injected with painkilling morphia 'to ease her passing', as Dr Bodkin Adams had said of his murders. Nevertheless, voyeurism *may* become addictive – not always in the sexual sense but to satisfy some other pathological need. I suggest that Shipman later developed an intensely morbid interest in death. I refer readers interested in this subject to Coltan Scrivner's article 'The psychology of morbid curiosity: Development and initial validation of the morbid curiosity scale' in *Personality and Individual Differences* (Vol. 183, December 2021). True, it is a lengthy paper, but it is of interest to anyone trying to fathom what might have made the lethal Dr Shipman tick.

Donneybrook

In 1977, Shipman began practising as a GP, this time at the Donneybrook Medical Centre in Hyde, Greater Manchester. He continued working there throughout the 1980s, in 1993, aged 47, establishing his own surgery at 21 Market Street, once again becoming a respected member of the community. Any normal person would have been content with having the support of hundreds of devoted patients, but not Shipman.

This narcissistic psychopath wanted much more and to this end he promoted himself to the media as a pillar of the community – which, ironically, he already was. In 1983 he appeared in a Granada TV *World in Action* documentary; the subject being how the mentally ill should be treated in the community. Smiling into the camera, he obviously felt it would be wrong for him to mention that he was murdering scores of his patients, or that he'd killed someone a few days before the interview and that he would be giving another elderly woman patient a lethal injection of diamorphine before the TV production company's cheque for his televised interview even arrived in the post.

Again with very strong echoes of the Bodkin Adams case, over the years doctors, funeral directors and even pharmacists had raised suspicions about Dr Shipman, but their concerns were swept under the carpet. Indeed, as early as 1988, police had investigated him. When Mikaela Sitford broke a story in the *Manchester Evening News* that a Dr Linda Reynolds of the Brooke Surgery had courageously spoken to the local coroner, Dr John Pollard, and told him that she was worried that Shipman was killing patients who were elderly, vulnerable, living alone, with *all* meeting premature deaths during home visits, one might have thought that the cops would have had a sniff around. They did, and they didn't, even though Dr Reynolds was also concerned about the large numbers of cremation forms for elderly patients that Shipman had asked Dr Pollard to countersign:

On the basis of [Dr Reynolds' concerns], I instructed the police to make an investigation [into Shipman] in what is now referred to as the 'failed investigation' because the police came back to me a fortnight later and said they had conducted their investigation and frankly said they could find nothing wrong.

– Dr John Pollard, Chief Coroner

The truth of the matter – the totality of this so-called investigation – is that on 17 April 1998 a police officer had paid a visit to Dr Reynolds and sternly told her that after some investigation she was 'mistaken'; that the much-loved doctor was a 'pillar of the community … she'd best be careful of what she said.' Doesn't that say it all? – because Shipman went on to kill three more women soon after that. He seemed to believe that the Hippocratic Oath had given him a licence to kill.

The true number of patients murdered by Shipman still remains unknown, but his roll call of victims eclipses many other serial killers' tallies, even to this very day. This man was a monster in disguise, carrying a black bag in which were his medical instruments of death. He was hiding in Hyde in plain sight,

Harold Frederick Shipman is an interesting case. The very remarkable nature of his case is the fact that he *is* remarkable. You could say 'He can't be a killer because he is just like us.' Harold Shipman fitted in with society to a great degree and this wasn't the very thing; the most important feature that made him go on and on to become one of the most prolific serial killers of all times was that *he was a doctor.*

> – Dr David A. Holmes, criminologist and forensic
> profiler: in *Born to Kill?*

Apart from the obvious point that Shipman was a general practitioner, a profession widely trusted by almost everyone, he also wore a mask of normalcy as *all* serial killers do. Indeed, during my lectures I always ask the audience to look around to see whether they can maybe spot a serial murderer in their midst. Of course they can't, but this simple exercise certainly drives the message home. So, have a bit of 'fun'. When *you* are in a public gathering, in a crowd or pub quiz, turn to *your* friends and ask out-of-the-blue: 'Hey, can any of *you* spot a psychopathic serial murderer among us?' That will give them pause for thought – and also to think that you are indeed crazy, too.

Kathleen Grundy

Earth provides enough to satisfy every man's needs, but not every man's greed.
> – Mahatma Gandhi (1869–1948)

Doctor Harold Shipman might have carried on killing for years if had not been for the suspicious death of Kathleen Grundy on 24 June 1998. The last person to see her alive was her GP when, early that morning, Shipman had called at Loughrigg Cottage, 79 Joel Lane, Gee Cross, Hyde, to take a routine blood sample.

The former mayoress had made a will to the merry-widow tune of £386,000 bequeathed to Dr Shipman and to the blanket exclusion of her solicitor daughter, Angela Woodruff, and her children. When Angela received a copy of the will she was absolutely astonished because it was so amateurish. As I am sure a reader might agree, if one is inclined to forge a will (which I am sure that you will never be), then even with a passing glance you'd say that Shipman would have scored two out of ten for forgery. The document, as leading police investigator Detective Chief Inspector Mike Williams confirmed, was 'fake and cack-handed', and something Angela knew that her mother could have played no part in. Indeed, Angela believed that her mother's signature was not hers. Consequently, this document needed to be examined.

The police officer assigned to the case talked to a couple of people whom Shipman knew; one of them being local undertaker Alan Massey, who reflected: 'I have been very worried about the number of cremation certificates, there are *so* many of them.'

Shipman's fingerprints were found on the will, yet at interview he denied that he'd even seen it. The fact that he owned the Brother typewriter that had produced the document left him morosely suggesting that 'Mrs Grundy used to borrow the machine', but he was unable to explain to police how she'd returned it to him straight after the will had been prepared in her own solicitor's office – as though solicitors did not have their own typewriters, no less. What a liar this man was. Even if his tongue had been notarised, everything he said would have been a lie.

Between proverbial rocks and hard places

When in doubt, don't.
    – Benjamin Franklin (1706–90)

Reluctantly, it was decided that Kathleen's body had to be exhumed so that her remains could be forensically examined to determine precisely *how* she had died, because the investigation into her death now raised bright red flags that all and sundry in Hyde were watching being hoisted. The rumours started, as most rumours do, with secretive over-the-garden-fence whispers, a twitch of net curtains, hushed gossip in the local greengrocer's, a little conspiratorial chitchat under the perm-drying hoods in hairdressing salons. Had Kathy passed away, as proclaimed on the terminal tin, through old age, or was there something more sinister afoot in Hyde?

In the knowledge that there had been an earlier investigation – the so-called 'failed investigation' of March 1998 – into Shipman's activities which had involved no fewer than 19 suspicious deaths, there now surfaced further information from a local taxi driver, John Shaw. The cabbie had previously told police that he'd suspected Shipman of murdering 21 patients. Shock, horror ... He had become suspicious because many of the elderly customers he took to and from the hospital, while seemingly in good health, soon died under Shipman's care. He might as well have placed a brass plaque outside his surgery reading: 'Dr Grim Sleep – surgery hours 24/7/365'.

I could now say that at this point Greater Manchester Police belatedly found themselves up the proverbial 'Shit Creek' without any paddles, but how dare I suggest such a thing? Yet maybe I *could* suggest that after trying to paper over the cracks in their previous, very brief, botched investigation into Shipman's medical comings and goings – when, inter alia, an inexperienced officer undiplomatically slapped Dr Linda Reynolds down – the police needed to act, and fast. The previous investigation had the knock-on effect of implying that coroner Dr John Pollard had been misguided; that cab driver John Shaw was deluded; that the local undertaker, who had lost count of the numbers of cremation certificates for elderly persons that had passed through his hands because there had been so many of them, was misguided; and that funeral directors Massey & Son – one of whom had actually said: 'I told people about this and no one listened' – were mistaken. Although it *is* fair to say that Dr Reynolds, Dr Pollard, Mikaela Sitford and just about everyone residing in the close community market town of Hyde now began to sense that their once-wonderful GP was about to have his Viyella shirt collar felt.

The problem as I see it was the fact that Shipman was from the medical profession, whose members are considered beyond reproach. For the police even to consider exhuming Kathleen Grundy – because the doctor's indecently hasty efforts to have her cremated had been dashed – required a lot of paperwork before they could even think about digging in Hyde Cemetery. This was no small matter. There still remained the possibility that there was nothing suspicious about Kathleen's death. But now the police had Angela Woodruff on their backs. She was a practising solicitor, and not one to be fobbed off. Decisions had to be made; a senior officer had to make the call.

The exhumation went ahead. Kathleen's body was found to contain traces of diamorphine (heroin), which is often used to control pain in terminally ill cancer patients.

Indeed, there was more than sufficient 'smack' in her body to have caused her death. A second autopsy revealed that she had not been suffering from a terminal illness, thereby forestalling any defence argument that Shipman had injected her to save her from further agony.

When questioned about this treatment, Shipman claimed that Mrs Grundy had been an addict (much along the lines of Bodkin Adams' mitigation). In an effort to throw detectives off the scent, he showed them comments he'd written to that effect in his computerised medical journal. Forensic examination of his computer proved that the entries were written *after* Kathleen's death. It was this bungling error that sealed his fate.

This is not quite up to Agatha Christie's standard of a criminology-inspired plot by any means … no motor yacht or de luxe hotel; no French Riviera; no Orient Express. Nope, I regret to say that shit happens even in the most ordinary of locations. I am NOT suggesting for a moment that some parts of Tameside, Greater Manchester, including Hyde, are not conducive to a damned good whodunit, but more importantly, *why* in God's name had Shipman dunit? So now is the time to look into the why, and *if* there was a motive, what *was* it?

Dr Death – Dr Jekyll and Mr Hyde

The Hyde community were absolutely behind Dr Shipman at this point. He had groomed that community so that they truly believed that he was looking after them when, in fact, he was killing them by the hundreds.

– Mikaela Sitford: in *Born to Kill?*

The kind of people he [Shipman] picked are what we place in the category 'less than dead'. In other words, the kind of people we don't actually notice so well. They are not the kind of people who are going to cause a big fuss, because it's almost expected. As a serial killer, Shipman is unique because he seems to be the only one who could get an undertaker or the local council to take the body away for him.

– Dr David A. Holmes: in *Born to Kill?*

The circumstance in which the victims were found was in itself quite disturbing, and here we find more red flags popping up. These should have raised the suspicions of local undertakers when they collected the bodies, because many of the victims were found in the middle of the day, fully clothed, sitting upright in a chair or on a sofa. In some of those instances Shipman had actually certified on the cremation form that he had carried out a full external examination of the patient's body, yet the victim had been found sitting there fully clothed, shoes on, sleeves buttoned down to the wrists, dresses buttoned to the neck. As coroner Dr Pollard later opined: 'How you could carry out a full examination under those circumstances, I don't fully understand.' But there wasn't just one deceased elderly person found in such a position; there were so many of them, *all* from the locality of Hyde, and *all* of them loyal patients of Dr Shipman, who had signed the cremation and burial forms.

Ann Alexander, solicitor for Shipman's victims, said on *Born to Kill?*: 'Often in the medical notes that he [Shipman] had made up for the families of victims, he suggested that these people had heart conditions, for example ... and then saying they must have had a heart attack, because someone having a heart attack doesn't just simply fall asleep sitting in a chair looking very relaxed and life isn't quite like that.' It is difficult to disagree with her.

More exhumations

When police investigated Shipman's medical records they found his book of death certificates and made a list of 15 deaths that needed to be looked into as a priority. Of the people on this list, nine had been buried, six cremated. More exhumations were ordered, turning sundry once freshly mown churchyards into sites for large holes and piles of soil. Police also learned through talking to the relatives of his victims that Shipman had subtly encouraged them towards evidence-destroying cremation. In each of the exhumations that took place a high level of morphine was discovered in the body, leading to a prosecution in relation to that particular death.

The police investigation would also reveal this serial murderer's modus operandi: he would often kill his victims – most of whom were elderly – with a lethal injection of morphine. With the patients assuming that he was taking a blood sample, they were none the wiser. Then medical executioner Shipman would return to his office to backdate their medical files on his computer so as to exaggerate their poor health. For Kathleen Grundy, he had backdated several entries suggesting that she had become addicted to morphine, which he intended for his own use.

Why Dr Shipman dunit is not a subject for criminology-educated, psychological debate among well-meaning liberals. No – when one takes off Shipman's metaphorical clothes, he stands naked before us as a non-person who committed medically induced homicide with a hint of financial gain in his mind. He had mentioned a few times that he intended to move to Australia and needed cash to do so. A quantity of his victims' stolen jewellery and gems was found by police in a box in the bedroom of the couple's Roe Cross Green house, which he claimed belonged to his wife Primrose. That smacks of 'trophy-taking', does it not? Primrose asked for around a hundred items to be returned to her after they had been seized by police following her husband's arrest. She said that she was able to prove that 66 items were her own, but later admitted that 34 items in the box found in the bedroom did not belong to her. Like almost everything else in this case, confusion reigned everywhere, with Primrose eventually getting some of the stuff back. The remainder was disposed of by the Asset Recovery Agency, sold at auction, with the cash going to Victim Support in Tameside.

Of course we will never know the entirety of Shipman's motive. He took that secret to his grave, yet when we reflect on the Dr Bodkin Adams case, and the obvious fact that Shipman attempted to forge a will in his favour, financial gain has to play some part, if only a small element of his overall pathology. While others are bound to disagree, I do not believe that he was playing at God. None of his elderly patients was in great pain; generally speaking, they were in remarkably good health for their ages. So the idea of Shipman compassionately putting them out of their suffering is a horse that does *not* run for me.

Dr Harold 'Fred' Shipman was convicted on 15 counts of murder and one of forgery at Preston Crown Court on 31 January 2000, and given 15 life sentences (plus four years for forgery), with a recommendation that he serve a whole-life tariff. Eleven days later, the GMC removed him from the medical register. On 13 January 2004, a day before his fifty-eighth birthday, he hanged himself in his cell at HMP Wakefield. Primrose Shipman, his wife of more than 35 years, continues to assert his innocence.

Nice cup of tea and a Garibaldi biscuit, anyone? Because shortly, we must pack our bags and cross the Pond to the 'Land of the Free'.

Nurse 'Jolly Jane' Toppan

They [the victims] are better off dead than alive.
— JANE TOPPAN: CONFESSION

Author's note

By its horrific nature, this is very much an historic case, but although reference material is not short in quantity, much of it is unreliable, and sometimes contradictory. What I will attempt to do is give the reader a thorough account after sifting through what is available, while occasionally striking a balance where accounts conflict. With echoes of British serial-killer nurses Beverley Allitt and Lucy Letby's crimes soon to ring in our ears, it would be remiss of me to dismiss 'Jolly Jane', for in examining her case we might gain a clearer insight into the minds of Allitt and Letby and other medical killers, whom we will meet soon enough.

Early days

No Agatha Christie mystery here. No Sherlock Holmes plot to be worked through. By my reckoning Jane Toppan was one of the most evil killer nurses in all of criminal history, with a cast of the deceased smacking of New England money; the elderly victims – very much like those in the cases of Drs Bodkin Adams and Shipman – falling prey to a nurse: in this notable case to a Massachusetts-born, bred and raised Lucrezia Borgia.

Jane was born Honora 'Nora' A. Kelley, the youngest of three (some sources say four) daughters to Irish immigrants in Boston, in the 'Bay State', Massachusetts. Her date of birth is listed on various documents and publications as 31 March 1854. This conflicts with primary sources such as those from the Boston Female Asylum and various census records, where her year of birth is attributed as closer to 1857. Of course, that fiddly difference does not amount to a hill of beans, but later it might.

Matriarch Bridget Finn died from tuberculosis when Honora was young, leaving her husband, Peter, to raise her and her sisters, Ellen 'Nellie' and Delia Josephine. According to the Lowell Historical Society: '... a Mary Kelley appeared in the newspapers after Jane's arrest as talking about being the child of the Kelleys, but no record of Mary's birth was found.'

To suggest that Jane was born on the wrong side of the tracks would be an understatement. Her father was well known as an eccentric and abusive heavy drinker. Brian Lane and Wilfred Gregg write in *The New Encyclopedia of Serial Killers*:

'[Peter] Kelley, either through overwork or a weak constitution, was not entirely right in the head.' They are not wrong. He was nicknamed 'Kelley the Crack' (from 'crackpot') by those with whom he was acquainted, an allegation stemming from an occasion when he was found in his tailor's shop trying to sew his eyelids together, although there is no affirmative evidence to support this. I lean towards the idea of a short-sighted man trying to thread cotton through a small needle while, as the Irish say, in a state of 'having drink taken'. Be that as it may, in 1863 he surrendered eight-year-old Delia Josephine and six-year-old Honora to the care of their grandmother before he was packed off to an asylum for the insane, never to see his children again. Then, when Grandma found caring for the two spritely lasses too much, they were committed to the Boston Female Asylum, an orphanage for indigent children.

Rescued from a very miserable home

Kelley, Delia Josephine, born 1855, admitted Feb. 1863.

Kelly, Honora A, born 1887, admitted Feb.1863. Nov. 1864 adopted by **Mrs. Ann C. Toppan**, Lowell. February 1863:

The Committee reported that two children had been admitted since the last meeting. They had no mother, had been offered by their father, **Mr Kelley**, whose habits evidently rendered him an unfit protector for his little girls. Their appearance indicated that they had been rescued from a very miserable home.

These circumstances having been heard, it was voted: That the act of the Committee in admitting **Delia Josephine** and **Honora Kelly** is approved by the Board.

November 1864: **Mrs. Ann C. Toppan** appeared before the Board and desired to adopt **Honora Kelley**. She seemed a very respectable woman and the home she offered to the child appeared to possess many advantages. It was therefore:

Voted: That **Honora A. Kelley** be bound to **Mrs. Toppan**.

– Boston Female Asylum Records, page 196

From the asylum Honora was taken in as an indentured servant by Abner and Ann C. Nestor Toppan, who had three children. Nothing is known of the siblings other than Elizabeth (1830–99), whom we will meet later.

Brian Lane and Wilfred Gregg state in *The New Encyclopedia of Serial Killers* that Honora was adopted by the Toppans. This is incorrect as she was never formally adopted, but this minor error springs from the fact that Honora took on the surname of her benefactors to distance herself from her sordid early years.

The Lowell Historical Society: 'According to Dr Henry R. Stedman who evaluated Jane Toppan pretrial, Honora was six at the time she came to live with the Toppans, and was "apprenticed to Mrs. T., on indenture papers"... little documented information exists about Honora's sisters and father after she entered the Asylum, but comments appearing in the newspapers stated that Delia became an alcoholic and sex-worker, while sister Ellen was also committed [to an asylum].'[12] Again, there is no firm confirmation that Ellen was committed, nor that Delia became an alcoholic prostitute.

Metamorphosing

In attempting to understand how such a young girl transformed into a serial killer we need to trace her early life. In 1865 Honora took on the new name of Jane 'Jennie' Toppan and appears as such in various documents from that time on in Lowell, a city just over 30 miles north-west of Boston, known as 'the Cradle of the American Industrial Revolution' because of its textile mills and factories. The Toppans lived in the city's Centralville area. 'Jennie' – as she appears in the 1865, 1870 and 1880 censuses – attended Lowell public schools and graduated from Lowell High; proving to be an intelligent child, quick to learn, who supported the household through work, as required by her indenture, which is a contract for one person to work for another.

In order to hide her Irish heritage, since there was still a stigma in Massachusetts from being so, the Toppans created a story about the loss of Jane's parents on an ocean crossing from Italy. Nineteenth-century Irish immigrants to the USA faced a combination of anti-immigrant, anti-Catholic, and specifically anti-Irish bigotry, all closely intertwined. This was especially true in Puritan-founded Boston and its environs, which had a predominantly Anglo-Saxon population. So up to this point in the young girl's narrative, I see her formative years as being almost a psychological car wreck,

---

12 https://www.lowellhistoricalsociety.org/lowells-ties-to-jolly-jane-massachusetts-female-serial-killer/

becoming a blessing in disguise when the strict Catholic Toppans acquired an indentured servant on the cheap, although a good education was provided as part of the deal.

The Lowell Historical Society: 'Jennie was recalled as being a regular gossip, fabricator of untruths and much more, though she had a charming nature... During interviews with Dr Stedman, she admitted that she told many tales which she knew to be sheer inventions; among them a story of her parentage, her alleged father having in reality lived in China for two years before her birth; another of her horror of the dead which was so great that she sometimes fell senseless at the sight of bodies.'

Dr Stedman opined: '... until Jane was a woman, she was under good moral and religious influences, home surroundings and discipline, and had good associates, but her incorrigible propensities for deceit, falsehood, and trouble-making [were] never absent from the first.' So where did this spring from?

To answer that we have to go back to Jane's very early days: a kid in her formative years having lost her young mother through illness and deprived of maternal love; a mentally unglued, unpredictable father who effectively abandoned his daughters; and Jane's year-long stint in a home for unwanted children, before being placed into strict indenture at about the age of six. I ask the reader to think about that for a moment or two, because I believe that she had been emotionally damaged by the time she went to live with the Toppans. No amount of love and care can *completely* repair a mind that has been subjected to so many negative influences so young.

I am not going soft on Jane Toppan, but we have to take all of that into account as her life moves on, with her 'inventions' being used as a form of compensatory self-protection. There is something else we might consider, too – her propensity for lying at the drop of a hat. Pathological liar signs can be symptoms of obsessive-compulsive disorder, antisocial disorder, borderline personality disorder, narcissistic personality disorder and Munchausen syndrome by proxy (MSBP) – the latter maybe also applying to Nurse Beverley Allitt, with whom we will acquaint ourselves later. For the reader interested, the National Library of Medicine in Bethesda, MD, publishes a first-rate paper online: *The Phenomenology of Lying in Young Adults with Personality and Cognition*, which makes for a very instructive read.

There are stories about Jennie/Jane having a beau who had agreed to marry her when she was around the age of 16, and that he gave her a ring in the shape of a bird. Soon after, the lad moved out west to find work, and there fell in love with his landlady's daughter, sending the bad news back to Jane. Their engagement was off. Rumours abounded that she destroyed the ring in a fit of pique, that this may have started her spiral into darkness with two attempted suicides and the 'withdrawing into herself to become a virtual hermit', as Lane and Gregg put it, although there appears to be no mention of attempted suicide at this time in her life in any documents. Nonetheless, on her eighteenth birthday, Mrs Toppan gave Jane $50 and encouraged her to find her way in the world, but for a time she stayed on as help, only leaving at the age of 24 when Mrs Toppan finally refused to let her remain any longer in her home.

The Lady of the Lamp

The very first requirement in a hospital is that it do the sick no harm.
Florence Nightingale (1820–1910)

An article published by *Penn Nursing* (University of Pennsylvania School of Nursing) gives us a valuable insight into hospital welfare during the period that Toppan was criminally active, so I rely perhaps a little heavily on it here with all credit due to the authors:

> Although women physicians in Philadelphia, New York, and Boston had already established formal training schools for nurses in the 1860s, the New York Training School at Bellevue Hospital in New York City, the Connecticut Training School at the State Hospital (later New Haven Hospital) and the Boston Training School at Massachusetts General Hospital in Boston, were the first nurse training schools to claim their organizations were based on the principles specified by Florence Nightingale. (https://www.nursing.upenn.edu/nhhc/ nursing-through-time/1870-1899/)

> I solemnly pledge myself before God and the presence of this assembly to pass my life in purity and to practise my profession faithfully. I will abstain from whatever is deleterious and mischievous, and will not take or knowingly administer any harmful drug.
> – The Nightingale Pledge for Nurses

Penn Nursing tells us:

> Nightingale's principles included an endowment
> ensuring the independence of the training school; a
> superintendent of nurses reporting only to the head
> of the hospital with a strong emphasis on sanitary
> knowledge; clearly defined lecture and ward time for
> students; an insistence on the importance of technical
> skill and a disciplined character in nurses. Few training
> schools – even Nightingale's own school at St Thomas's
> hospital in London – met all these criteria, and most
> reported to medical directors. Nevertheless, the idea
> of shaping a school around Nightingale's principles
> became an animating spirit for the experimental idea
> of formal nurses' training in hospitals and accounted in
> large measure for its success.

The direct antithesis of Florence Nightingale

In 1885, 26-year-old Jane enrolled as a trainee nurse at
Cambridge Hospital in Cambridge, Massachusetts. Apparently a well-liked, eager student and having a cheerful
disposition, she was nicknamed 'Jolly Jane'. If her fellow
nurses had been asked to name any faults, however, they
might have been inclined to refer to her 'unhealthy, morbid
fascination' with what went on at autopsies, and her trouble-making. Some articles suggest that she killed a number of
patients during her time (her first time) at Cambridge. To
be honest with the reader, no one is entirely sure about
that. Nonetheless, Jane was later listed in Lowell's 1901 City
Directory under 'Nurses'.

Massachusetts General Hospital

In 1889 Jane Toppan was recommended for a post at the prestigious Massachusetts General Hospital in Boston, an endorsement not given lightly. Again she started off quite well, working 12-hour days without complaint. However, the nursing staff at the hospital kept a closer eye on their cases than they did at Cambridge. The high doses of medication Toppan was giving to patients were spotted by her superiors. Even so, rather than suspecting foul play, administrators simply put it down to ineptitude.

During her time at Massachusetts General, a strange new angle slowly developed. Jane Toppan had a penchant for telling ever more imaginative tall tales, for gossiping and for spreading unwarranted rumours about the nurses and patients she disliked. Woe betide those who made a complaint, for she would then take the matter into her own hands. So while they described her as both 'brilliant' and 'terrible', those around her grew wary of Nurse Toppan. There appeared to be a dangerous side to this pleasant-faced young woman, although no one seemed able to be more specific than that. But let's drill down a little more here. During her residency, Jolly Jane often became close to patients – she picked her favourite cases, who were normally elderly as well as ill – and she used them as guinea pigs. *Wikipedia*: '... in experiments with morphine and atropine, she altered their prescribed dosages to see what it did to their nervous systems. However, she spent considerable time alone with patients, making up fake charts, medicating them to drift in and out of consciousness, and even getting into bed with them.'

While wanting to keep her favoured patients as long as possible, she would overdose them and then bring them back from the point of death.

An example of this point-of-death revival is the case of Mrs Amelia Finney, who was in Toppan's care following an operation. Amelia later recalled that the nurse gave her a 'sour-tasting drink', causing her to convulse and drift in and out of consciousness; whereupon Jane climbed into Amelia's bed, stroked her hair and face, saying, 'It will be all right soon,' but was disturbed by someone and fled the ward. Amelia survived to give her account, believing that her experience was some kind of 'fever dream'. So, taken in the round, despite Jane Toppan's initial bright start at Massachusetts General, her reputation among her fellow nurses – very much like the sour-tasting drinks she administered to patients – quickly became unsavoury.

The Lowell Historical Society: 'Her mischief-making of her early years at Cambridge Hospital continued. It is reported that her fellow workers were concerned because of her unfounded and absurd suspicious, tale-bearing, slanderous gossip, and consequent trouble-making, as well as her pleasure in inventing fabulous tales.' Some sources mention that Nurse Toppan misreported information, removed patients to other institutions (the latter being highly unlikely, it has to be said), prolonged the illness of her favourite patients by reporting symptoms that had never occurred. During her term of service – and she was never awarded her nursing licence – many articles went missing, including sums of money, stationery, aprons and uniforms. That she was thought to have stolen cash and jewellery from staff and patients was all just strong suspicion, despite the strong circumstantial evidence against her. Yet, despite her pathological nature, generally her friends spoke very well of Jane Toppan. She was so adroit, such a plausible liar, that any suspicions were swept under the carpet, and haven't we noted this behaviour with the narcissistic medical killers considered thus far in this book? Indeed we have, but one day in 1890, when she decided to leave the ward without permission, her supervisors seized the opportunity to dismiss her.

Hope springs eternal

At this stage in her life one might have prayed on bended knees that the medical profession would have banned Jane Toppan from nursing *anyone* for ever. Alas, any prayer was less than a whisper in a gale-force wind, because after a short stint as a private nurse she had the nerve to return to Cambridge Hospital, whose senior staff were clearly oblivious to this highly dangerous nurse's behaviour. Here, she continued her vicious practices. Besides elderly patients she also attempted to poison a trainee nurse named Mattie Davis.

One day a patient under her care – a man previously recovering – unexpectedly died. Another patient passed away shortly thereafter. Jane was summoned to the chief surgeon's office to answer a few questions: namely, why had she been recklessly administering opiates? No official accusations were made against her, but she was discharged from her post. Of course it had not gone unnoticed that a large number of patients had inexplicably died under her care while their health had been improving, but no autopsies were conducted. Instead, the administrators, fully aware that Nurse Toppan had been administering lethal doses of drugs, thought it best quietly to dismiss her. After all was said and done, any scandal might have resulted in large endowments being withdrawn. 'God forbid that a student nurse is murdering patients on our watch. This *will never* do!'

There, that should give readers pause for thought, as we have already established. The turning of blind eyes. The ostriches' heads buried in the sand. The closing of ranks. I suggest that in some rare instances not much has changed to this very day. But at last Nurse Toppan was gone. We can thank the Lord for that … but not quite yet, for reasons I now reveal.

Licence to kill

Because Jane Toppan had not served enough time at either hospital to have earned her nurse's licence, and with all chances dashed of ever setting foot inside a hospital again, she turned to private nursing. We don't need a degree in probability theory to figure out what was going to happen next … Yes, having distanced herself from the Nightingale principles and the watchful eyes of colleagues and administrators, she could kill at will. After all, as a freelancer, who would keep an eye on her? What did it matter if a large number of her patients died? 'They are better off dead than alive,' she would later callously claim many times.

Between 1880 and 1901, on the recommendation of many experienced physicians, she served in a number of New England nursing homes while keeping undertakers busy into the bargain. There was no CV to suggest anything other than her being a devoted trained nurse. Hey, look, she is even listed in Lowell's 1901 City Directory, under 'Nurses', and if that's not good enough for anyone, what is?

Freelancing proved to be a prosperous venture for Jolly Jane. Despite numerous claims of her stealing from patients, by 1895 she had become one of the most successful private nurses in Boston, yet this outward mask of professional nursing respectability did nothing to deter her murderous ways, indicating a fully emerged criminal psychopath. Her blatant lying, constant mischief-making, followed her from caring position to nursing post. There were numerous instances of theft, of not returning borrowed money and other dodgy issues aplenty; however, many families still felt that Jane was a competent and caring professional. Unfortunately, her penchant for stealing items that didn't belong to her, combined with her selfish nature, soon led to her stealing the lives of many vulnerable Massachusetts residents.

Israel and 'Lovely' P. Dunham

Mr Israel Dunham, late of 17 Wendell Street, passed peacefully away at an early hour Sunday evening, after a brief illness of five days.
– *The Cambridge Chronicle*, Vol. L, No. 22, 1 June 1895

Jane Toppan appears to have committed homicide for a number of reasons: her motives varying with circumstance, including opportunity, frustration, failure to clear a debt, employment, marriage prospects and more, but at this point in her narrative she is now lodging at 17 Wendell Street, Cambridge.

'Wendell Street?' a reader might enquire. Once called

'prime real estate', and well might it have been back then, for it had gold written all over it. Gold because when Charles F. McClure returned from the 1849 California Gold Rush, he bought an extensive tract of land off Massachusetts Avenue (then known as North Avenue) and commemorated his 'Forty-Niner' prospecting fortune by naming streets running through his property. One of these was Wendell Street, so named for Katherine Brattle Wendell, a daughter of Major General Wendell Cushing Neville (1870–1930) of the US Marine Corps: a Medal of Honor recipient with many other gallantry awards to his name. Similarly, Garfield Street was laid out and named shortly after the assassination of President James A. Garfield in 1881, while Everett Street was named for Harvard University president Edward Everett. Jane Toppan was now in residence in Wendell Street; the owners of the property being Israel Dunham and his wife 'Lovely' – which she may well have been. Jane later said that the couple seemed to be 'well-liked in the area', those possibly being the nicest words that she *ever* said about *anyone*.

Israel had lots and *lots* of money. He had been born in Maine in 1812, and after their marriage in 1835, the couple settled in Cambridge, where he established himself as an architect and builder. Many of the houses in Old Cambridge were built or remodelled under his direction. Some say that Israel built the entire area. He didn't, but the couple did build three sons and two daughters. However, in 1895, 83-year-old Israel had become feeble, fussy and, with his mind deteriorating, he became Jane's next victim. After falling ill for five days, he was murdered on 26 May 1895. Alleged cause of death: 'strangulated hernia'. Two years later, on

19 September 1897, 87-year-old 'Lovely' met the same fate. Alleged cause of death: 'old age'.

The Untouchable

By now Jane Toppan must have felt invincible. Murder had become second nature to her. She had metamorphosed into a fully emerged homicidal psychopath exhibiting no compassion for anyone; consumed by greed, callous to a fault, without any moral compass, much less a conscience. Yet while her victims to this point had no real connection to her, her next victim was much closer to home. As for her motive for killing old Israel? I'd put that down to money. She had either borrowed cash from him and could not repay the debt, or he had caught her stealing and was on the verge of kicking her out. As for 'Lovely', being herself elderly, she had come to rely on Nurse Toppan, who had 'cared' for her husband during his very short illness. So out of necessity she allowed Jane to stay on for a further two years as a nursing companion, until Jane had no further use for her, and into a coffin 'Lovely' did go.

Elizabeth Stanford Toppan Brigham

I felt rather bitter against Elizabeth after Mother Toppan's death, because I always thought she destroyed the will that left me some of the old lady's property. Elizabeth came down to visit me at Cataumet on Buzzards Bay, where I was spending the summer of 1899 in one of the Davises' cottages. That gave me a good chance to have my revenge on her.
    – Jane Toppan: confession

★

In 1899, Jane went on vacation, renting a cottage in the grounds of the Jachin Hotel, Cataumet, Cape Cod; a summer getaway for her, thereby avoiding the hustle and bustle of city life. The specific reason for *this* visit to Cataumet, however, wasn't for rest and relaxation along the Cape's sunny shores. Far from it: this time she had invited her foster sister Elizabeth to stay with her, and Liz would not be leaving any time soon because, 20 years her senior, she represented everything that Jane was not.

Liz was delighted with the opportunity to spend some time with Jane because she was very fond of her, having always regarded her as a real sister. Jane saw things differently. Mrs Toppan had never been backward in telling Jane exactly where she stood in the household pecking order. Elizabeth was her biological daughter, while Jane would always be an Irish cast-off who had been God-given lucky to be indentured to the Toppans to become little more than a loud-mouthed skivvy. So, although Elizabeth never felt this way towards Jane, unknowingly she became a symbol of the anger and bitterness Jane felt towards her foster mother, as Jane later told Dr Stedman before her trial.

On 26 August, the day after Elizabeth arrived on the Cape, Jane suggested that a picnic on the beach might lift her guest's spirits, because for several weeks her foster sister had been suffering with a mild but persistent case of melancholia.

Writer and internet blogger Sue Coletta, author of the brilliant *Pretty Evil New England* (2020), provides us with a perfect word picture:

... Basket in hand, Jane escorted Elizabeth down to Scotch House Cove, where the two women spent several hours chatting away while munching on corned beef and taffy. Salty ocean breezes swept its fingers through their hair as they basked in the summer sun. But deep within Jane a volcano of resentment was about to erupt.

Here is what Jane Toppan coldly said in her confession: 'She [Elizabeth] was really the first of my victims that I actually hated and poisoned with a vindictive purpose. So I let her die slowly with griping tortures. I fixed mineral water so it would do that and then added morphia to it.'

Sue Coletta describes what happened next:

All that sun drained Elizabeth of energy, so she retired early to her upstairs bedroom. The following morning, Jane called Elizabeth down for breakfast. When she didn't respond, Jane rushed to the home of her landlord, Alden Davis, and asked if he could summon the doctor because her 'sister had been taken sick'. Toppan then telegrammed Elizabeth's husband, O. A. Brigham in Lowell, informing him that his wife was in a grave condition.

Grave? Well, yes, because Liz would soon be in one.

I held her in my arms and watched with delight as she gasped her life out.

– Jane Toppan: confession to the murder
of Elizabeth Brigham

Liz had suffered what the doctor ascribed to an 'apoplectic stroke', leaving her in a coma from which she would never awaken. We can only imagine what spiteful words Jane may have whispered into the dying woman's ear as she convulsed into death. Or did her foster sister seize this moment to voice a lifetime of indignation? We could be forgiven for thinking that with the murder of the last person connecting her to an unhappy childhood, Jane Toppan's lust for killing might have been satiated. If so, we would be wrong.

Edna Bannister Brigham

I have to confess that it is tempting to take a liberty with the chronology of events here, because Toppan's murderous involvement with the Brigham family is so similar to her killings among the Davis family of Cataumet, which ultimately led to the nurse's arrest. That was eighteen months in the future, however, as I will describe later.

Having disposed of Elizabeth, this very antithesis of a Florence Nightingale-trained nurse returned to Lowell in an attempt to woo and comfort the grieving widower, Oramel A. Brigham (1830–1920), moving into his house. Readers will discern Jolly Jane's modus operandi: the murder of Elizabeth to get her claws into her wealthy husband's home and wallet, like the proverbial cuckoo in a nest. Then quickly into a hole in the ground went Oramel's sister, 77-year-old Edna. According to her headstone – which one prays *is* correct – she was murdered on 29 August 1899. Assuming that she wasn't murdered twice, that is, because the Lowell Historical Society gives an incorrect date of death of 27 August – after two days' illness, with the cause of death ascribed to heart failure. It is probable that Jane was trying to bring Edna to death's door then revive her, as she had previously done with her hospital patients. This time, however, she failed: in trying win over crotchety O. A.'s affections, whoops, Edna's heart gave out.

Florence 'Florrie' M. Calkins

The next victim to fall foul of Jolly Jane was O. A. Brigham's protective 45-year-old housekeeper, Florence, who, after falling ill for three days, died on 15 January 1900; cause of death ascribed to heart failure. Toppan was present at the time. It is believed that Florrie was targeted because she was interfering with Jane's ability to court Mr Brigham, whose frustration with her pushy and complicated nature now led him to ask her to leave. As a result of his request, Jane attempted suicide by giving herself a dose of morphine, which is interesting in itself. Jane obviously knew what constituted a fatal morphia dose, so I suspect that this was merely a ploy to gain Brigham's sympathy. Nonetheless, the Brighams' regular physician, Dr W. H. Lathrop – who had recommended Jane in the past to people seeking a private nurse – had her admitted to Lowell General Hospital, where allegedly she attempted suicide again.

By now, however, detectives were on Toppan's trail. One of them had himself admitted as a 'patient' at the hospital to keep an eye on her, but could find no probable cause for an arrest – nothing to see, nothing to hear. As a result, after she was discharged, Jane travelled to Amherst, New Hampshire, to kill once again.

Backtracking a tad, who was the heavily whiskered

Oramel A. Brigham? Sue Coletta offers this word portrait: 'a well-liked, highly regarded Deacon of the First Trinitarian Congregational Church in Lowell, and depot master for the Boston & Maine Railroad … alarmed over Elizabeth's sudden illness, O. A. took the first available train to Cape Cod. By the time he arrived the next morning, Monday August 28, Elizabeth had fallen into a coma.'

Following this murderous plotting, Mr Brigham married Martha Cook, who died from natural causes on 18 June 1925, O. A. having predeceased her five years earlier on 21 September 1920. Martha and Oramel are in the same plot with Elizabeth, being buried — I say this most respectfully — as a threesome in Glidden Avenue, Lot 1245, Lowell Cemetery, Middlesex County, Massachusetts, and may God bless them.

At which point, let us take a break and look at another aspect of Jane Toppan's modus operandi.

★

Dependency in the elderly

The definition of dependency is as broad as it is unsettling, but it can be summarised as describing people who need help to carry out their daily lives. This includes assistance with personal hygiene, eating, going to the bathroom, getting dressed, even just getting out of bed. The hospital patients under Nurse Toppan's care fitted this vulnerable demographic exactly, as did many other patients of the nurses, doctors and carers who feature throughout this book. One must also take into consideration factors such as a fear of being left to live alone, the loss of family or friends, disability, chronic illness and loss of hearing and/or sight. Indeed, loneliness is the feeling of being alone *regardless* of social contact. We have seen echoes of this in the patients of Dr John Bodkin Adams and Harold Shipman, because I think we covet a reliance, in many cases *total* reliance, on, and complete trust in, the caring doctor, the caregiver or private nurse – especially when we get old and sick.

In placing Jane Toppan's psychopathology under the glass we see that she was well schooled, even trained in the methods established by Florence Nightingale, thus enabling her to exploit the vulnerabilities and dependencies of the elderly with whom she came into contact. If a potential elderly victim had money, she would zero in, often gaining the added bonus of bed and board to whet her killing appetite. So I suggest that her principal motive was one of financial gain. I also suggest that anyone who stood in the way of her satisfying this narcissistic greed-need was lethally poisoned as a sort of by-product. These kills were completely incidental to her dreadful homicidal enterprise, as though she viewed them as nuisance rivals – the murder of her foster sister Elizabeth and the housekeeper Florrie Calkins being just two examples.

Well, break's over, so let's move on.

★

William H. Ingraham

Quite where William fits into Jane Toppan's chronology of fatal poisonings is unclear.

The Lowell Historical Society doesn't tell us much except that he was from the city of Watertown, about nine miles west of Boston, that he died on 27 January 1900, of 'heart failure', and that Jane Toppan nursed him. Burial records confirm that he was born in 1899, making him 90 at the time of his death.

Miss Sarah E. 'Myra' Connors

I kid you not, this research business is like wading through molasses, with the Lowell Historical Society providing a grounding of solid material about Jane Toppan and a pick-and-mix of other facts, some perhaps more reliable than others. Sorting rumour and legend from hard facts can be a labour of love at the best of times – at worst, it's a nightmare. Prior to Mr Ingraham going through the pearly gates, Jane had already been setting her sights on her next victim. Moving on from ending the lives of those she viewed as serving little or no use, her motive for the next kill is again all too evident.

The soon-to-be decedent Myra Connors had believed that she had a good friend in Jane Toppan. I use the past tense, *had*, advisedly, because Myra had also been the matron of St John's Seminary in Boston, a position providing a regular salary, an apartment and a maid – which it is claimed Jane secretly coveted. When Myra died, she was quick to offer her services, so it may come as no surprise to learn that Myra's condition quickly deteriorated after she fell ill, dying on 11 February 1900. Cause of death: 'complication of Diseases', with apologies that I cannot be more specific, although we might assume that Jane made a contribution to this sad event.

At Myra's funeral, busy bee Nurse Toppan played the role of bereaved and grieving friend. Speaking to the Dean of St John's, she explained that Myra had been planning to take an extended break and had intended to recommend that Jane was to stand in for her while she was absent. Despite the fact that Myra hadn't told anyone else, least of all the Dean, of her vacation, he took Toppan at her word. How could he turn down such a kind offer from a close friend of the dearly departed? Jane was a trained nurse; that she had never gained a nursing licence never came into it. With a steady salary, with a seminary roof over her head and a maid very much in the front of her mind, what did a fib here or there, or a sudden lapse of memory, matter in her cunning scheme of things?

The Dean offered Jane the job. After a few moments' reflection she coyly accepted, stating that she 'owed Myra'. But what Jane *owed* could be interpreted in several ways. From our knowledge of her motives to date, killing for a pecuniary advantage featured heavily. Always borrowing money from patients and friends and unable to pay back the loans strongly suggests that a monetary debt to Myra was long overdue. We also know that Jane Toppan stole pretty much anything that wasn't nailed down, and there was a job to steal here too. While it has been claimed that Jane had coveted Myra's job at the seminary, this does not fit with her cold-blooded psychology. She did not like taking responsibility for tough tasks such as that of matron, for which she was not even remotely qualified. Nevertheless, her nefarious plan worked and she assumed the role once occupied by Myra Connors. It wasn't to last. She was asked to resign after a year due to poor management skills and misappropriation of funds. This setback would have left her seething with rage. Woe betide anyone who dared to get on the wrong side of Jane Toppan.

Mary McNear

In terminal order came 70-year-old Mrs Mary McNear of Cambridge. We know little of her except that she was a wealthy widow to whom Jane probably owed money. She died on 28 December 1900, after two days' illness, with Jane nursing her for three hours before her passing. Cause of death: ascribed to apoplexy (almost certainly what we would now call a stroke).

Mary Louise 'Mattie' Stebbins Davis

Now let's up the ante.

The Davises owned the holiday cottage at Cataumet, Cape Cod, where Toppan had previously murdered her foster sister Elizabeth. After Liz's death Alden Davis and his wife Mattie compassionately waived the rent owed for that year 1899 – and it was by now 1901. Whether it was from pride or determination to clear the debts owed to her, Mattie travelled the 73 miles from Cape Cod to Cambridge, where Jane was staying, hoping to collect the outstanding sum for the time she had spent summering in Cataumet. But 62-year-old Mattie had a mishap when she fell down and injured herself, but insisted on making the trip to settle this account. Once arrived at Cambridge she collapsed and, after Jane's 'nursing', passed away within two days on 4 July 1901. Alleged cause of death: 'chronic diabetes'.

Jane then travelled with Mattie's body to Cataumet, where she met the Davises' married daughters, Mrs Anna Genevieve Davis Gordon and Mrs Mary Eliza Davis Gibbs, as well as the grieving widower, Alden P. Davis. She seems to have made efforts to ingratiate herself into becoming the next Mrs Davis, in almost a mirror-image of her later attempts to woo Oramel Brigham.

Jane Toppan would later become known for dosing her victims with morphine, atropine or strychnine. Typically, she gave the morphine with a fatal dose of atropine in Hunyadi water, a remedy generally accepted by patients and doctors alike. The bitterness of the poisons was disguised by the strong taste of the mineral water, which was used as a curative for the digestion, and had been since 1863.

On 7 July 1901, Jolly Jane was among the group of mourners in Cataumet's small cemetery. When the service was over, she participated in the age-old custom of scattering a handful of damp soil on Mattie's coffin as it rested in the grave. How touching, people must have thought, the nurse so devoted to the last. One can envisage the scene: a not unattractive woman dressed all in black, head bowed, a sad smile, hands clasped in grief as taught at 'the Undertaker's School for Fake Condolence'. Can you picture Jane now? I can, and so loyal and devoted a nurse did she *appear* to be that the deceased's entire family begged her to stay on and look after the rest of them, who were unaccountably falling ill too. Talk about some turkeys voting for Thanksgiving. One couldn't make this up if one tried, but it would only get worse!

Anna 'Annie' Genevieve *Davis* Gordon

After Mattie's funeral, Jane felt that she ought to leave her employer's home; 'after all she was becoming something of a jinx on the health of its occupants,' as authors Lane and

Gregg succinctly put it in *The Encyclopedia of Serial Killers*, but the family would not hear of it. 'How could anyone doubt this highly trained nurse, devoted to caring for and saving lives, would do anything to hurt anyone' must have crossed their minds, but next to be airbrushed from the family group photo was 30-year-old daughter Annie Gordon. She died following a short illness on 31 July 1901, with Jane nursing her. Somewhat conveniently for the latter, no death certificate was issued, as had often been evident in the previous cases. The upshot was that Annie had become sick and confined to her bed, so a doctor was summoned because Jane thought that her patient appeared 'restless', as she later said at trial, adding, 'I obligingly gave her an injection.' When Dr Walters arrived, Jane told him, 'I think she is sinking.' The doctor took the frail woman's wrist, seeking a pulse, then looked up to say, with medical precision, 'This young woman *is already* dead!'

Alden P. Davis

The lethal nurse's next victim was the suffering widower, for whom the funerals were proving too frequent and a bit too much. Owner-landlord of the property in Cataumet where Jane had holidayed, as well as the Jachin Hotel in nearby Pocasset, he became depressed … so depressed, indeed, that he called for Jane to give him a nightcap. The following morning, 9 August 1901, 65-year-old Alden Davis was found stone-cold dead in his bed. Again no death certificate was issued. 'He died of a stroke,' Jane told his surviving daughter, Mary, who had got on well with her father while her husband was at sea. During this period, three small fires mysteriously occurred in the house, with all being doused with water without too much destruction – it is now thought that these were started deliberately by Jane.

Mary 'Minnie' Eliza Davis Gibbs

Just like her late father, Mary, also known as Minnie, soon became depressed, unsurprisingly after the deaths of her mother, sister and father, so she asked a cousin, Beulah Jacobs, to come to stay with her. A few days later, on 13 August 1901, 39-year-old Mary died, with Jane nursing her. Again no death certificate was issued.

It is impossible to view the previous medical oversights, *and* the earlier red-flag warnings the medical profession had so patently brushed under the carpet, over Nurse Toppan with anything other than disdain. To put no finer point on it, the entire Davis family had been wiped out in just six weeks, and that after three other siblings, Allie, Henry and Bessie, had previously had died of natural causes. When Mary's husband, 39-year-old Captain Irving Foster Gibbs, returned from his voyaging he found his wife dead, with her cousin explaining that Toppan had refused an autopsy because such a practice was against the religious beliefs of the devout Catholic family and the Church. Captain Gibbs smelt a rat, however. He lost no time in sharing his suspicions with the police, and the body of Mary was exhumed and found to contain enough morphine to murder six people.

Nurse Toppan's collar is felt

Jane, meanwhile, travelled to Amherst, New Hampshire, to stay with an old friend, Sarah Nichols, and her husband,

George. On the night of 29 October 1901, a Detective Whitney stood at the door of the Nichols' home in the rain and asked: 'Are you Jane Toppan, the nurse?' 'Yes.' 'You are wanted in Massachusetts for questioning in connection with the deaths of Mrs Henry Gordon and Mrs Irving Gibbs.' Jane went in handcuffs, apparently bemused by the thought that anybody should think her capable of murder: 'I have a clear conscience. I would not kill a chicken, and if there is any justice in Massachusetts, they will let me go', she said.

Now police throughout New England began to exhume dozens of bodies – all former patients of Jane Toppan. Autopsies proved that all had died of morphine and atropine poisoning. Meanwhile, from the Barnstable County Jail (Cape Cod lies within the county's boundaries), Jane was beginning a triumphant confession to as many as 70 murders:

Yes, I killed all of them. I might have killed George Nichols and his sister that night if the detective hadn't taken me away. I fooled them all – I fooled the stupid doctors and the ignorant relatives; I have been fooling them for years and years. I read [the prosecutor's] statements about me poisoning people with arsenic. Ridiculous. If I had used arsenic my patients would have died hard deaths. I could not bear to see them suffer. When I kill anyone they go to sleep and never wake up. I use morphia and atropia, the latter to hide the effects of the former. It took days sometimes to kill them.

– Jane Toppan

In a quote attributed to her confession in the *New York Journal* in June 1902, Jane often lamented that her killing spree took place because she had never married: 'If I had been a married woman, I probably would not have killed all those people. I would have had my husband, my children and my home to take up my mind.' On the evidence, that seems extremely unlikely.

On 25 June 1902, Jane stood trial in the County Courthouse in Barnstable, having admitted to 31 murders (the actual figure may have been nearer 100). Dr Henry Stedman, the forensic psychiatrist, gave evidence: 'Jane Toppan is suffering from a form of insanity that cannot be cured,' to which with an indignant cry the defendant shouted, 'The alienist [i.e. psychiatrist] lies. I'm not crazy and you all know it. I know that I have done wrong. I understand right from wrong … that proves that I am sane.' The not–so Jolly Jane was found not guilty by reason of insanity and subsequently confined to the Taunton State Asylum for the Criminally Insane, where her behaviour alternated between the docile, almost morose and raging fits of paranoia, during which, ironically, she would accuse the nursing staff of trying to poison her. She continued to live a long and healthy life, dying on 17 August 1938, aged 84.

Morally insane

'Moral insanity' used to refer to a type of mental disorder consisting of abnormal emotions and behaviours in the apparent absence of intellectual impairments, delusions or hallucinations. This was an accepted diagnosis in Europe and America through the second half of the nineteenth century. Dr Stedman stated that Jane Toppan's 'form of insanity that cannot be cured', which when taken within his overall diagnosis can only mean that Jane was a calculating psychopath, a person who knew right from wrong; a person who exhibited no remorse whatsoever for the terrible deaths and untold suffering she'd caused. Indeed, her own words tell us this much. My 2024 book, *Talking with Psychopaths: Guilty but Insane*, covers in depth the issue of criminal insanity and the application of the so-called defence known as the M'Naghten Rule, so even at a glance, it should have been obvious to almost everyone that Jane Toppan was sane.

It somewhat comes down to the 'Moral Insanity Defence' *v.* the 'M'Naghten Rule'. Did this diagnosis of moral insanity mentally incapacitate Jane Toppan to the degree that she could no longer recognise that her crimes were legally wrong, and was she suffering from a disease of the mind? The answer has to be 'no', because she knew the difference between right and wrong yet carried on regardless. Her principle motive was financial gain. She was stealing and filching from the start of her nursing training and probably much earlier while living with the Toppans; she befriended patients whom she thought might be of some worth – bringing them to death's door and reviving them, for which they were expected to be thankful, while killing those who were more of a hindrance on her time. To Jane, they were better off dead than alive.

Capital punishment in Massachusetts

'The Bay State' or the 'Old Bay State' has a long history of capital punishment ever since it was founded as an English colony in the seventeenth century. The reason I raise this subject here is because until capital punishment was abolished in the state in 1984, Massachusetts had never been shy of executing people. More to the point, between 1788 and 1951, any man or women convicted of first-degree murder received the death penalty. Even a person convicted of just *one* capital murder would die in the electric chair. Jolly Jane Toppan was convicted of *12* capital murders (she confessed to a total of 31 killings), so why was she not strapped into Ol' Sparky and fried?

The interesting thing is that medical serial killer Jane Toppan never entered into a plea-bargain agreement to save herself from execution. Indeed, she was smart, savvy, streetwise. She laughed in the face of the forensic psychiatrist who labelled her 'insane' – a diagnosis as far from the truth as it is possible to get. Some say that she claimed to have had some kind of sexual fetish that she indulged by murdering helpless patients. I don't buy into that at all as any type of motive for her crimes. What *is* reliable is a quote in Colonel Robert Barr Smith's article 'The Modest Ambition of Jane Toppan', in his 2015 collection, *Outlaw Women*. He cites Jane as saying that her ambition was 'to have killed more people – helpless people – than any other man who ever lived', and that seems entirely plausible to me.

Afterword (almost . . .)

Looking back through her homicidal narrative, we find in Jane Toppan a woman as cunning as a fox, with a heart of ice, a soul as cold as a wintry day, so was her final disposition in an asylum preordained? As I see it, and some readers might disagree, how on earth could the state execute a former nurse who had been trained in the highly respected Nightingale principles and had served in two of the most prestigious teaching hospitals? Of course it could not is the bald answer. Never mind some perturbed colleagues telling senior staff that trainee nurse Toppan spent time at autopsies and in the mortuary, apparently fascinated by cadavers, or that many patients under her watch were dying like flies, where was any oversight? Why were the police not contacted to make enquiries during her time in those hospitals? Why on earth during her residency were no post-mortems held on the deceased, many of whom, while in fragile health, were on the road to recovery? And, to cap it all, she left the official nursing profession all prim and starched proper with any stain on her dodgy character washed out. This allowed Jolly Jane to move with ease into the private sector with a stream of well-known doctors recommending her to vulnerable people, only for her to kill again and again!

I know that this is a well-documented historic case, but has the medical profession learned anything from Jane Toppan? Possibly not, at least in part. Ask any hospital administrator whether they have studied the psychology of Nurse Jane Toppan and they might well reply with: 'Er … Which ward is she presently on?' before returning to sucking a pencil while shuffling some paper around. A few nurses of Toppan's ilk may still be among us today, and God help you if one of them is at your bedside right now.

Jolly Jane Toppan is buried in grave 984, Section 34, in the Potter's Field at Mayflower Hill Cemetery, Taunton, MA. I am reliably informed that she's still there today.

A psychiatric conundrum

In 1983 Richard J. Bonnie published a paper in the *American Bar Association Journal* called 'The Moral Basis of the Insanity Defense' (Vol. 69, No. 2, February 1983, pp.194–7), of which an extract can be found online.

In 1891, the psychiatrist Julius August Koch sought to make the moral insanity concept more scientific and suggested the phrase 'psychopathic inferiority' – later changed to 'psycho personality'. An extremely readable paper, 'Moral insanity and psychological disorder: the hybrid roots of psychiatry' by David W. Jones, published by the journal *History of Psychiatry* (10 April 2017) and available online via the National Library of Medicine, is also well worth studying. Nevertheless, I rather think that it all comes down to one's own perspectives. There are hundreds of homicidal psychopaths on death row in the United States of America today, and no doubt a great number of them – including multiple child killers – shovel out some form of moral-insanity defence to get themselves off the hook. But here's the thing: none of them will end up in a cushy prison being waited upon hand and foot like the nurse whom we will meet next. Period!

Nurse Lucy Letby

She is not the first National Health Service (NHS) serial killer and Lucy Letby is unlikely to be the last. Beverley Allitt, Harold Shipman and Colin Norris were all convicted of murdering their patients. The authorities were asked 'Why they were not stopped sooner?'
– BBC Two: *Newsnight* (21 August 2023)

From birth through to death, life is a journey with good times, bad times; a rollercoaster ride in between, as evidenced by the narratives of the medical killers previously laid bare in this book. And what did they all have in common? They stole memories, happy days, bad days, adulthoods, futures with loved ones while enjoying the most selfish of lives themselves. So too did Nurse Lucy Letby.

It will be the most un–Christian thing to say, yet I am obliged to in the context of this chapter, for it comes down to a matter of degree. The murder of an elderly person easing towards a natural death; or of an individual who has already lived a fulsome life; or one who is approaching their sell-by date with no going back to fresher times might seem a lesser business than taking the life of a baby not long from the loving mother's womb. That helpless infant, so vulnerable, so reliant for their life at its start, with so many prospects, dreams and joyous days to be had for perhaps eight decades, is cruelly snuffed out like a candle before it starts to glow.

One can view the headstones of some of Jane Toppan's victims online and what *do* you see?: grimy weathered limestone; chiselled names barely readable after the passage of time, damp earth sinking, their life's narratives reduced to yellowy paper, the ink slowly fading away, and just maybe some mention on the *Find a Grave* website. Nothing more, nothing less, these victims now mere footnotes in the annals of murder most foul. Fast forward to the present. The murdered child in a small white coffin, pallbearers in tears, the tolling of the bell, and the parents' hopes and dreams for that baby gone too. And somewhere the killer sits, all smug, snug and warm, having destroyed many innocent lives with a 'fuck you, fuck them' attitude, having already enjoyed a good life while callously stealing the very start of the lives of others.

Phew! That was heavy-going, I have to say, so let's move on.

What can I say...

... that has not already been said? What can I write that has not already been written about NHS neonatal nurse Lucy Letby? Not much, I am bound to say, so she is included in this book more in passing than in depth. The details of her convictions are so well documented elsewhere that it would be tedious for the reader to have me wade through her narrative all over again, since there is already more than enough material online and in the media, with often conflicting professional opinions and a lot of educated and uneducated guesswork thrown in for good measure. Similarly, I will not go down the 'Establishment's blame-game road' either, because it has already been well-signposted, chewed over and spat out like bitter medicine many times.

NHS serial killer Dr Harold Shipman targeted elderly patients who trusted him, lethally injecting them with morphine. He killed them because to his mind they needed to be killed/executed. Elderly patients were also the target of young NHS nurse Colin Norris, who went rogue. In 2008 he was found guilty of murdering four elderly patients and trying to kill a fifth because he despised old people. His warped psychology dictated that he needed to kill them.

But the closest comparison to Letby is NHS nurse Beverley Allitt, also in her twenties and who also worked on a children's ward, in this case in Lincolnshire. In 1993, Allitt received 13 life sentences for the murder of seven infants and the attempted murder of seven others. As set out earlier, giving patients lethal injections of drugs amounts to executing them, so let's not dress these homicides up as *anything* less for fear of upsetting those who take a more liberal view of such crimes. That simply wouldn't do, would it? For the purposes of this chapter, however, I propose to look into Lucy Letby's childhood to see whether there are any indicators that might have pointed to a serial killer in the making.

A serial–killer breed

The FBI defines a serial killer as any individual who kills three or more people with cooling-off periods in between the 'events': John Wayne Gacy; Ted Bundy; nursing assistants Gwendolyn Graham and Cathy May Wood; Peter Sutcliffe; Andrei Chikatilo; Myra Hindley; Carl Panzram; Rose West – on and on ad infinitum. Pick up any compendium volume and you will see that 'serial killer' is an all-encompassing term. No psychological icing sugar can sweeten their horrific murders, no matter what sex, age or ethnicity their luckless prey may be, or what their sickening motives or methods of killing. Words such as gross; sickening; evil; abominations and monsters leap from the black pages of criminal history and if anyone feels any compassion for them in their hearts they should think again, for it could be one of *your* very own beloved who falls prey to a serial killer. Don't ever think 'This could never happen to me'.

Lucy Letby, join the serial–killer club!

The person who kills within a healthcare setting has already developed the desire to kill before they join the healthcare setting. And if you want to kill of course you're going to identify people who are vulnerable.... People whose deaths won't be noticed, *so guess what?* The people who serial killers target by and large are older people or they target very, very young people, specifically in a neonatal unit in this case [Letby] where again small babies with chronic underlying health problems are vulnerable.

– Professor David Wilson: BBC Two *Newsnight*

I hold a deep respect for the noted Professor Wilson. Although we have both appeared in the television documentary series *Born to Kill?*, I have only met him briefly in person – we did a grip-and-grin photo at CrimeCon UK in 2023. I admire him, and so should anyone. (Oh, and if you have never heard of CrimeCon UK, it's an annual event for true-crime enthusiasts held in London and in Glasgow, so look it up online and book a ticket ASAP. Endorsement done and dusted.)

Formative years – in brief

Unlike serial-killing nurse Jolly Jane Topman, who was born on the wrong side of the tracks, the same cannot be said of serial-killing nurse Lucy Letby. There is no evidence even to suggest that she endured a brutal or disadvantaged childhood, far from it. Unlike the American serial killer Aileen 'Lee' Wournos, who went through Hell and back *even before* she had turned 12 years old, suffering the most nightmarish child abuse that one can only dare think about. I wrote about this in my book *Monster*, the basis for the 2003 movie starring Charlize Theron, but even this brilliant film skipped Lee's formative years as being far too disturbing for public consumption.

> Of all human activities, education is the one most likely
> to give rise to cant, pomposity and fraudulent expertise.
> – John Rae: the *Observer*, 1983

'Those who know the Letbys say that 77-year-old former shop manager John and 63-year-old retired accounts clerk Susan doted on their daughter. Some might even say too much so,' wrote Barbara Davies in the *Daily Mail* (22 August 2023).

Lucy was born on 4 January 1990, six months after her parents married and not long after they bought a semi in a cul-de-sac in Hereford. Lucy, said neighbours, was always a 'delight to her parents', who watched her thrive at Aylestone Comprehensive School and then at Hereford Sixth Form College, one of the most successful sixth forms in the UK and officially graded 'Outstanding' in all aspects of its work. So Lucy Letby had a first-rate education.

Her first part-time job was as a teenager at high-street booksellers WH Smith, but she had plans for her career, telling a schoolfriend that she'd had a very difficult childbirth and was 'very grateful for being alive to the nurses who would have helped save her life'. This, her friend mentioned, had led Lucy to want to be a nurse all her life, and that 'everything that she did was geared towards the ultimate goal of becoming a nurse'. When, in 2011, she graduated with a BSc in Child Nursing from the University of Chester, her parents were so delighted that they took space in the local paper, telling all and sundry: 'We are so proud of you after all your hard work.' They did the same again when she turned 21; this time accompanying the birthday notice with a photograph of their daughter as a sweet-looking child. Although they were said to be unhappy about her moving away from Hereford to start her new job at the Countess of Chester Hospital in Chester, they helped her buy her first home: a £179,000 three-bedroomed semi – just a mile from the hospital – where she lived alone with her two rescue cats, Tigger and Smudge. There will be many young adults across the world who would love their parents to buy them a three-bedroomed property and rocket them up the housing ladder.

So there she is, at the beginning of her career: personable, well educated, well provided for, and about to start her dream job.

Mind control/Psychological manipulation

Allow me to place a bit more of Letby's younger years under the glass to ask, were there any homicidal indicators to be found in her mindset? Perhaps I discern overbearing parental imprinting entering the picture we are now painting of young Lucy Letby. There is nothing wrong in parents being very proud of a child, that's a given, but taking out birthday greetings and notices in newspapers congratulating their pretty daughter while adding a photo of her as a 'sweet-looking child', as though she is a precious piece of bone chinaware only to be brought out on special days is, I think, a little over the top. Had every proud Hereford parent done this, the local newspapers would have been as thick as Long Island telephone directories, and they are VERY BIG, as I can attest. Besides, for a teenager this vainglorious advertising might well have been an embarrassment to her; inviting ridicule from peers who had less fortunate childhoods and educations than hers. (I can also attest that if my mother and father had stuck a photo of me in the local rag – and I have never been 'sweet-looking' from day one, with my ears looking like a London taxicab with its doors wide open – I'd still be a laughing stock across Planet Earth many decades later, social media being what it is today. Yes, my parents used to take me and my sister Elizabeth on summer bucket-

and–spade holidays to the seaside. Elizabeth told me quite recently that our mother, Mary, once scolded Dad with something like: 'Christopher is not in the car', to which he replied: 'Never mind, I'm sure some idiots will adopt him.')

We find other small indicators of possible discontent elsewhere. During her 2022 trial, the emergence of texts that Letby exchanged with colleagues hinted that sometimes she felt 'smothered' by her parents, while at the same time feeling guilty about moving away from them. Nonetheless she continued to holiday with them, going on the thrice-annual trips to Torquay, the south coast resort the family had enjoyed since her early childhood. Torquay? And she once told a doctor who was moving to New Zealand that she would never have been able to make such a move because it would 'completely devastate them [her parents]', adding, 'They find it hard enough being away from me now and it's only a hundred miles.' Another time she messaged: 'My parents worry massively about everything and anything, [they] hate that I live alone, etc. I feel bad because I know it's really hard for them, especially as I am an only child, and they mean well, just a little suffocating at times and constantly feeling guilt.' Ironically, given the nature of Letby's crimes, maybe the key to understanding her sometimes claustrophobic relationship with her parents might well lie in her infancy. So what are the psychological effects of controlling parents if, indeed, hers really were a little too inclined in that direction?

A 2019 study of 762 children reported that those who perceived their parents to be more controlling had a significantly higher risk of internalising issues. This includes emotional problems, such as depressed mood, apathy and psychological stress. Controlling or overbearing parents are often referred to as authoritarian. If a parent is strict, they may not let a child have much autonomy or independence, as was the case with young Harold Shipman. Dr Jennifer Litner, a certified sex and relationship therapist, endorses Marissa Moore's 2 August, 2022 online piece: 'Dealing with an overbearing parent can feel like walking on eggshells.'[13] There is no suggestion from me that Mr and Mrs Letby were strict authoritarians; indeed, quite the opposite. Perhaps they were overinvesting in their daughter by wanting the best for her; being overprotective and somewhat restrictive at the same time because of her difficult birth. In this regard her parents' perceptions might well have differed from their daughter's mindset, thereby introducing some tensions.

If Letby's comment, that she wanted to become a neonatal nurse because she had survived a traumatic birth *is* true, this *might* go some way towards explaining why her parents had a tendency to overprotect their only child. What effect this might have had on Lucy as she entered her adult years is another matter entirely. I somehow feel that many psychologists, including Professor Wilson, might say that I am barking up the wrong tree. I will let readers judge me on this.

On the subject of psychologists, some have suggested that Lucy Letby was/is a covert narcissist; that having been the centre of her parents' universe for so long she still craved the attention she'd received since childhood and, once living away from them, needed to find it elsewhere. There might be some truth in this because other text messages sent

---

13 PsychCentral website: https://psychcentral.com/relationships/understanding-and-managing-your-controlling-mother

throughout the period of her NHS killings reveal how she sought sympathy and admiration from colleagues – a sort of neediness, both clingy and attention-seeking. Several factors can cause a person to be needy, including low self-esteem, a negative self-image, past traumas, or an anxious attachment style. We will see this neediness trait in Beverley Allitt.

But does any of this answer the question: 'How could a child raised by such adoring parents have been convicted of being one of the worst child-killers in modern British history?' As my late friend, Professor Elliott Leyton, once bluntly told me, 'Millions of children have good and bad upbringings but they don't turn into serial killers, do they?' He had a point.

After the death of Letby's first victim, 'Baby A', in June 2015, a colleague sent her a message: 'I hope you are OK, you were brilliant.' The murderous nurse responded with a short, cold reply: 'It was the hardest thing I've ever had to do... Just a big shock for us all. Hard coming in tonight and seeing the parents.' Yes, it must have been hard for Letby having to face a dead infant's mother and father. Yet she did not seem to harbour any emotional feelings, no remorse towards the deceased infant *or* the grieving parents in that reply.

According to Dominic Willmott, a lecturer in criminology at Loughborough University, some of the nurse's texts suggest that she wanted to 'garner sympathy' after the babies' deaths. 'She [Letby] may have been motivated by a pathological desire for attention and sympathy' (quoted in the *Daily Mail*, 21 August 2023). To bolster this, another key prosecution argument throughout her trial was that she wanted to gain the sympathy of a doctor with whom she had become 'infatuated'. I find that idea a little hard to swallow. We could poll thousands of young women who wanted sympathy from a doctor because of a doe-eyed crush on him, but who would never dream of murdering babies in order to win him over – at least, I hope not!

There have even been suggestions that Lucy Letby was suffering from Munchausen syndrome by proxy – the condition in which, for instance, carers may sometimes intentionally harm children to gain attention for themselves. 'Harm' can be interpreted in several ways, but there is a vast difference between a little slap and intentionally stopping hearts, isn't there? Furthermore, one is straying into the territory of 'moral insanity' here, and there are claims that Letby became animated after some of the murders, as though revelling in the medical drama that she had created.

Not seeing the wood for the trees

It is a shocking indictment that killers such as the murderous psychopaths John Bodkin Adams, Harold Shipman, 'Jolly Jane' Toppan, Beverley Allitt, Edward William Pritchard, William Palmer, Thomas Neill Cream and Marcel Petiot had worked hand-in-hand with many of the most talented professional doctors, surgeons, consultants, psychologists and psychiatrists of their day, *and no one even suspected* that there was a cold-blooded serial killer in their midst. These colleagues often canteen together, socialise together, party together, sometimes have sex with one another, even go and work abroad together (where they can earn a decent salary), yet these murderous doctors, nurses and caregivers remain invisible, hiding in plain sight. And where are the managers and administrators when a whistle-blower dare raise concerns? I will leave that question hanging in the air while the reader considers the medical establishment's cover-ups in the cases of John Bodkin Adams, Harold Shipman and the ever-smiling Jane Toppan.

As for law enforcement, these days the police have enough problems with their own whistle-blowers – and I am not referring to the shiny whistles that they used to carry in their tunic pockets either. Flippant? Perhaps, but as we have already know, police are reluctant at the best of times to meddle with the medical profession, if not even more reluctant to question one of their own. Yet these medical killers have sworn the Hippocratic Oath or have pledged to uphold Florence Nightingale's principles, have they not?

I am not suggesting that we should be living in some Utopian society; one where we 'spy' on everyone with whom we come into contact. That would be a step too far, but there *are* the behavioural red flags that these medical monsters subconsciously raise to advertise their intentions, so we might educate ourselves as to what those warning signs mean when presented, and not be persecuted when we report them.

Afterword

As mentioned from the outset of this chapter, I had no intention of rummaging through Letby's crimes ad infinitum. The reader will be better served by looking elsewhere, with *Wikipedia* doing a first-rate job as a starting point. There are YouTube videos aplenty and TV documentaries too, as well as endless press articles and several books. But I would like to end this chapter with some high notes and low notes.

John and Susan Letby come from good stock. Law-abiding, hard-working folk who only wanted the best for their only child, so their hearts were certainly in the right place. It must have come as an earth-shattering shock to their good morals and sensibilities that Lucy metamorphosed into a serial-killing nurse, so they too have become victims – albeit to a much lesser degree than the bereaved parents. I have seen this familial victimology echoed in the countless cases I have studied or worked on in my long career, including Jeffrey Dahmer's father and Joanne Dennehy's parents. As for Lucy Letby, did she truly love her parents? Of course she didn't. Her so-called love and respect for her mother and father was all a sham, with no consideration for their feelings at all. Lucy Letby only loves herself.

Wikipedia tells us that she is presently incarcerated in HMP/YOI Low Newton, Brasside, County Durham, of which notable inmates have included:

Rose West – former wife of serial killer Fred West

Sharon Carr – the youngest female murderer in modern British criminal history who killed aged 12. (She has since been moved to some other facility after a violent incident with another inmate.)

Tracey Connelly – known for her part in the abuse killing of 'Baby P'

Anne Darwin – wife of John Darwin, who faked his own death in an initially successful bid to fraudulently claim insurance

Bernadette McNeilly – leader of a group that tortured 16-year-old Suzanne Capper (released in 2015)

Barbara Salisbury – nurse convicted of the attempted murder of two elderly patients in order to 'free up beds', and also charged with, though not convicted of, other attempted murders of patients

… and serial killer Joanne Elizabeth Dennehy – formerly of HMP Bronzefield

If you have read *Love of Blood*, my definitive book about Dennehy, you might be dismayed to learn that HMP Low Newton offers: 'some level of personalisation'. According to the *Daily Mail* (21 August 2023): 'At the top security prison, killer women get the chance to pet sheep and goats and look after a rabbit and birds as a way to keep them "calm".' Truly, one could not make any of this up however desperately one tried: 'Letby will likely have access to the 'Rags to Riches' shop which sells clothing to inmates... photographs from a previous inspection show pink towelling and beauty products.' But to end this chapter, there are many liberal-minded people who will say that spending the rest of her life in jail is punishment enough for Lucy Letby. Not to me it isn't. She's still breathing. Her victims are not.

For us, however, it's time to move on with our murdering medics' travelogue, some 4,500 miles; to the country that is a hub of the call-centre industry and where millions of people seem to enjoy riding on top of rickety trains, frequently falling off. Yes, India!

Dr Bukhtyar Rustomji Hakim, aka 'Buck Ruxton'

Red stains on the carpet. Red stains on the knife. Oh,
Dr Buck Ruxton, you cut up your wife!
– News of the Times – Unlocking the Vaults of Historic
Crime: podcast hosted by Robin Coles

Anyone who has watched online the 'long drop' hanging of Saddam Hussein will understand what it's all about: a loud bang; a millisecond of weightlessness; a numbing jolt, a moment of anoxia, dizziness, a kick of the legs, then death. Saddam wasn't smiling.

One of his murderous sidekicks, Ali Hassan al-Majid al-Tikrit aka 'Chemical Ali', was hanged at Camp Justice, Iraq, on 25 January 2010. The execution was botched. His head was torn off and rolled across the floor. 'Chemical Ali' wasn't smiling either.

On 12 May 1936, an unsmiling, terrified Dr Buck Ruxton briefly acquainted himself with hangman Albert Pierrepoint at HMP Manchester. The Bombay-born Parsi with a pathological jealousy disorder provides a notably historic case to be sure, but what fascinated me out of the scores of crimes I have reviewed is not so much Ruxton's dismemberment murders, but it is his psychopathology and backstory that are so intriguing. The more so because what follows has more twists, turns and permutations than Rubik's Cube, with the added puzzle of a morbid Cyclops eye as the finale to what was then billed as 'the Greatest Murder of the Century'.

The Parsis

Bukhtyar Rustomji Hakim, aka Buck Ruxton, was born in Bombay, now Mumbai, on 21 March 1899, into a prosperous Parsi family of Indian/French origin. Parsis are descended from Persians who fled their country in the eighth century to escape persecution by Muslims. Initially they settled in the Indian state of Gujarat, but with the growth of European trade in the seventeenth century, they flourished as merchants to spread to other parts of the country and played a major role in the growth of Bombay. Parsis, followers of the Zoroastrian faith, have a strict religious outlook on life, and are described as conscientious and skilful in their mercantile pursuits. (The tale 'How the Rhinoceros Got His Skin' in Kipling's *Just So Stories* features a Parsi 'from whose hat the rays of the sun were reflected in more-than-oriental splendour'.)

As befitted his background, Buck Ruxton received a thorough education. A thoughtful, sensitive youth, he studied at Bombay University where, in 1922, he qualified as a Bachelor of Medicine, and later as a Bachelor of Surgery. As expected, great things were foreseen for the handsome young doctor by his family, friends, colleagues and many other Parsis, in view of the first-class honours awarded him in medicine, midwifery and gynaecology. With a start like that in life, what could possibly go wrong? Indeed, from university he joined the staff of a Bombay hospital, later becoming a medical officer to the Malaria Commission. On 7 May 1925, in an arranged marriage, he wed Motan, a young woman from a well-to-do Parsi family. Despite the happiness of their betrothal ceremony in Bombay, however, his preparations for marriage to Motan did not proceed smoothly. Her parents, extremely strict followers of the Parsi faith, appear from entries in his diary to have raised objections to her marrying the young doctor, on the grounds that he was more a Muslim than a Parsi. Ruxton's diary entry for 24 April 1925 reads: 'As usual, went to Motan's place when she told me her parents suspected me to be following Mohammedan customs. I felt small and determined not to go to her place till they were satisfied about me.'

By 5 May 1925, however, all seems to have been resolved and young Dr Ruxton records his satisfaction with his bride-to-be's substantial dowry. Two days later, he writes of his 'Happy Marriage Day' and records that he spent 2,500 rupees for 'marriage purposes'. I'm not sure what the exchange rate rate for the rupee against the pound sterling was back then, but Indian weddings are some of the most lavish and expensive in the whole wide world. They are grand affairs with family and friends coming together to celebrate the union not only of two people, but of two families and all their relations, as well as friends and neighbours and their families, so they don't come cheap: around 50 lakh (5 million rupees – about £43,000 at the present exchange rate) might get you by for a middle-range union. Anyway, the wedding was such a fantastic success that Motan is no longer mentioned in his diaries beyond the few days' celebration of the marriage itself. Thereafter, what became of her no one seems to know, but the marriage was *very* short-lived and a complete waste of money if you ask me, for the soon to be renamed young doctor came to England alone, determined to conceal all evidence of wedlock and his Parsi faith for fear that this would affect his social and professional standing.

At this point in our travels into Dr Ruxton's mind, it would be remiss of me not to explain that once I visited India to meet the murderous sisters, Seema Gavit and Renuka Shinde. They were on death row at the time, although their sentences were commuted to life in Pune's Yerwada Jail, but that's a story for another day. While in India I had wanted to visit the Taj Mahal, dip my feet in the Ganges, and see other iconic places, but in the end I skipped all that and caught the next plane home.

I digress, but already at this early stage in Ruxton's narrative we see insecurity creeping into his fragile ego. What would it matter if he had been married in Bombay or not because at the time of his marriage, Dr Ruxton was employed in the Indian Medical Service for which he had worked in Basra and Baghdad, in Iraq, as well as in thriving Bombay, and by the time he set foot on English soil, he had also served as a ship's doctor? What more could Motan, her parents and many relations have expected – sainthood, maybe? With the help of a grant from the Bombay Medical Service, he attended courses at London's University College Hospital, going under the name of Dr Gabriel Hakim: 'Gabriel' is a given name derived from Hebrew meaning 'God is my strength', and one would certainly need strength, as well as a strong stomach, to dismember two bodies and heave them over a bridge into a waterfilled ravine – which Ruxton would later do!

Isabella Kerr

Isabella was born in 1901 into a hard-working family in Falkirk, Scotland. The 26-year-old manageress of an Edinburgh restaurant had disastrously married a Dutchman named Van Ess but after a few weeks she left him and continued to use her maiden name of Kerr. In 1927, after a brief spell in Paris, Ruxton moved to Edinburgh – a major centre of the medical world – where he studied to become a Fellow of the Royal College of Surgeons. He failed the entrance exam on no fewer than three occasions, but was allowed to practise by the General Medical Council on the strength of his excellent Bombay degrees. And it was while in Edinburgh that he fell in with Isabella. A stormy courtship followed, but one initially based on a genuine mutual affection, and when Ruxton went south to work as a locum to a London doctor, Isabella followed shortly afterwards. By now, he had changed his name by deed poll to 'Buck Ruxton'. This, he suggested to a friend, 'tripped off the tongue' and was more likely to prove palatable than his birth name of Bukhtyar Rustomji Hakim in sober medical circles which, like other aspects of his supposedly devout background, he'd jettisoned as inconvenient baggage, so perhaps he had a point there. In a nutshell, Ruxton was reinventing himself, as though he was ashamed of his background and formative years and his Parsi faith and heritage.

In London, in 1929, Isabella gave birth to their first child, Elizabeth, a name he chose as a nod to Queen Elizabeth I. The following year, the family moved to Lancashire, where Ruxton acquired a substantial practice in a solid-looking terraced house at 2 Dalton Square, Lancaster. In 1931, Isabella gave birth to a second daughter, Diana, and two years later, to a boy, Billy, and the couple took on a nursemaid named Mary Rogerson to look after the children. At this point it is fair to say that Dr Ruxton was a kind and caring GP. More than once he waived his fees for patients who could not afford to pay for treatment, and all in all, his practice was thriving.

> Do I look like a murderer? It's not in my nature and my religion would not allow it.
>
> – Dr Buck Ruxton

Behind curtained windows

The first glimpse of a smart home is very much like that of a well-dressed person. We may see a smile or a frown, but we cannot know what lies behind that stylish front. We see a nice-looking grey stone residence sitting in an upper middle-class street. A glossy painted front door, perhaps a maid coming out to polish the brass plaque beside it, which reads: 'Doctor Buck Ruxton. Hours: 2–4 p.m. 6.30–8 p.m.', and we pause to watch as a young woman, perhaps as young as 20, bustles giggling children to school. 'Ah, how nice,' we murmur as we move on our way.

Think about this. How many Norwood Park Township residents walked past serial killer John Wayne Gacy's house at 8213 West Summerdale Avenue, Chicago, oblivious to the fact that this monster had tortured and killed some 34 young lads and buried them in the crawlspace? 'John Wayne is such a neighbourly guy. He's a builder; a respected member of the Jaycees, and he's met Rosalynn, the First Lady of President Jimmy Carter, you know.'

How many folk strolled past serial killers Fred and Rosemary West's home, 25 Cromwell Street, Gloucester, ignorant of the terrible atrocities going on inside? 'Fred always has a cheeky smile and Rosemary never says a bad word against anyone, you know.'

How many Londoners looked at the frontage of 10 Rillington Place, Notting Hill, without ever suspecting that John Christie was one of the worst serial killers in history? 'Oh, yes, "Reg" was once a policeman and he has medical knowledge. So polite, too.' Or glanced up at Dennis Nilsen's top-floor flat at 195 Melrose Avenue, Cricklewood, London, completely unaware that he was strangling young men, dismembering them and trying to flush the remains down a drain? 'Den is very polite. A bit shy. He was once a police officer, you know.'

Countless murder houses hold many dreaded secrets and ghosts aplenty, it's just that we never have a clue as to what's going on behind those walls. A closer peek behind the stolid facade of Dr Ruxton's home would reveal loud arguments taking place between the couple, which tended to centre on Ruxton's unfounded belief that Isabella was unfaithful to him, so that jealous accusations regularly flew.

Weary of the arguments, Isabella would frequently pack up her things as well as those of their children and move, back lock, stock and barrel, to her Scottish family home. Panicking and in tears, the insecure Ruxton would telephone, begging her to return, with Isabella eventually caving in, only for the cycle to repeat itself again and again.

Police records document accusations by Isabella of physical abuse. On several occasions both parties were brought to the police station, where a sobbing Ruxton was recorded as rambling in speech, while Isabella made complaints stating that her common-law husband was beating her. As the excellent podcast *News of the Times* reports: 'Isabella was generally considered as attractive. She was vivacious. She enjoyed socialising. She enjoyed going to events. At one town hall function she spent the whole of the evening dancing with different men as Ruxton watched, so the dramatic ups and downs continued.'

In 1932, Isabella attempted suicide by asphyxiation, which ended with a miscarriage. After the birth of their third child the already tempestuous relationship between the couple grew even more so, with constant allegations of infidelity and mistrust. I have no intention of speaking ill of the dead: Isabella was a doting mother and faithful to her partner. Any talk of infidelity came only from Ruxton's lies in his statements to the police.

The Edmondsons

The Edmondsons were known within the Lancaster community of the time as a respectable upper middle-class family. Son Robert Edmondson was a strapping, handsome young man and considerably younger than the drab Ruxton and his 36-year-old outgoing partner. It can be said that Robert, who worked at the Town Hall, and Isabella were considered to have a friendly relationship, nothing more and nothing less, and although rumours flew – as they are inclined to do in such close communities – that their relationship was illicit, these were never substantiated. It was all just idle gossip. However, the green-eyed Dr Buck Ruxton was convinced in his own mind that the affair between Robert and his common-law wife was real and had been going on for some time.

Pathological jealousy

Pathological jealousy is an extreme, irrational form of mistrust that can have a profound impact on an individual's life and relationships. It extends beyond what is considered usual and takes the form of a conviction that a spouse or partner is being unfaithful. It can result in extreme distress, emotional instability, even violent behaviour – including murder most foul. Pathological jealousy is also known as 'morbid jealousy' or 'delusional jealousy', and frequently involves excessive suspicion, mistrust and intense emotional reactions such as anger, hostility and aggression irrespective of the actual situation within a relationship.

With that in mind, I tend somewhat to view Dr Buck Ruxton as an insecure man scrabbling to compete with his English colleagues, and this sense of inferiority, with its roots formed almost as soon as he had arrived in England, could lead to extreme anxiety and on to controlling behaviour. Instead of using healthy coping skills – he was a physician/ surgeon, after all was said and done – he wanted to control free-spirited Isabella in order to feel better himself. It is all about power and control, so what we see in the relationship between these two people is a clear-cut example of domestic violence and abuse. Not much has changed today, that being one of the reasons why I have included Ruxton in this book.

Dismembered bodies

On 29 September 1935, Miss Susan Johnson was enjoying a quiet Sunday afternoon stroll near Moffat, a popular town in Dumfriesshire, Scotland. As she walked across a stone bridge spanning a fast-moving stream called the Gardenholm Linn, she paused to look at the waters below, and found her attention attracted by something odd protruding from some sort of wrapping and caught up in the undergrowth. Looking more closely, she recoiled in horror when she realised that it was a human arm, so she hurried straight back to the hotel where she was staying to tell her brother of her grim discovery.

He accompanied her to the stream and uncovered other parts of a human body wrapped in newspapers and pieces of a sheet. The police were called. The stream and ravine were initially searched by Sergeant Sloane of the Dumfriesshire Constabulary, who found a further four bundles of human remains; some were wrapped in clothing (including a blouse and a pair of child's rompers) and some in a pillow case and another piece of sheet. An intensive search was then organised and within a few days, several other pieces of human flesh had been found in the Gardenholm Linn, and also in the Annan, the river into which the linn flows. A few days later, a left foot was found south of the bridge over the Annan at Johnstonebridge, some nine miles south of Moffat, on the Edinburgh–Carlisle road.

Human jigsaw

In an echo of the case of Dr Marcel Petiot, the first task of the medical team called on to assist the police in their inquiries had been to reconstitute the bodies from the varied remains found at or near Moffat. Initially it was not certain how many bodies they came from, such was the damage caused by putrefaction, or even what sex they were. Despite the state of the remains, however, it quickly became apparent how thorough the murderer had been in removing any identifying marks: facial features and virtually all the fingertips had been removed. This could only mean that someone with skills like those of a surgeon or a doctor could have done this, possibly someone who was 'forensically aware'. Yet, with insufficient knowledge of what he needed to do to conceal his involvement, Ruxton was already revealing clues to his identity.

Markedly different in size and form, the two heads were first designated 'Head Number One' (later shown to be Mary Rogerson's) and 'Head Number Two' (later revealed as Isabella's). In investigating what became known as the 'Jigsaw Murders', the heads formed the basis for the assignment of other parts in the reconstruction of the bodies. Professor John Brash of the Anatomy Department of Edinburgh University was able with increasing confidence to apportion parts to one or other of what became clear were two bodies. The pelvic trunk of 'Body Number Two', for example, could be seen as part of the same body as the upper portion, since the latter had two lumbar vertebrae attached to it while the former had three. Together, these two trunk portions completed the proper total of five lumbar vertebrae and when placed together, articulated perfectly. X-ray examinations in which the bones could be compared exactly with regard to shape, size and texture confirmed the initial finding.

When the two bodies had been reconstructed as best they could, Professor Brash was joined by the Scottish forensic scientist Professor John Glaister[14] and Dr Gilbert Millar (elsewhere Miller), Lecturer in Pathology at the University of Edinburgh. If Ruxton had only been aware of what was going on he would have been quaking in his shoes, for the very medical people he had striven so hard to emulate were on track to provide the evidence with which to hang him – ironically, to fracture the second vertebra towards the top of his neck, close to the skull, designated as C2.

Determining the sex of the two victims did not trouble the experts unduly. In Body Number Two, female sex organs were still intact, while in the head of the other body, a small and obviously female larynx was discernible. Additionally, pieces of facial skin from Body Number One showed no signs of stubble. If that were not horrific enough, now comes the bad part. The fact that both bodies had been drained of blood and viscera on dismemberment – which delayed the usual process of decay – meant that some pieces of flesh *could be* identified under microscopic examination. Three pieces were found to be female breasts, although Glaister could not say to which of the bodies they belonged.

Without wishing to ruin your dinner, the appearance of the bones enabled Glaister and his colleagues to reach fairly firm conclusions about the ages of the two women. In Body

---

14 1892–1971, Regius Professor of Forensic Medicine at the University of Glasgow

Number One, for example, sutures in the bones of the skull were not completely closed, calcification of the extremities of bones and teeth were not complete, and wisdom teeth had not erupted. All these features pointed to a female considerably younger than the more mature Body Number Two. Eventually, Glaister and the other medical experts were able to compile rough descriptions of the two women whose bodies they had examined. They assessed Body Number One as being aged between 18 and 25 years old (Mary Rogerson was 20) and between 4ft 10in and 4ft 11.5in (she was 5ft). Body Number Two was estimated to be aged between 35 and 45 years of age (Isabella was 34) and about 5ft 3in tall (she was 5ft 5in). The fact that the vertebrae in Body Number Two had been separated relatively skilfully gave further weight to the notion that some medical knowledge must have been applied in the dismemberment process.

Causes of death

The next question was how did these women get to die? With Body Number One it proved impossible to determine a cause, but in Body Number Two, broken hyoid bone in the neck and small haemorrhages in the lungs suggested asphyxia. If strangulation was indeed the cause of death, it would have left certain indications at the point of the tongue and in the eyes, ears and nose. Ruxton had skilfully removed all these parts of the body in what appeared to be an attempt to destroy any means of determining the cause of death of both women. But, although he didn't know it, in doing this he was inadvertently putting his own signature on the human remains, indicating, inter alia, that the victims

were more than likely to have been known to their killer –
and intimately.

The forensic team next considered the apparently indiscriminate mutilation of certain parts of the bodies. The leg
of one body had been completed flayed of the soft tissue and
skin while the other three legs were intact. The fingers and
toes of one body had been removed, but had been left alone
on the other body. Similarly, the skin had been removed on
just one of the upper forearms.

The dead *can* talk!

It was only when, at a later date, a list of known identifying
features of the two women was compared with the mortal
remains that a pattern became clear – namely, that the
mutilations coincided with the location of distinguishing
marks. Isabella's legs, for example, had been nearly the same
thickness from the knees to the ankles, hence removal of the
soft tissues. Her bevelled, squarish fingernails had also been
distinctive, so they, too, had been removed. Isabella is now
talking to the pathologist. She is saying, 'I know my killer
very well, and he knows me very well, too!'

The removal of skin on Mary's upper forearm had been to
conceal her conspicuous birthmark. She also had a squint in
one eye. Mary is also talking to the pathologist. She is telling
him, 'I know my murderer and he knows me very well!'

One of the specialists whose findings were to prove of
particular forensic value was Dr Arthur Hutchinson, Dean
of the Edinburgh Dental Hospital. He was able to determine
from the sockets of the missing teeth in the two bodies that
while some had been extracted some time ago, others had

been removed not long before or after death. That it *was* possible to date the extraction of the teeth from the condition of the sockets and gums appeared to have been overlooked by the murderer. Isabella had rather prominent teeth, which would have been a clear clue to her identity, thus leading the police to her husband – a doctor and surgeon. Professor Glaister estimated that the dismemberments could have taken about six hours to complete and, after due consideration after examining the remains on 1 October 1935, he pro-pounded that death had occurred some ten to 14 days earlier. Where this gruesome work had been carried out had yet to be established.

Locard's Exchange Principle

We saw above that under autopsy even the dead can talk in much the same way as a crime scene can 'speak' to SOCO (Scenes of Crime Officer) investigators through the French criminologist Edmond Locard's Exchange Principle, usually rendered as 'Every contact leaves a trace'. Actually Locard, who became known as the 'Sherlock Holmes of France', didn't say that at all. He stated '*Toute action de l'homme, et a fortiori, l'action violent qu'est un crime, ne peut pas se dérouler sans laisser quelque marque.*'[15] Translated, this means that any action of an individual, and obviously the violent action constituting a crime, cannot occur without leaving a trace.

Locard's Exchange Principle can be reverse-engineered and modified to apply to many other aspects of human behaviour, as I have explored in my 2023 book, *Letters from*

---

15 Locard, Edmond (1877–1966), *La police et les méthodes scientifiques* (1934), page 8.

Serial Killers. Over time, correspondence can reveal much about a person's mindset. Not only is the graphology of interest, but the content is so important because on every occasion when a killer puts pen to paper, he is consciously or subconsciously revealing more about himself than it might be wise for him to do so.

We could, if we wish, apply a similar principle to how the 'body language' and speech of an accused person under police interrogation reveal clues about truth and lies. Yes, I realise that I have wandered a bit off our intended route here, but Ruxton is leaving so many contacts – both physical and psychological – almost like his own unique fingerprints, the trail of which will eventually lead him to the gallows and a noose in a length of previously stretched hempen rope. 'Previously stretched?' you may enquire. Yes, hangmen previously stretched their ropes using a weighted sandbag to avoid a 'bounce' that could tear a person's head off, which someone would then have to reattach as best they could before the corpse was buried behind prison walls.

Last seen alive

On Saturday, 14 September 1935, leaving Ruxton to attend to his business, Isabella drove to Blackpool to meet her sisters, Mrs Nelson and Mrs Madden, and to see the illuminations for which the seaside town is famous. She left her home in the early morning for the 35-mile drive and returned to Dalton Square at about 11.30 p.m. Her car was found in Lancaster the following day, but Isabella had vanished. And Dr Ruxton? Well, he had two line of reasoning:

1. Isabella went to Blackpool in her own car with Robert

> Edmondson, although her two sisters did not confirm that Robert was with her, or
>
> 2. She took the nursemaid Mary Rogerson, which her sisters also did not confirm.

It's something of a mess, really, because published accounts vary. To my mind it seems highly unlikely that Mary accompanied Isabella on that trip, because her duties were more or less confined to caring for the children at 2 Dalton Square.

Mary Jane Rogerson

Mary was 20 when she went missing on Saturday, 14 September 1935. She was employed by Dr Buck Ruxton principally to look after the three children, although her duties extended to other work around the house. She had a simple outlook on life, was well liked, and she spent all her free time with her father and stepmother, and had never gone away without their prior knowledge. When on holiday she used to write home nearly every day, so her disappearance on this occasion was completely out of character, and even more so because she would have been thrilled to tell her parents that Isabella was taking her to see the famous Blackpool illuminations. So the reader can see that Mary, even post-death, is now offering some clues to why she has mysteriously gone missing.

Home help

As was her normal practice, charwoman Mrs Elizabeth Curwen would have called at 2 Dalton Square on Sunday the 15th to begin work at 10 o'clock; however, she had been told by Ruxton the previous Friday not to come to the house until the Monday morning. This indicates that Ruxton planned the murders in advance and did not, as he claimed at trial, commit them in a rage, a spur-of-the-moment sort of thing.

Charwoman Mrs Agnes Oxley was also expected that Sunday morning but stayed at home after her husband received an early morning visit from Ruxton, who explained that Isabella had gone on holiday to Edinburgh with Mary Rogerson and that Agnes would not be required until the following day. It is clear from this that the so-called holiday trip to Edinburgh was the doctor's invention, a ruse to keep the home helps from entering the house. By then Isabella and Mary had already been murdered and dismembered piecemeal.

Among the deliveries to be made at 2 Dalton Square on that Sunday morning, in addition to Dr Ruxton's copy of the *Sunday Graphic*, were four pints of milk brought by another helper, a Mrs Hindson. She normally carried them through to the scullery, but on this occasion Ruxton asked her to put them down on a table just inside the front door. He then told Mrs Hindson the same story – that Isabella and Mary had gone away with the children. Before she left, Mrs Hindson noticed that the doctor's hand was bandaged; he told her that he had jammed it in a door.

At about 10.30 that morning, with the house now clear of home help, Ruxton left in his Hillman car to buy two cans of petrol, later calling at a second garage to have four gallons of fuel put in the tank. From this, my dear Watson, I conclude that he had two purposes in mind for the petrol he'd bought, and would use it for something other than topping up his car for what would appear to be a long drive. Then, shortly before midday, Ruxton drove his three children to the house of a Mrs Anderson, the wife of a Morecambe dentist whom he and Isabella knew well, and asked her to look after them for the day. Mrs Anderson enquired as to the whereabouts of Mary but Ruxton avoided giving an answer, then described how he had cut his hand on a tin of fruit while preparing the children's breakfast – a completely different excuse from that given to Mrs Hindson.

At just before 4.30 p.m. on Monday, 16 September, Ruxton called on a Mrs Hampshire, a patient who was prepared to do some housework for the doctor and his wife, and later one of the prosecution's most important witnesses at his trial. The account Ruxton gave Mrs Hampshire of Isabella and Mary's absence differed again from previous versions. Mary, he said, had gone away for a holiday, while Isabella was in Blackpool. He explained that he needed help about the house because he had cut his hand badly while trying to open a tin of fruit, and was trying to prepare for the arrival of decorators the following morning in accordance with arrangements which, he claimed, he had made some months previously.

When Mrs Hampshire arrived at 2 Dalton Square she found that the stair carpet had been removed. The stairway was very dirty. Straw littered some parts of the floor and protruded from under Ruxton's locked bedroom door. In the doctor's waiting room, she noticed rolled-up carpets, stair pads and a badly stained man's suit. In the back yard she came across two carpets from the landing and stairs and some partly burned towels. Cleaning up as best she could, Mrs Hampshire asked for her husband to be called to help her, and on his arrival, Ruxton told the couple that they could take away the stair carpets and suit. On the following morning, however, Ruxton called on the Hampshires and asked for the suit to be returned to him so that he might have it cleaned. Inspecting the suit, he came across his nametape and told Mrs Hampshire to cut it off and burn it. When the doctor had gone, she looked more closely at the carpets and found that they – like the suit – were stained with what looked suspiciously like blood. Twenty to 30 buckets of water later, the colour running off the items was still reddish.

On returning to Dalton Square, Ruxton suggested to Agnes Oxley that Isabella and Mary had simply made up the story of their trip to Edinburgh. Mrs Hampshire was told later that same day that Isabella had, in fact, gone to London. Pressed on the subject, Ruxton claimed that Isabella had run off with another man, whereupon he broke down and started weeping. Unbeknownst to him, however, his problems were only getting worse. The various women who helped him in his domestic tasks could hardly avoid noticing that something peculiar was going on, for here we can see suspicious behaviour indicative of guilt.

On 18 September, a Mrs Curwen found a heavily stained blanket being soaked in a bowl of water in a recess in the back yard, and she and Agnes Oxley were offered what remained of the carpets as gifts. When a Mrs Smith arrived to start stripping paper from the wall near the stairs, she noticed that the curtains of the window below the top landing had traces of blood on them. Ruxton's response when she took the curtains down was to tear off and burn the bloodstained portion, remarking that the police would soon be accusing him of murdering a Mrs Smalley – a woman who in a completely different incident had recently been found dead in Morecambe.

Fictitious journeys

During this period Ruxton made several often clumsy attempts to cover his tracks, only to draw more attention to himself. For instance, on Tuesday, 17 September, he called on decorator Arthur Holmes and asked his daughter why her father had not been to Dalton Square, when in fact all that had been agreed was that he should call *at some time* in September.

Later that same day, Ruxton was involved in a road accident at Kendal, knocking a man off his bicycle. His explanation for what he had done and how he came to be in the Kendal area was contrived and convoluted. His account of the collision with the cyclist on 17 September would prove to be one of the best examples of the damaging fabrications he offered in trying to avert suspicion. When the cyclist, Bernard Beattie, reported Ruxton's car registration number to the police after the driver failed to stop, they intercepted the doctor at Milnthorpe, a few miles south of Kendal. Questioned about the accident some weeks later, the doctor was asked whether he'd been to Carlisle on that occasion. We will come to the reason *why* the police asked him this pointed question soon enough. Nevertheless, Ruxton denied it all, claiming that Beattie must have made all this up because he, Ruxton, had been to the Grange-over-Sands area, his route making it impossible to have been in Kendal without a detour of some 11 miles.

On Thursday, 19 September, Ruxton parked his car close

to the back door of his house and closed the kitchen door on Mrs Oxley, who was preparing his breakfast, and made several trips between the car and the upstairs rooms. He then drove off, after which she noticed that some of the upstairs rooms previously locked were now open and there was an unpleasant smell coming from the doctor's room.

Since the Tuesday of that week, Ruxton had instructed Mrs Smith and Mrs Curwen to keep fires alight in the back yard, on which he had burned papers. Now the two cans of petrol have significance, and on the Thursday, while sweeping out the yard, Mrs Curwen noticed pieces of burned blue and red material and a bloodstained swab of cotton wool. The material she found resembled a coat and an old-fashioned dressing gown that young Mary Rogerson used to wear. On Friday, 20 September, Ruxton told Mrs Curwen to buy eau-de-Cologne to rid the house of its nasty smells.

At 2 Dalton Square later that Friday evening, Ruxton arranged for the children to be taken out by Miss Bessie Philbrook, who was one of his patients and who knew Isabella socially. While driving her over to Dalton Square, Ruxton asked if she had known that young Mary was pregnant; the first of several attempts to stop enquiries being made concerning the maid's whereabouts by suggesting that Isabella had taken her away to have an abortion. Indeed, he tried to convince Mary's very concerned parents of the truth of this story when he called them the following Wednesday, cruelly claiming that Mary had been seeing a laundry boy, an explanation that utterly failed to assuage their growing fears. I think that the astute reader will now see where all this is going, and for Dr Ruxton, things were now about to get a lot worse.

Inside Dr Buck Ruxton's head

I killed Mrs Ruxton in a fit of temper because I thought
she had been with a man. I was mad at the time. Mary
Rogerson was present at the time. I had to kill her too.
     – Dr Buck Ruxton: confession written in HMP
     Manchester shortly before his execution

Quite apart from the fact that Ruxton was as guilty as sin,
there still remains unanswered the question as to why he
murdered Isabella and Mary, because I do not believe that his
scribbled note written while in prison was the whole truth,
and nothing but the truth – or even half of it.

There is not much to be gained by reflecting on his
formative years and through his teens, for they show Ruxton
to have been a highly intelligent individual willing to learn
and better himself in the medical profession. We can't fault
him for that.

It is true that his first marriage to Motan didn't work out,
and there is nothing unusual in that either. We know that his
relationship with Isabella had its up and downs so there is not
much to see there either, but he had a fatal character flaw:
he was capable of flying into an almost uncontrollable rage
on the slightest pretext, with Isabella once telling her sisters:
'We can't live together nor live apart.' When asked about
his relationship with Isabella at trial, he added to his answer a
quotation in French: 'Who loves most chastises most,' which
is without doubt the attitude of a narcissist.

Among Ruxton's attempts to divert attention away from
himself he suggested any inquiry directed at him could only

be the result of professional jealousy from other doctors in the area – which I believe tells us that he held a very high opinion of himself – while at the same time suggesting that a Bobby Edmondson, a friend of Isabella's who worked at the Town Hall, might know where his 'missing' wife was, implying that the two had been lovers. Slamming his fist down on the table, Ruxton stormed, 'The blighter! I could murder him.'

> In the witness box Ruxton, insignificant in appearance and pathetically nervous in manner, cut a sorry figure under cross-examination.
> — Sir Sydney Alfred Smith, forensic scientist and pathologist (1883–1969)

Ruxton's trial opened at Manchester High Court on 2 March 1936, when he pleaded not guilty to a charge of murdering Isabella. Among the first prosecution witnesses called was Isabella's sister Mrs Jennie Nelson, who described some of the lower points in Isabella's relationship with Ruxton and the latter's jealousy of Bobby Edmondson. Various other police witnesses also appeared to give details of the occasions dating from April 1934, when Ruxton had appeared at a police station complaining of his wife's behaviour and threatening her with violence. Eliza Hunter, a former domestic servant at 2 Dalton Square, described how she had seen the doctor with his arms around Isabella's neck, and she found a 'revolver under his pillow'. Bobby Edmondson's testimony revealed how Ruxton had talked in a roundabout way of the former's relationship with Isabella and his subsequent emotionally charged denial of any accusations of impropriety. As we have seen, Ruxton told Mary's parents that their daughter had been seeing a laundry boy, and he also claimed to others that Mary was pregnant, and that Isabella had taken her off to arrange an abortion, which was illegal in those days.

Ruxton spent what he must have realised was to be his last day of freedom in something of a mental nosedive. Clutching at straws, he tried to distort certain individuals' recollections of events that had occurred on and about 15 September in order to support his own version of events. He first asked the Andersons' maid whether she would say he had called every day since his wife had gone away, a request with which at first she felt obliged to comply, but later rejected.

Charwoman Agnes Oxley was asked to amend certain details about her arrival at work on the morning of 16 September but refused. Ernest Hall, one of Ruxton's patients occasionally engaged by the latter as an odd-job man, was asked to say that when he called at Dalton Square to repair a fuse on the night of Saturday, 14 September, the door had been opened by Mary Rogerson. Despite Ruxton's encouragement, Hall pointed out that he had been in bed on that day.

Motive for murder

Buck Ruxton and Isabella Kerr had lived together in what some might describe as a volatile and sordid relationship; while unable to live together or apart, they had three children. He was an excitable lapsed Parsi with a religious chip on his shoulder and a sense of low self-esteem among his medical peers. Life with the emotionally unpredictable Dr Ruxton must have been somewhat problematic for Isabella at the best of times, while she faced physical violence at the worst. No reliable statistics are kept of crimes arising from motives such as sexual jealousy or psychological derangement. How often do we hear of couples opting to stay together for the sake of their children or a partner's career, until a final straw breaks the camel's back? I suggest that this case resonates with similar unhealthy domestic arrangements to this very day.

A master of disinformation and of the juggling of facts, given to pathological lying at the drop of a hat, and to trying to mirror his own failings in others, these were ultimately Dr Ruxton's downfall via the hangman's trap. Moreover, I do not think for a moment that a fit of jealous rage over a man whom the doctor *imagined* was seeing his common-law wife was the final straw, because all those close to Isabella knew her to be a doting mother and faithful to a fault. Is it not possible that young Mary was pregnant with Ruxton's child, that she told her mistress and when both women confronted the doctor, he flew into a murderous rage?

It is interesting to note that despite overwhelming evidence that he killed Mary, Ruxton was tried *only* for the murder of Isabella. Counsel for the Crown, Mr J. C. Jackson, KC, claimed that Isabella had arrived back from Blackpool, where she had seen her sisters, and had then been beaten around the head and probably stabbed by Ruxton for her supposed unfaithfulness, and that Mary Rogerson had witnessed the incident and was also murdered to silence her. Mary's skull had been fractured by blows to the head, but she had been killed by 'some other means'. In this readers will have to decide for themselves, for this *was* a case of the more you see, the less becomes visible. Perhaps it is all hiding in plain sight?

The Cyclops Eye

If all the aforegoing hasn't put your own mind in a spin, try this: for many observers the most intriguing aspect of the entire case was the discovery with the rest of the remains in the ravine of a Cyclops (or Cyclopean) eye. Named after the Cyclopses, the one-eyed giants in Homer's *Odyssey*, the organ was a sort of fusion of two eyes. Remarkably, there was no medical proof whether it was of human or animal origin, but Professor Brash believed that its state of preservation differed from that of the other gruesome discoveries. The point was not pursued, but if it was the case that the eye was better preserved and bore a remarkable resemblance to a museum specimen, this would have emerged, perhaps? Since Ruxton was known to be interested in ophthalmology (the scientific study of the eye), it is possible that he owned such a specimen, although it is still hard to explain how it came to be found with the dismembered remains of Isabella and Mary Rogerson.

Think about that for a moment. What on earth was Dr Ruxton doing with a possible museum exhibit on his person when he committed murder most foul or disposed of his victims' bodies? The defence suggested that the Cyclops eye may have been from a deformed baby born to Mary Rogerson. If she had been killed in the course of an illegal abortion, then, the line of argument went, the abortionist would have had to murder Isabella, who had accompanied the younger woman to wherever the procedure was carried out. No one took this theory seriously, however. The Cyclops eye was really no more than a mysterious red herring. Several people were cross-examined about it, and Ruxton denied that it was his property, but no conclusion was ever reached about how it came to be in the ravine – and in the same wrapping as some of Mary's other mortal remains. (For anyone interested in the congenital disorder known as cyclopia the National Library of Medicine has published a paper, 'Cyclopia, a newborn with a single eye, a rare but lethal congenital anomaly: A case report', which can be found online.)

It seems fair to ask here what became of Ruxton's children? Author Jeremy Craddock writes: 'But I think what has lingered with me is writing about Ruxton and Isabella's children – Elizabeth, Diana and Billy. It is easy to lose sight of them. For them this was an unfathomable tragedy. They were left as orphans and put into care. The truth of what became of them is locked away in Preston's archives until 2035.' (*The Jigsaw Murders: The True Story of the Ruxton Killings and the Birth of Modern Forensics*, 2021.)

Considering sweet Mary Rogerson and her squint, if the Cyclops eye and a first-rate hanging don't keep readers up at night, then nothing will. Dr Buck Ruxton's punishment was, one might say, a case of an eye for an eye, a tooth for a tooth – *lex talionis*, the law of retaliation.

But now it is time to change time and place, to late-1960s Corby Glen, to be precise.

Nurse Beverley Gail Allitt

I know you don't believe me.
– BEVERLEY ALLITT: TO POLICE ON
HER ARREST IN 1991

Formative years

This shocking woman, dubbed by the media the 'Angel of Death', was born on 4 October 1968 and raised in the quintessential English village and civil parish of Corby Glen, about nine miles south-east of Grantham, a market town now well known as the birthplace of former British prime minister Margaret Thatcher. Set in the rolling Lincolnshire countryside, Corby Glen, until 1956 just 'Corby', boasts a fine Grade I-listed Church of England church founded in the twelfth century and is famous for its Sheep Fair, which dates to 1238. Now, sadly, also famous as the birthplace of serial-killer nurse Beverley Allitt.

Beverley is one of three sisters and a brother. Their father Richard worked in an off-licence (better known to our American cousins as a liquor store), while her mother was a school cleaner. As for her schooling, Beverley failed to get into Kesteven and Grantham Girls' School, the grammar school where the woman who was at the time about to become prime minister was a star pupil. Instead, Allitt attended the Charles Read Secondary Modern School (now Academy), a good school and certainly not one that might in any way have shaped Beverley Allitt's future …

So you see, young Beverley's background was nothing out of the ordinary and I am struggling to find where in Miss Allitt's formative years things started to go south. Was she so bitterly disappointed to have been turned down by the Tory leader's old school that resentment against mankind rankled within her? It does not seem likely, but there have been hints at a strong vein of attention-seeking within her. How early this behaviour began is unknown but attested reports from her school indicate that she would often arrive there wearing plasters and bandages, even plaster casts, and bask in the sympathy she received – while refusing to let anyone look at the supposed injuries. The school put her fictitious injuries down to 'clumsiness'. She apparently even managed to convince doctors that she had appendicitis, which led to her undergoing a quite unnecessary operation. It never occurred to anyone at the time that she might have a mental disorder known as Munchausen syndrome, named after the fictitious comic character who told incredible tales of his extraordinary exploits to seize the attention of and impress all who would listen.

Grantham and Kesteven Hospital

Moving on, Allitt left school at the age of 16 and enrolled in a pre-nursing course at Grantham College. At home, she appeared to be the model daughter, taking on babysitting jobs and saving the money she earned from them. She was, though, frequently absent from college due to various mystery illnesses: between 1987 and 1990 she presented herself to the casualty ward of Grantham and Kesteven General Hospital 24 times. Her nursing course ended in early 1991, by which time she had had 93 days off sick, and had unsurprisingly poor results to show for her training, but Grantham and Kesteven General were so understaffed at the time that when she applied to work there, they offered her a six-month contract on the children's ward, starting in February 1991.

Between the last week of February and the last week of April 1991, 22-year-old State Enrolled Nurse Allitt murdered three infants and a severely disabled 11-year-old, attempted to kill three other children and caused grievous bodily harm to a further six on the children's ward at Grantham and Kesteven General. Her means of killing were easily to hand: insulin – or just air. She administered massive doses of insulin to at least two children. A large air bubble was found in the body of another child at autopsy.

A high level of insulin in the blood lowers the blood sugar level (causing hypoglycaemia), which, if mild, leads to symptoms such as anxiety and hunger, but, if severe, leads to seizures, coma, even death. An air embolism specifically is a bubble, or bubbles of air or gas trapped within the blood vessels. This will, at some point, cut off the blood supply to a particular part of the body and can easily cause significant and permanent damage to the central nervous system. An injection of 2–3ml of air into the cerebral circulation can be fatal. Just 0.5–1ml of air in the pulmonary vein can cause a cardiac arrest. Direct-injection embolism was one of the methods used by Belgian murderer Roman Catholic deacon Ivo Poppe, his other method being to inject an overdose of Valium. But who was he? Let's take a moment to check Ivo out.

★

Ivo Poppe

Married father-of-three Ivo Poppe, who was 61 at the time of his trial in 2018, worked as a nurse and, once ordained a deacon, as chaplain at the Hôpital du Sacré-Coeur in Menin, west of Brussels, for some 30 years. Nonetheless, quite obviously, bless him, he wasn't a happy bunny; telling investigators that at the times of his murders he was particularly stressed after an operation on his wife, his sister's divorce, renovations on his house and his training to become a deacon. It seems he didn't get on well with his mother, his stepfather and two great-uncles. He murdered them too!

Poppe was arrested in 2014 after police were told that he had confided in his psychiatrist that he had 'euthanised dozens of people'. It seems that he had nightmares and told the psychiatrist that he 'could no longer deal with having "in good faith" ended the suffering of up to 100 patients by injecting air into their veins'. In court, the murderous nurse-cum-deacon modified this number to between 'ten and 20, 20 maximum. This is an approximate figure … It is an order of magnitude.' Somewhat plaintively, he told the court:

'I wanted someone to help me with my nightmares, I really needed therapy. That's why I talked to the psychiatrist who had also treated my wife.' As for the killings, he claimed they were on the grounds of compassion: 'I wanted to end their suffering; these people weren't really living any more.'

So back to Nurse Beverley, whose motives have never been fully explained, not that we need to find any motive at all.

★

Factitious disorder

In Allitt's case, Munchausen syndrome, which is also known by the less colourful term of 'factitious disorder', was manipulated by her into what is, or was, known as Munchausen's syndrome by proxy – another form of factitious disorder, now more boringly called 'fabricated or induced illness' (FII). This is when someone falsely claims that another person in their care shows physical or psychological signs or symptoms of illness, or causes injury or disease in another person in their care with the intention of deceiving others to attract attention to themselves. The other person is usually, though not exclusively, a child.

The National Health Service website states:

Fabricated or induced illness (FII) is a rare form of child abuse. It happens when a parent or carer exaggerates or deliberately causes symptoms of illness in the child. The parent or carer tries to convince doctors that the child is ill, or that their condition is worse than it really is.

The parent or carer does not necessarily intend to deceive doctors, but their behaviour is likely to harm the child. For example the child may have unnecessary treatment or tests, be made to believe they're ill, or have their education disrupted.

... FII covers a wide range of symptoms and behaviours involving parents or carers seeking health-care for a child. This ranges from exaggerating or inventing symptoms, to deliberately making the child ill.

Those with the disorder are assiduous in trying to make healthcare professionals (or, indeed, their own colleagues) believe that a healthy child is ill. This they do by exaggerating the child's symptoms, and even creating symptoms by such ploys as adding glucose to the child's urine to suggest diabetes; adding blood to the child's urine or stool; withholding food from the child so the child does not gain weight; heating up thermometers used for the child, or giving the child unnecessary medication, or other substances, to induce sickness. Sometimes, older children come to believe that they are invalids when they are not, which can cause psychological problems in later life.

Specifically relevant to Beverley Allitt is that, according to the American website *Medline Plus*:

The caretakers often work in healthcare and know a lot about medical care. They can describe the child's symptoms in great medical detail. They like to be involved with the healthcare team and are well-liked by the staff for the care they give the child. These caretakers are very involved with their children. They seem devoted to the child. This makes it hard for other health professionals to see a diagnosis of Munchausen syndrome by proxy.

We can now see how such a serial killer nurse, a pathological liar, a psychopathic individual can cover their tracks while wearing a fake mask of humanity. Allitt was – like so many of the previously mentioned killer doctors and nurses – hiding in plain sight. It was only following the death of her final victim that Allitt's colleagues became suspicious of the number of cardiac arrests on the children's ward. Police were called in and it was determined that she was the *only* nurse on duty during all the attacks on the children *and* that she had easy access to the drugs used.

From our examination above of the condition FII or Munchausen syndrome by proxy, it is clear that the death of the victim is not sought: Allitt, however, seems to have taken matters further and allowed her victims to die – why? It seems unlikely that the killings were accidental. Her victims were mostly too young or incapable of pointing the finger at her, so she had no reason to kill them, yet kill them she did. She had nothing to gain by their deaths – except perhaps more sympathy from her colleagues. In her babysitting days she had seemed genuinely fond of her charges so she could not claim some deep psychological aversion to babies. The question is, is Munchausen syndrome by proxy a viable defence for committing serial homicide?

Which takes us to the next question: which is preferable – a mainstream prison, locked up with hardened criminals such as spree killer Joanne Dennehy or serial killer Rosemary West; or the supposedly easygoing confines of a secure mental hospital such as Rampton or Broadmoor?

It was revealed in the 2018 TV documentary, *Trevor McDonald and the Killer Nurse*, that Allitt told close friends before her trial that she would never go to prison. Indeed, after just one week in prison, she refused to eat or drink, and lost a great deal of weight – which is the playing-for-attention card from the bottom of the honesty deck once again. Nonetheless, with this alleged Munchausen syndrome idea in her purse, and giving some psychiatrists pause for thought with: 'let's err on the safe side now', Allitt was diagnosed with anorexia nervosa, a psychiatric condition, rather than with manipulativeness and shipped off to Rampton high-security psychiatric hospital in Nottinghamshire.

Rampton Secure Hospital

Rampton is one of three high-security 'hospitals' in England and Wales. Among the well-catered-for clients, according to *lincolnshirelive.co.uk*, are: 'Mark Rowntree, the spree killer who, in 1976, admitted murdering four people in West Yorkshire; Eltiona Skana – who stabbed to death a seven-year-old girl in Bolton Park in March 2020, and Deividas Skebas – found guilty of the 2022 murder of nine-year-old Lilia Valyute.'

An awful hand of cards, to be sure, and lest I forget, people are detained in Rampton under the Mental Health Act 1983, for, among other things, learning disabilities, mental illnesses or sundry non-specific psychopathic disorders.

As is par for the course, the psychiatrists involved in

diagnosing on what planet she lives, could not agree on Beverley Allitt's mental condition. The *Daily Mail* of 24 October 2018 reports: 'Professor Todd Hogue, Lead Psychologist at Rampton Hospital between 1995 and 2008, said it is "very difficult" to convince experts of mental health problems.' Professor of Forensic Psychiatry Jeremy Coid told Trevor McDonald on the 2018 documentary: 'She doesn't sound like somebody who has a severe mental illness or a personality disorder so severe that she needs to go to Rampton.' And the criminologist Professor Elizabeth Yardley was quoted in the *Daily Mail* as saying: 'When we start talking about mental ill health, we're looking at people who aren't in control of their actions, but Beverley Allitt knew exactly what she was doing.' Both concluded that Allitt *was not* mentally ill and should be in prison and not a hospital, to which I fully agree, and anyone looking into her eyes would say the same as me because she is a homicidal psychopath and is 'working the system'.

That view was not shared by the mental health assessment panel before whom Allitt had appeared to be considered, as reported by the BBC on 3 October 2023, for a transfer to a mainstream prison – if she were, she could become eligible to apply for parole in a matter of six or so months. Two months later, it was reported that her request had been denied and that she was to remain in Rampton. She will not be eligible for another assessment until 2026 at the earliest.

Dr John Dale Cavaness

*The wicked is overthrown through his evildoing, but the
righteous finds refuge in his death.*
– Proverbs 14:32 (ESV)

Saline County (and that name is not intended as a medical pun), in southern Illinois, a region sometimes called 'Little Egypt', is about 300 miles south of Chicago, which it formerly exceeded in two regards: churchgoing and homicide. At the heart of Saline County is Eldorado, not so named because it was ever a place of gold and unbelievable riches, but after its two founders, Samuel Elder and Joseph Read; legend blames a sign painter for the misleading spelling. Known as a 'sundown town', it was a place of unrest, racial segregation and racism until the late 1960s, and was once said to have had a murder rate that was twice the US national average or about equal to that of the Chicago. This was the birthplace of John Dale Cavaness.

John Dale Cavaness was a natural fighter. His Bible-thumping momma, Noma, was a 'Dale': one of the first English families to settle in Ozark hill country, a lonely, wooded area that had become scarred by coal tips and open-cast mines. By the way of digression, in folklore, the 'Howler' is a legendary creature said to dwell in the Ozarks. Some describe it as a large, nocturnal animal resembling a panther or canine. Some say that it's as big as a bear but as lithe and stealthy as a leopard, while others claim it has sharp horns growing from its head with glowing red eyes, long black fur and a blood-curdling cry. I guess that the Ozarks are not the sort of place to pitch a tent in the dead of night.

Cavaness's father, Clarence Mark 'Peck' Cavaness, worked on the railways, which enabled the little family to avoid the worse of the Depression years when the mines were closed down and their neighbours were reduced to living on watered-down gravy. His mother Noma liked to boast of her only child, born 15 October 1925: 'He was a breech birth, and he's been doing things the hard way ever since.' When she forced her son to go to school in fancy knickerbockers and insisted that he learn the violin, the other boys bullied him. Then one day the diminutive Dale faced his tormentors and discovered that he could fight better and dirtier than any of them. Encouraged by his father, he became famous as a scrapper, making up in aggressiveness for what he lacked in height and weight.

When he left school in the late 1930s, Cavaness joined the US Navy as the Second World War rumbled on. He joined the battleship, the USS *North Carolina*, in the Pacific in time to see action against Japanese kamikaze attacks, and was honourably discharged after two years' service — a US

Navy veteran at only 21. He then married his childhood sweetheart, a local physician's daughter named Helen Jean Pearce. And it was her father who, chatting with Cavaness, encouraged him to enter the medical profession and so he attended Carbondale's Southern Illinois University and SIU Champaign-Urbana for his undergraduate studies, moving on to Washington University School of Medicine in St Louis. His fellow students reportedly found him to be a braggart and know-it-all, but he was competent and dedicated throughout medical school. It was reported that his father-in-law, who was building a new hospital in Eldorado, was planning to name it the Pearce-Cavaness hospital in anticipation of his son-in-law joining him in practice. It lasted as the Pearce Hospital until 1989.

Mariann Newberry

Before Cavaness had even left St Louis to start his residency, Helen left him for one of his friends. He was, it was said, devastated, but soon found comfort with a nurse at a St Louis hospital. Mariann (or Marian), who had been a friend of Helen's, was at first reluctant, but the two began to date, and when Dr John Dale Cavaness began a residency in Baltimore, she took a job with an airline based in New York.

Mariann, who was from St Louis and loved dancing, opera and wrote romantic poetry, and was used to big city life, was unimpressed with Southern Illinois when she went with John to meet his parents in Eldorado. But she was captivated by his confidence and energy and they were married in St Louis on 3 October 1952. After a short spell away, the couple returned to St Louis so that John could finish his education at the Maternity Hospital of St Louis. Rightly so, Mariann expected her new husband to scale the heights of medicine and was stunned when, in 1954, he abruptly chose to become a country doctor; at first working at Hamilton Memorial Hospital in McLeansboro, a small city in so-called Little Egypt, and then transferring to Eldorado and to Pearce Hospital, 'Cavaness' having been dropped from the name for obvious reasons; in spite of his divorce from Helen, he remained on good terms with Dr Pearce. Cavaness became an excellent physician and surgeon, putting long hours into his job. Mariann, however, was not thrilled about living in Southern Illinois and on their first wedding anniversary, after a few glasses of wine each, she mentioned *maybe* moving from the Midwest back to city life. Her husband responded by punching her in the face – a sign of things to come.

Children and spouse abuse

On 15 August 1954, Cavaness delivered their first child, whom they named Mark Dale. Another son, Kevin Dale, was born less than two years later, on 20 May 1956.

For the next 30 years, the legend of 'Doctor Dale' was to grow in Saline County, where people came to regard him as a cross between Superman, Mother Teresa and Robin Hood. He could do anything and remained good-humoured and cheerful while banishing their ills. There was nothing pretentious about their Dr Dale – he was one of them, Saline-County born and raised, and just to visit him was enough to cure most Eldorado people, so great was their faith in him. A long queue outside his surgery would wait uncomplainingly for hours. It was said that he never turned anyone away, and once a year he'd throw out the bills of those he knew could not pay.

Of course, as a fully trained doctor and the chief surgeon at Pearce Hospital in Eldorado, Dr Cavaness ensured that his patients came first: he saw nothing wrong with cheating an insurance company or the Prairie State to help out a patient or indeed himself, and any such misdemeanours would be noted with a chuckle and a wry smile. In Eldorado, and for miles around, Dr Cavaness could do no wrong even when he screwed up. Those who dared say a bad word against 'Dr Dale' had his army of grateful patients to answer to. What they did not see was the narcissist within Cavaness – the man who was always right, whom everyone admired, could never ever be contradicted or even stood up to. Any transgression of his rules at home would be met with unreasonable fury and violence. He was drinking heavily at the end of the day and would often become abusive towards his family, apologising profusely when he sobered up. Mariann would dutifully forgive him, but must have despaired as he grew more and more controlling and vindictive. One of his son Kevin's earliest memories was of being locked in a cupboard by his father and left there, crying, only to be told roughly not to be a baby.

The public image that Cavaness cultivated was that of the dedicated doctor who would work late, come into his surgery early, do house calls for free when needed, and even, unlike most practising physicians, take 'workman compensation' cases, which made him extremely popular. As time went on, however, this facade began to slip, especially as his various enterprises on the side, such as a catfish farm and a cattle-breeding project, began to falter financially and debts began to mount. His outbursts of temper increased as his drinking became heavier. Like his family, his office staff came to see his flip side, as he urged them to falsify documents and get into other fraudulent activity. If someone quit or upset him, he would get angry very quickly, especially if he had been drinking – as time went on, he was often knocking back bourbon at the office and *even before* performing surgeries.

Unfaithful

On one occasion Mariann found her husband at one of his properties with Martha Culley – a married woman who had left her husband to continue to see Dr Cavaness. Despite this, in 1962, another son, whom they named Sean, was born. The couple were now firmly rooted in Eldorado, with Mariann now having given up all hope of returning to city living.

Cavaness was given to playing what he termed 'pranks', which were no more than malicious tricks to control the emotions of the victims of these practical jokes. Among his favourites was to inform a patient that she was pregnant with twins, which would cause either consternation or joy, or to exchange X-rays, so that a patient was led to believe for a time that they had a fatal malignancy. These practical jokes grew more cruel with the years. He also carried around a loaded .357 Magnum pistol with a hair trigger, which he would sometimes fire into the air to startle people. On one occasion he reportedly shot dead his prize bull with the cry: 'Now it's a hamburger!' Nevertheless, the community still saw only the persona he presented to it of the caring, big-hearted doctor.

Ticking time bomb

Intermittent explosive disorder (IED), as the Mayo Clinic describes it, involves repeated, sudden outbursts of aggressive, violent behaviour or angry verbal outbursts, often disproportionate to whatever caused them; examples being road rage, domestic abuse, throwing or breaking objects, or other temper tantrums. IED can be caused by many things, including stress and financial issues. For some it may be caused by an underlying disorder, such as ADHD, or external factors such as alcoholism. With Dr Cavaness we can now see the dark side of his personality: the loud-mouthed, narcissistic braggart with his heavy drinking, a wife-beating husband, a controlling bully to his family; a conman and fireraiser willing to commit financial crime when his medical practice income fell short of his needs. Still, all the locals loved him. And, Cavaness's explosions of temper became less controlled, as did his drinking. He was said to keep an oxygen bottle handy, just to clear his head before an operation. His womanising became intemperate.

Taking a deeper dive into Dr Caveness's narrative, life with her husband must have been almost unbearable for Mariann. A mother with three boys, she must have had the patience of a saint for he was never around for his sons, but the two remained married even after he left her: she was later to find out that he'd never actually completed signing the divorce papers. Then Mariann gave birth to *another* son in 1966: Patrick Dale Cavaness. She was now living with her family in a house Cavaness owned – which mysteriously burned down (apparently because three-year-old Sean had been playing with matches). They moved into a trailer on the property while Cavaness collected the insurance to rebuild the house. He collected the money but did not rebuild the house. Eventually, after ten years of marriage, tired and frustrated with everything going on around her, Mariann moved with her sons to St Louis.

As for the fire and the insurance money Cavaness collected – this was used towards paying back the debts he incurred from foolhardy financial ventures and his catfish and cattle-breeding enterprises that were not profitable. The debts continued to rise, more mysterious fires occurred, more fraudulent medical claims were presented, more insurance money was collected until the companies grew wary. In 1980 Dr Cavaness was convicted of persistently making false health insurance claims. The penalty was a small fine.

Skewed justice

Cavaness's drinking almost led to his downfall. In 1971 (elsewhere 1972), Dr Cavaness was convicted of 'reckless homicide and drunken driving', after killing a young father and his ten-month-old daughter in a car crash. He didn't even lose his licence. It was night time on 8 April, and Cavaness, driving on the wrong side of the road, side-swiped one car and careered into another. Local cops found the baby impaled on the wing mirror, its mother unconscious and gravely injured, her husband dead on the road. Cavaness was unhurt and babbling incoherently. In his car was a nearly empty bottle of Scotch, a loaded .357 Magnum pistol and a 12-gauge shotgun. When told that two people were dead, he mumbled: 'Everybody's got to get dead sometime.' He pleaded not guilty. A year later he changed his plea and paid three $500 dollar fines – just $1,500 for three lives. Where is there any justice in that? Was he struck off the medical register? No.

Mark Dale Cavaness

Mark Cavaness as the oldest of four sons was known as the 'Doc's Boy'. Popular and good-looking, but incurring his father's wrath by doing poorly at school, he eventually drifted into casual work. His father was coldly indifferent to his welfare; his oldest son was a disappointment to him because he did not shine at school, left school early and had no qualifications. None of this is surprising when you consider how Cavaness belittled and bullied his sons. Loud and hearty with his favoured drinking companions – he called them his 'rudies' – he would tell them that their sons were 'real men', not 'pussies like Mark'. Cavaness grew even louder and more abusive with his family, especially with his firstborn. Often, the abuse became physical.

It was April 1977, and Mariann had arranged an Easter get-together with her husband and all four of their boys. Mark, who had had trouble finding and keeping jobs, had sought employment from his father, and had recently approached Cavaness who had agreed to employ him tending to his tanks of catfish. When he did not show up to greet his mother and brothers, Kevin decided to go and look for him. The others joined him, with 15-year-old Sean bounding ahead. The first thing he spotted was Mark's belt buckle in the grass. Twenty-year-old Kevin was right behind and tried to cover his younger brother's eyes, but it was too late.

There was not much left of Mark Cavaness. Mostly

freshly gnawed bones; one eyeball stared out from its socket and a fine set of teeth and a shock of long auburn hair gave a ghastly lifelike look to the young man's skull. As for the rest of the body, only the lower legs and feet were intact in their tightly laced boots – which was enough for a tissue test that would indicate that death had occurred the previous evening – Good Friday, 8 April 1977.

There are no wolves in southern Illinois, so investigators could only that wild dogs had got to the body, perhaps possums or turkey vultures. The remains lay in thick grass next to the pickup truck Mark had been using. The driver's door was open. There was a shotgun in the vehicle. There was blood on the driver's seat and door. This, together with a ragged, bloody hole in the front of a tartan shirt, told some of the story but not the *whole* story, so we must back up a bit because the circumstances leading up to the discovery of this horrific scene could not have been more upsetting.

Guns were as common as Bibles in the depths of rural Illinois back then, and where there are guns, there are accidents. But what the police found when they reached the scene was out of kilter. A 12-bore Browning, known locally as a 'goose gun', was lying on the passenger seat of the pickup truck, pointed towards the open door and propped across an axle handle, which had the effect of raising the angle of the barrel, thus the aim. The gun was still inside its well-worn case, with its muzzle poking through a hole, and through another hole the hook of a wire coat hanger snagged in the trigger guard. Draped on the hanger was a camouflaged hunting jacket, the tail of which was caught in the closed passenger door.

Thinking at first that this must have been a terrible accident, police discovered that the gun's safety catch was off, so it *was* possible to picture Mark opening the truck door, reaching for the gun case and getting blasted in the chest when the trapped coat hanger tripped the trigger; an extraordinarily bizarre accident, or just a fiendishly clever booby-trap. The sheriff and his deputies accepted that it had been an accident.

The sleuth

Special Agent Jack Nolen of the Illinois Department of Criminal Investigation was sceptical. It was his business to know more about the residents of Saline County than they knew about themselves. And Jack Nolen knew about Mark: that he was an experienced hunter who would be as unlikely to leave off a safety catch as to reach across and grab the dangerous end of a loaded shotgun. He reasoned that if a self-loading gun had been fired *inside* its case, that is where the ejected cartridge had to be. It wasn't. The cartridge was found lying under the steering wheel, thus Nolen concluded that this was a straightforward homicide rigged to look like an accident. The murder had been staged, but for the moment he said nothing to the cops muttering nearby.

Motive

From the beginning of this book we learned that one doesn't need a motive in the solving of a crime, although it can help if one could be found, so who would want to murder Mark Cavaness was a question in Nolen's mind. Mark was good-looking and liked by everybody, a favourite with the girls, but too laid back, too easy-going for any jealous rival or outraged father to have him in his gunsight. For his part, Dr Dale Cavaness seemed anxious for people to believe that it was an accident, saying to Nolen that he had warned Mark against drugs, hinting that the young man took drugs – a cynical ploy to lead Special Agent Nolen off the scent.

But Nolen hadn't earned his gold shield by being a dumb fuck, so he checked his network of informers, shook a few of them down, rattled some cages and came up with nothing. Apart from a little pot smoking, Mark Cavaness had led a wholesome life, and on his meagre earnings could hardly have afforded to do otherwise.

After six months of painstaking investigation, Special Agent Nolen filed a confidential report that put on record his initial conclusion of homicide, but listed no suspect for the obvious reason: Dr Dale Cavaness was, after all, the local doctor, an excellent surgeon and worshipped by his community. However, among the loose ends that Nolen kept in mind was his discovery that the doctor had taken out a double-indemnity life insurance policy on Mark a couple of months before the tragedy. That he had a rap sheet and had defrauded several insurance companies in the past Nolen noted too. Thus, the case was kept open as 'unsolved' but not allowed to go completely cold.

Life now moved on for Dr Cavaness. Eldorado rallied round its doctor in his time of anguish. Out of an apparently twisted sense of grief, he took to berating his dead son: 'I never did like Mark,' he was heard to declare. 'He was no good.'

Sean Dale Cavaness

While Kevin became morose and obsessed with finding his brother's killer, it was Sean who took it the hardest; dropping out of school at 16, he began drinking and putting on weight; drifting in and out of labouring jobs. As his drinking grew worse, he would try to phone his father at all hours, but Dr Cavaness seemed to be put out by his son's need for emotional support and constantly berated Sean as a failure, an overweight one to boot.

At 22 – the same age as Mark when he was blasted to death – Sean lacked Mark's casual air and self-confidence, and clung to his mother while his father rejected him. Late in 1983, Sean entered an alcoholics treatment centre. After he left, he seemed to improve. He found a girlfriend. To his delight he began to get calls from his father. Cavaness invited Kevin and Sean to participate in an insurance investment – that is, he would insure their lives. He told them that he would pay the $1,000 monthly premiums, so he would gain from the tax deduction, while they would benefit in the future because of the borrowing power the policies would accumulate. He did not add that, of course, if one of them were to die, he, the grieving father, would be better off by well over $100,000 …

As the harsh Midwestern winter set in, Sean found occasional work shovelling snow, and was looking forward to a family Christmas reunion in Eldorado.

Fourteen stiff drinks

At 7.45 a.m., on Thursday, 13 December 1984, police discovered the warm corpse of a portly young man lying between the carved gateposts at the entrance to a misty pasture in the Meramec River Valley, about 20 miles west of St Louis. The body was on its back, arms by its sides, as though laid out for burial. It was clad in brown corduroy trousers, a cream V-neck sweater and blue tennis shoes. The pockets were empty. There were no personal effects of any kind, making early identification very difficult.

Death had been caused by an execution-style shot to the back of the head at point-blank range, followed by another behind the right ear, fired from within two feet. Either shot would have been fatal according to crime scene investigators, who judged the weapon to be a .357 Magnum – a firearm so powerful that it can fire a round through the engine block of a Mack truck and stop it in its tracks. At autopsy, it was established that the victim had been drinking heavily; the blood alcohol count being 0.26: the equivalent of 14 stiff drinks.

Initially all the signs pointed to a classic mobster hit, but an initial search of criminal records found no match for the victim's fingerprints, so for a while the police were at a loss as to the young man's identity. But then a match was made with a set of prints that had been taken when the victim was stopped for a minor traffic violation more than a year earlier. It was Sean Dale Cavaness, born 20 May 1962.

Location-wise, the body had been found next to one of the most shunned spots in the US – an argument for the murder having been planned. It was only a few yards from the sealed entrance to Times Beach; a ghost town, once home to 2,000 people who had been evacuated by order of President Reagan early in 1983 due to contamination by TCDD (a type of dioxin). This was the largest civilian exposure to the compound in the history of the United States and this action followed the discovery that a spray used to keep down dust on the township's roads was laden with the active ingredient of the Vietnam War 'Agent Orange'.

Drunk as the proverbial skunk

Dr Dale Cavaness got the news of Sean's murder then slammed the phone down when he returned home in the early hours of Friday morning from a long and lively Christmas party, and Eldorado churchgoers prayed for their doctor that Sunday. The funeral was held in St Louis and Sean was buried next to his brother Mark in Hamilton County. Dr Cavaness wanted 'Onward, Christian Soldiers' and 'The Battle Hymn of the Republic' to be played, but they were deemed inappropriate. The minister's eulogy was based on the text from Proverbs 14:32 (ESV) – 'The wicked is overthrown through his evildoing, but the righteous finds refuge in his death. When calamity comes, the wicked are brought down, but even in death the righteous seek refuge in God.'

After the service Dr Caveness's mood brightened when he introduced the detective in charge of the investigation to fellow mourners. 'This is my buddy, Detective Dave Barron,' he told them. 'He's the best damned detective in St Louis. He's gonna solve this damned thing.' Detective Barron smiled politely, because solve it he damn well would! The very next day, Barron stopped Dr Cavaness as he was setting off on the 150-mile drive home to Eldorado and placed him in cuffs for Sean's murder.

A lucky break

The events had gone like this. Soon after the discovery of Sean's body, Detective Dave Barron had set about tracing the dead man's last address – a bleak apartment in a rundown corner of St Louis. Telephone, electricity and gas were all disconnected, with only a tiny paraffin stove as the source of heat and light. The lad had been living in squalor.

Thinking outside of the box while we take Sean's living conditions into account, what does this tell us about his father, the highly respected surgeon/physician so well loved and respected by the entire community? Clearly Dr Dale could not give two fucks about his son's welfare; no decent father would allow his boy to get into such a state.

Dirty clothes and an empty vodka bottle completed the dismal scene in Sean's room. Barron had children himself. Feeling his anger rising, he questioned the downstairs neighbours – a couple named Kroeck – who had let Sean use their phone, and who had grown fond of him. On the night before the body was discovered, they had seen a car prowling up and down the street and became suspicious enough to take down its registration number when it parked under a streetlight. Barron held his breath. 'You wouldn't still happen to have that number?' he ventured. The Kroeks rummaged around in their kitchen, where they found a brown paper bag with scribbling on it: 'Ill AVT-183'. This could be a lucky break, thought Barron – the kind of miracle that only happens in fiction. Over his car radio, he immediately traced the vehicle: it was an Oldsmobile Toronado. It was owned by Dr John Dale Cavaness, and the Kroeks were able to identify the doctor's mugshot as the driver of the car. Of course, the doctor knew nothing of this when he boasted that the detective was his 'buddy' at Sean's funeral. Now that he had Cavaness under arrest, Barron asked the big question: 'When did you last see your son?' Barron held his breath. The reply was relaxed: 'Let's see . . . about four weeks ago.'

The doctor displayed remarkable resilience when he dismissed his attorney and withstood 15 straight hours of interrogation. He began by insisting that he had been at home in Southern Illinois on the night of the killing but had no alibi to support the claim. With the screw now turning, he changed his story; admitting that the Kroeks were correct. Yes, he had driven up to see his son, he said, stayed with him until about 1.30 a.m., then drove home through the night. 'So why did you lie?' 'Because I didn't want to be thought of as a suspect … it just seemed logical,' he replied.

Interrogated again on Christmas Eve, the doctor changed his story once more. He did shoot his son, he said, but only when he was already dead! This seemed incredible to Barron. Now digging himself even deeper into guilt, Cavaness explained that he had taken Sean drinking on the Mississippi waterfront until 3 a.m. They had driven around St Louis, and as the sun came up, they found themselves in the country. At this point I suggest that there was some truth in this ride-around ride-along because Sean would have been pleased to see his father when he called unexpectedly that night and suggested that the two of them should go out for a drive and have some drinks. Never would the lad have expected that his father would murder him. But now in the country with dawn breaking, the doctor told Barron that Sean had asked to see his father's gun, a Smith & Wesson .357 Magnum. Dr Cavaness told the detective that he thought nothing of it and handed it over, and was fetching a soft drink from the car when he heard Sean say, 'Tell Mom that I love her,' followed by a shot. He turned in time to see him fall to the ground.

His eyes growing moist, the doctor maintained that once he realised his son was dead, his only thought was for the boy's mother, not that he cared a damn about her in any event: 'Suicide would have been too much for her to bear, so in order to make it look more like a murder, I fired a second shot.' Cavaness, it seemed, had thought of everything: removing the jacket, wallet and keys from his boy's body to simulate a robbery and wiping the dead lad's hands with a damp cloth to remove the tell-tale gunpowder blowback residue. But with all of that said and done, the police didn't believe him – Dr Dale, the guy who had sworn the American equivalent of the Hippocratic Oath would go on trial for murder most foul.

Some sort of justice

A mistrial was declared in July 1985 after the jury was mistakenly handed the results of a lie-detector test because polygraph evidence is inadmissible in Missouri. A second trial began mid-November in a courtroom packed with the doctor's loyal supporters – the Cavaness trial was notable for the strength of hometown support for the accused physician and his indictment was, they said, with little or no sympathy for the victim, 'a diabolical plot to frame him', the *Chicago Tribune* of 20 January 1985 reported. The support even extended to those few who accepted the remote possibility of guilt. 'If he [Cavaness] did do it, I hope and pray that they can't prove it,' a reader told the Eldorado *Daily Journal*. A local storekeeper felt that if the doctor had indeed murdered his son, then 'he probably deserved it'.

As the trial unfolded, some saw it as a contest between the pure values of rural America and the corruption of big city life.

Dr Cavaness looked haggard. His suit hung limply as he mustered a steady, hostile glare in the direction of his former wife and two remaining sons. He took the stand to argue that his hundreds of thousands of dollars in debts were no more than a mere 'cash-flow problem'. He recalled his family life as 'beautiful', which it wasn't. However, in a trial without eyewitnesses, the crux of the case was the ballistic evidence. Which shot was fired first? For suicide to be credible, it had to be the one to the side of the head. Experts for the state used X-rays and blood-spatter patterns to demonstrate that it was the other way round: the first shot had been discharged into the back of Sean's head while his left arm was raised as if the terrified lad knew what was coming. While Sean was lying in the dirt, he was shot again. This was damning evidence. The jury – most if not all them being ardent gun-owners themselves – got it in a microsecond and they gasped unbelievingly when the doctor brusquely assumed the cross-examination himself and without a flicker of emotion, made technical observations as he sifted dismissively through the gruesome colour photographs of Sean's shattered head 'like a pack of cards', recalled one of the jurors.

On 19 November 1986, the jury took a little over two hours to return a verdict of premeditated murder. In demanding the death penalty, the prosecution called the doctor's third son as its only witness, an action believed to be unprecedented even to this very day. 'As long as he's alive I can't feel safe,' said Kevin Cavaness. Judge Drew Luten agreed and sentenced the doctor to die in the gas chamber. Back in Eldorado, a clear majority still believed Doc Cavaness to be innocent.

Motives

The appeal process is automatic in all US states, so Dr Cavaness became inmate No. 40 on death row in a grim nineteenth-century penitentiary on the Missouri River. Once settled in, he initiated legal proceedings to try and recover his double-indemnity life insurance on the son he had been convicted of killing. At 7a.m. on Monday, 17 November 1986, Cavaness was found hanging from the door of his cell by electrical cord greased with Vaseline to make the slip knot slide strangle-tight. With a supreme act of will, he had tucked his knees up to keep his feet off the ground. Efforts to revive him failed. He was pronounced dead an hour later.

It is clear that, immersed in debt, the violently out-of-control wife beater and serial womaniser Dr Cavaness – one well familiar with making fraudulent medical claims, when his patients were not lawfully qualified to receive them – turned his con-artist expertise to line his own pockets. He had taken out two policies on Sean totalling approximately $140,000. He had also received $40,000 following the death of his son Mark. Financial gain was quite plainly the motive.

Dr Cavaness was meticulous about his suicide. He left 13 notes and letters of instructions, including thanks to his guards for being 'considerate'. In none did he make any mention of his sons or their mother, and this 100 per cent true sociopath blamed his fate on his attorneys: 'If the initial treatment is bungled, the patient has nothing to look forward to except a lifetime of agony,' he wrote. Cavaness also had a $200,000 double-indemnity insurance policy on his life. He killed himself on the day after expiry of a clause rendering it invalid in the event of suicide.

It has been claimed that Kevin Cavaness scattered his father's ashes near the spot where he and Sean had scattered Mark's ashes ten years before. Mariann Cavaness remarried and settled in Wisconsin with her two surviving sons. Kevin married a nurse who had worked briefly at his father's hospital. In 1987 they had a daughter they named Shannon, with Kevin saying: 'I'm glad it's not a boy.'

Conclusions

Dale Cavaness was a prime example of the little fish turning into a killer pike in a small pond. Everybody in Eldorado respected the 'Doc' whatever he chose to do and eventually there was no curbing his self-indulgence.

Cavaness had felt free to commit drunken manslaughter and to fake fires for the insurance. When he got around to shooting his two sons for the insurance, only his ill-considered arrogance tripped him up. He invented an alibi when he had no need to. His over-inflated ego assumed the police would not question it. He was a physician, after all – he'd sworn an ethical oath, when all was said and done!

Surviving son Kevin had a chilling explanation. Pointing to his father's keen interest in rare cattle breeding, and for his contempt for the way Mark and Sean were turning out, Kevin speculated that their father decided to turn a profit on what he regarded as genetic failures: 'I guess he was culling the herd,' he said, and he still believes to this very day that, at one time or another his father would have murdered him too! The *Chicago Tribune* reported that Kevin and his wife were sleeping in a trailer on Cavaness's property when visiting his father. They woke up fortunately early in the morning to find the gas stove's taps were on. It would have taken little for them to have died in a fire. A few months later, apparently, that same trailer went up in flames. Cavaness collected the insurance money.

But all that I have written so far somewhat misses the point of this book: if one can't trust a doctor then who can one trust? All the patients of the physicians and nurses previously mentioned were trusted by hospitals and medical practices to the nth degree, yet killers lived in their midst, and throughout historic times until the present day, this remains true. Yet, in most respects Dr John Dale Cavaness is unique in the black annals of homicidal history: he showed every sign of caring for his patients – while killing his own sons.

Nurse Stephan Letter

I wanted to help the victims, out of spontaneous sympathy, although now I know how catastrophically wrong my actions were.
— STEPHAN LETTER: STATEMENT TO THE
KEMPTEN DISTRICT COURT

In a goodwill attempt to save readers travel costs in flying Lufthansa to Deutschland, I can tell them as we move on through baggage reclaim that *Krankenpfleger* (nurse) Letter was born on 17 September 1978, in the town of Herdecke, in the state of North Rhine-Westphalia, Germany. He is now serving a full-life term for killing upwards of 29 elderly patients between January 2003 and July 2004, and is presently incarcerated in a prison at Straubing, a city in Lower Bavaria, on the Danube. Very much in the manner of Nurse Toppan's playbook, more than 800 deaths occurred during his shifts. Letter might have come straight out of the pages of Dr Harold Shipman and Dr John Bodkin Adams' apocryphal

How to Kill Elderly People and Try to Get Off Scot-Free Handbook. Officials exhumed the bodies of more than 40 patients, but another 38 had already been cremated, thus destroying any evidence of a lot more murders most foul.

Statistics

I will confess to a weakness for this sort of thing, but even so it is instructive to look at the stats regarding Nurse Letter: 80-plus suspicious deaths, and all committed between January 2003 and July 2004, at the Sonthofen Hospital, situated in the Bavarian Alps, some 90 miles south-west of Munich. One might have supposed that at least *one* whistle-blowing colleague would have thought: 'WTF is going on here with Nurse Letter … his patients are dying like flies?' It seems, however, that the merest suggestion that Letter was killing patients was deemed *verboten*, or words to that effect. To try and keep this in some sort of perspective, let's imagine a guy who is the *only* driver of a bus of which 40 or more of his passengers have been murdered over a period of about a year. Same guy, same schedule, same MO, with *all* the bodies dumped along *his* route. Let's figure this out, shall we? – because Letter's colleagues could not, and did not, figure him out … period!

Letter, who had been working at Sonthofen Hospital for less than a month before he started killing patients, *only* became a suspect after staff noticed that large quantities of potentially lethal drugs, including Lysthenon, had gone missing from the hospital and unsealed medicine containers were later found by investigators in Letter's apartment. Lysthenon, also known as suxamethonium chloride (Scoline), is a drug used to cause short-term paralysis as part of general anaesthesia. It is administered by injection into a vein or a muscle, and that is how the young nurse murdered his elderly patients.

In February 2006, Letter stood trial in Kempten, Bavaria, for the deaths of 29 patients, including 16 counts of murder. Most of his patients were aged 75 years or older, but overall, their ages ranged from 40 to 94. Trotting out the euthanasia mitigation, Letter claimed that in some of the killings he had acted out of sympathy and a humane desire to end the suffering of sick patients. His attorney, Juergen Fischer, argued that his client was 'motivated by compassion for seriously ill patients', while presiding Judge Harry Rechner said that the accused was an active proponent of assisted suicide and appeared to want to put an end to what he deemed to be senseless suffering. The judge added a rider, however: 'The evidence showed he [Letter] was interested, at best, superficially in the state of health of the patients.' Nor did the prosecution buy into the euthanasia defence, not least because Letter also reportedly gave an inappropriate injection to a 22-year-old female soldier who had suffered minor injuries after a fall. She lost consciousness but luckily recovered. *Wikipedia* also informs us that the prosecution indicated that 'Letter was not the assigned nurse for some of the patients, and that some of them were in a stable condition and due to be released from hospital.'

Following the trial, German forensic doctors demanded higher standards in the investigation of unexplained cases of death, especially when it later came to light that there had been numerous 'unexplained deaths' at Letter's former workplace – a hospital in Ludwigsburg, Baden-Württemberg. A 21 August 2004 article written by Annette Tuffs for the

British Medical Journal and available via the *National Library of Medicine*, highlights other important failings:

> Professor Wolfgang Eisenmenger from Munich University, president of the German Society for Forensic Medicine, estimates that between 1,200 and 2,400 murders in Germany had not been registered because post-mortem examinations are done in just 5% of cases of suspicious death.

It seems, therefore, that financial costs feature greatly here because this is all, 'exacerbated by fears of additional costs among the police and prosecuting attorneys.'

So how may we sum up Letter's psychopathology? For a considered answer, I think I will leave this to Professor Karl-Heinz Beine, a psychiatrist from Hamm, near Dortmund, who has published papers on hospital staff who kill:

> Most of them kill to try to diminish their own fears of suffering and death. Although unstable, they are mostly inconspicuous and often valued as reliable but introverted colleagues, but their initial motivations of healing and helping have been overcome by aggressive fantasy and obsessions. Suspicions are rarely raised, and the murders often pass unnoticed in a place where unexpected death is common.

Perhaps this is also applicable in the cases of Dr Harold Shipman and Nurse Beverley Allitt, too?

Betrayal in Care Homes

Every one of the doctors and nurses featured in this book so far broke the trust of their patients. The saddest thing about betrayal is that it almost never comes from one's enemies, but from those one trusts the most. As the saying goes: 'Trust is like a mirror: once it's broken, you can glue it back together but you can still see the cracks'.

The doctors and nurses so far mentioned gave solemn undertakings to do no harm, not to injure others, and not to to be immoral or iniquitous, for that was their sworn duty. Hundreds of innocent people were betrayed by them. So before going any, I think that the reader who wishes to study further the psychologies of such evil people in more detail might refer to Karl-Heinz Beine's paper published in the *Deutsche Medizinische Wochenschrift* in September 2022 (available online via the *National Library of Medicine*): 'Serial murder in medical clinics and care homes'. When it comes down to the nuts and bolts of this subject it makes for a fascinating yet very grim read, because one can extend all that Professor Beine says to doctors, nurses and carers in nursing homes as well.

Alpine Nursing Home

What may seem at first to be a mystery very often becomes the mechanics of what actually happened. Many years ago I interviewed, for the TV documentary series *The Serial Killers*, Catherine 'Cathy' May Wood and Gwendolyn Graham at their respective prisons, the Federal Correctional Institution, Tallahassee, and the Women's Huron Valley Correctional Facility, Michigan. I have written extensively about this evil couple of murderous nursing aides before, so I will not labour over them again. For further reading, my colleague Lowell Cauffiel's 1992 book, *Forever and Five Days*, is a first-rate read, while the *Wikipedia* article, 'Gwendolyn Graham and Cathy Wood', offers a pretty thorough grounding in the case, too. However, we are talking about the breaking of trust here, not so much about their murders of five elderly patients at the Alpine Nursing Home, Grand Rapids, Michigan.

The obese Wood and her lover, the slightly built Graham, 'burked' their victims by kneeling on their chests, pinching their noses closed and stuffing cloths into their mouths until, after a great deal of struggling, these much-loved elderly folk expired. The two lovers then went out to party and drink themselves stupid.

After serving time in prison, Wood, the prime instigator who had worked a plea-bargain deal, was released in January 2020 and is now free to walk the streets. Graham is still locked away, a complete mental wreck who self-harms, with cuts and burns week after week. I was interviewing her when she showed the film crew evidence of this on camera. Their motive: a lesbian love pact. It was as sick as that. Michigan does not have the death penalty, but if did, and if one of those frail and trusting people had been a member of my family, I would have been first in line to pull the switch, no question about it …

Parkfields

Back in the county of Somerset in the UK, in 2007 a British husband and wife were arrested for the murders of five care-home residents. Fifty-year-old Leigh Baker and his 46-year-old wife Rachel were initially questioned after the death of 97-year-old Lucy Cox in January at the 16-bed private Parkfields home, in the village of Butleigh, near Glastonbury. Rachel Baker had run the home for 19 years.

The *Guardian* reported: 'During the investigation, detectives also had the remains of three other residents exhumed for toxicology tests to establish whether they had been poisoned.' The remains of Nellie 'Mary' Pickford, 89, were removed from Glastonbury cemetery on 5 June. Marion Alder, 79, a grandmother of four, was exhumed from the churchyard of St Leonard's, Butleigh, a week later. The remains of Fred Green, 81, were removed from a graveyard in the village of Kingsweston, near Somerton, about six miles south of Butleigh, on 11 July. Three other residents whose deaths the authorities were treating as suspicious had already been cremated. It was later proved that at least 12 of the elderly residents had been murdered.

God bless her, Nellie Pickford had been admitted to Parkfields after she became unsteady on her feet. In her heyday, she trod the boards with her local amateur dramatic society with 'great aplomb', recalled a close friend. 'By all accounts, she was an accomplished – and enthusiastic – singer and actress,' reported Paul Bracchi in the *Daily Mail* on 11 October 2008.

Serious concerns

The registered owners of Parkfields during the period that the residents were murdered were Malcolm and June Baker, who were often to be seen walking their two golden retrievers near their Georgian country home in nearby East Compton. As Paul Bracchi noted, however: 'But Parkfields was actually run by their daughter-in-law Rachel, along with their son, Leigh Baker, a chef.' 'I always thought Leigh was a nice man,' remembered one elderly woman who lived at the Parkfields care home. 'Whenever I saw him, we always had a chat. I didn't see Rachel as much, but she was always friendly and ready to help. I was very happy with the standard of care.' All of which goes to prove what I have said so many times: medical murderers wear reassuring smiles and offer comforting chit-chat even when they are committing homicide.

But things for this murderous couple started to come unstuck when, in June 2006, Parkfields received an impromptu visit from the (now defunct) Commission for Social Care Inspection (CSCI). 'There was a comfortable and homely atmosphere,' the report glowingly stated. 'Staff were friendly and were observed being kind and caring towards residents.' Unfortunately, this false presenting was all a facade. In early January 2007 a phone call to the CSCI revealed a very different state of affairs. It was made by a brave whistle-blower at Parkfields, who raised serious concerns about the standard of care. The name of the recently deceased resident Lucy Cox came up. As a direct result of that conversation, the police were called in. Rachel and Leigh Baker were arrested on suspicion of murder, perverting the course of justice and the theft and unlawful possession of controlled and prescribed drugs.

There are thousands of care homes in the UK and overseas, of which by far the majority are thoroughly devoted to the care of residents, where staff go beyond the call of duty when the need arises. In the UK, however, the CSCI did not have the resources to monitor each care home week after week. Even their own inspectors could be fooled by cunning, psychopathic, pull-the-wool-over-one's-eyes individuals such as Rachel Baker, thereby proving that Professor Karl-Heinz Beine is right on the nail with his work.

'A number of Parkfields residents, who had families forking out fees in excess of £20,000 a year, had "suffered weight loss"... ' wrote Paul Bracchi in the *Daily Mail*. '... They weren't eating properly or receiving a balanced diet at mealtimes. Portions at mealtimes were small, and there was little or no choice. If you didn't like what was on your plate, you went without.'

A number of the elderly were 'isolated in their bedrooms for long periods. Standards of cleanliness and hygiene left much to be desired,' the CSCI now reported. 'One man could not reach the (emergency) bell call from his bed. When a bell was rung, there were sometimes no staff at hand to respond.' Yes, dear reader, I know this is depressing, but I am making a point here, because 'lights were not working, tiles were coming off in the bathroom, hot pipework was left exposed which posed a "risk" to the most vulnerable'. And it was further reported that 'some staff treated residents in a way that did not respect their dignity'. So here were elderly folk, many of whom had served their country in past wars and paid their taxes, only for their families to get stiffed for the so-called 'care' of their loved ones by the owners and managers of Parkfields: 'Staff did not always knock on doors before entering residents' rooms. Lights were often left on in the front bedrooms and curtains so anyone could see inside, and Parkfields kept residents' money in a safe.' Records for six 'service users' (politically correct term for residents) were examined by the CSCI.

Residents' money had gone missing. The balances for two years were found to be 'less than the amount recorded. There was no evidence of any receipts to account for the missing monies,' reported the CSCI. In a word: stolen. I would have truly liked to have lightened the reader's load here, but the most shocking concerns highlighted in the CSCI report were over the way medication was managed for the elderly inmates who lived at Parkfields: 'Unlabelled prescription-only medicines were found to be unsecured in the bottom of the medicine trolley and in the various cupboards, drawers and around the home... these included unlabelled prescription-only medicines for "service users" no longer resident, and it was not always possible to determine the actual dose that have been administered from the records or what stocks of medicine had been taken back to their own homes by staff '. There used to be a time when drug addicts burgled pharmacies for pills and other mind-blowing substances, but I guess that they wouldn't have had to bother when they could have simply ambled into Parkfields and helped themselves, and had a cup of tea and a biscuit while they were at it.

Macabre House of Horrors

'Homicide in a care home' is not a compelling phrase. Effectively, it describes the wilful snuffing out of lives. As Patricia Evangelista puts it in her book, *Some People Need Killing*: 'Slaughter dressed up in bureaucratese dulls the senses, and over time can anesthetize an entire population to the horror happening right where they live. Objective reality is winnowed down by each succeeding government report. The dead perish once again into nonexistence, having once been loved only to have been betrayed.'

We may never know what goes on behind closed curtains and locked doors, any more than we can see the deviancy that can exist in a human mind. (My book, *Letters from Serial Killers*, looks into this subject in depth.) The 'Parkfields' name was designed to reassure the vulnerable in their remaining years, suggesting green grass, perhaps some trees, maybe daffodils springing up, birdsong, quiet strolls with loving families in the summer sun ... tranquillity. You may be offered some palliative care while at the same time your money is being stolen and your carer is about to kill you, because to their mind your sell-by date has long expired. There is no more worth in the keeping and feeding of you. So, confined to your room, it's too bad if the paint is falling off the walls and anyone passing your window can see you getting undressed.

The upshot

In April 2010, registered nurse Rachel Baker was convicted of the manslaughter of resident Lucy Cox, aged 97. She was cleared of the manslaughter of resident Frances Hay, aged 85. Both women had 'died' in November 2006. Baker was cleared of murdering both residents and admitted ten counts of possessing Class A and C drugs, and one of perverting the course of justice. On Friday, 21 May 2010, the *Guardian* reported: 'Nurse Rachel Baker jailed for 10 years for giving a lethal dose of painkilling medication to Lucy Cox while abusing drugs herself... "She was living a life of lies, forgery, and deceit," Bristol Crown Court was told... Sentencing her, Mr Justice John Royce said that she was caught in the "vice-like grip of drugs"... Her dependency on prescription drugs had turned her from a caring nurse into a woman capable of a "gross and appalling breach of trust." During her trial it emerged that Baker stole thousands of doses of drugs such as diamorphine and tramadol prescribed for residents and took them herself. It was also alleged in court that Rachel Baker may have got a "perverted" kick out of being in control of elderly people's lives. In the witness box she said she enjoyed feeling "needed" when she was around people close to death.'

Mrs Cox was frail but spirited. She was frail, confused at times. On occasions she was in severe pain. She loved coming downstairs for a glass of sherry. She had a very loving, caring family, who visited her on a daily basis. She may have been in the winter of her days but her long life should not have ended this way. Relatives of people who lived at the home felt great betrayal and bitterness and worried about whether their nearest and dearest did receive a proper level of care.
– Mr Justice Royce

Pleading not guilty in April 2010, Rachel Baker's husband was cleared of perverting the course of justice. Leigh Baker had been accused of helping his wife in doctoring medical records in a bid to try and cover up her drug habit. The upshot was that at Bristol Crown Court the Crown Prosecution Service offered no further evidence against him, with Judge Neil Ford accepting the decision.

Dr Louay Omar Mohammed al-Taei

There is no presence of American infidels in the city of Baghdad.

— Muhammad Saeed al-Sahhaf,
aka 'Baghdad Bob', aka 'Comical Ali'

The preceding chapter was certainly somewhat grim, so to set the scene here, let's first look at 'Comical Ali' — a play on 'Chemical Ali', whose execution was described earlier — for his notable and colourful television appearances as the Information Minister under Saddam Hussein during the US-led invasion of Iraq in 2003. He surrendered to the American 'infidels', was interrogated, cosied up to his captors and was then released without charge, some say with his bank account full of millions of US dollars. In March 2008, it was reported by *The Times* that 'Baghdad Bob' was living free as a bird in the United Arab Emirates. It is amazing how fast politicians jump ship when they come undone, but one wonders what Comical Ali would have made of his fellow countryman,

Dr Louay Omar Mohammed al-Taei, because he was certainly no laughing matter.

> I made a mixture of drugs and injected them. They were dead in three hours.
>
> – Dr Louay: quoted in the *Guardian*,
> 17 April 2006

Information about Louay's early life is hard to come by, other than that he was born in Iraq, qualified as a doctor, worked in a hospital in Kirkuk, in northern Iraq, at the time of his murders, and was in his mid-twenties when he was arrested in March 2006. I *almost* wanted to visit Iraq at one time but was deterred by the thought that had I been injured or taken ill, I might have encountered Dr Louay Omar Mohammed al-Taei who, it is said, murdered 43 people between October 2005 and March 2006. By my reckoning that's around seven kills a month, which easily catapults him into the serial-killer category. His motive and his defence – in trying to excuse himself for his wicked crimes, Louay claimed to have been recruited into the insurgent organisation Jamaat Ansar al-Sunnah – I will come to later. According to Iraqi police, he administered anticoagulants to injured pro-Coalition soldiers, police and officials brought into the Al-Jumhuriya Hospital for treatment, only for him to exacerbate their bleeding and bring about their deaths.

Michael Howard, who reported for the *Guardian* in Kirkuk, gives us a remarkable account of this evil doctor's crimes, beginning with:

Lieutenant Arjuman of the Kirkuk police lay uncon–

scious in the recovery room after a successful operation to remove an insurgent's bullet from his chest. His weary surgeons had gone home for the night, satisfied a life had been saved.

Al-Jumhuriya Hospital – Kirkuk's largest and busiest – was quiet. At 10.30pm, a doctor moved along the corridor on the second floor and entered the recovery room. He leaned across the bed and turned off the oxygen supply. Half an hour later, Lt Arjuman was dead.
– *Guardian*, 17 April 2006

Jamaat Ansar al-Sunnah

The name translates as the 'Assembly of the Helpers of Sunnah', although it was also known as Jaish Ansar al-Sunnah – Ali ibn Talib Battalion' was an Iraqi Sunni insurgent group that fought US troops and their local allies during the Iraq War that followed the invasion and occupation of the country in 2003. Based mainly in northern and central Iraq, it consisted of mostly Iraqi (including Arab and Kurdish) fighters. To give the reader a little more background, Jaish Ansar al-Sunnah claimed responsibility for several suicide bombings in Iraq, including the devastating attacks on two main Kurdish political parties, KDP and PUK in Irbil (Erbil), the capital of Iraqi Kurdistan, on 1 February 2004, which killed more than 100 people. It also had a strong presence in Mosul in northern Iraq, the country's second largest city, where it launched an offensive in November 2004, along with other foreign fighters and militant groups. It claimed responsibility for a major suicide bombing of the dining hall at the US base in Mosul on 21 December

2004, which killed 22 people, including 14 US servicemen.

Like numerous other insurgent groups, Jaish Ansar al-Sunnah was, since 2005, banned in the UK under the Terrorism Act 2000, but it split up and changed its name in 2011. So how, you might ask, did Dr Louay, a member of this extreme terrorist outfit, get to work in a hospital and be allowed to treat pro-Coalition troops and local police, because whatever version of the Hippocratic Oath might exist in Iraq, it is patently obvious that he didn't sign up for it.

Medical executions

The deputy commander of Kirkuk's Miqdad police station was the first of the 43 victims Louay murdered. Over a six-month period this Iraqi 'Doctor Death' waded through puddles of blood and crowds of well-wishers in Al-Jumhuriya's hectic emergency unit, quietly murdering pro-Coalition police officers, soldiers and officials, some only lightly injured in insurgent attacks. As we have seen often in this book, there was no apparent reason to suspect Louay. He was an enthusiastic 26-year-old who had graduated from Mosul University in 2003. He was always on hand whenever there was a major incident, such as a bomb attack or a gun battle, that resulted in mass casualties.

> They [the injured] came to the hospital to be cured but instead they were killed. I can understand a doctor may have personal sympathies with the insurgency but to use his professional position to become an instrument of death turns sense and any humanity on its head.
> – Yagdir Shakir, Kirkuk's police commander

As Michael Howard explained, ten days after he killed Lieutenant Arjuman, Louay struck again. This time he used a method that would become his favoured MO: an injection of a lethal mix of drugs. His victims were four members of the Iraqi National Guard brought to the hospital after being wounded in a roadside bomb attack. After Louay's arrest in March 2006, it was determined by the authorities that he was an active member of an insurgent cell; indeed, he was picked up following the arrest and confession of a senior member of Jaish Ansar al-Sunnah. He confessed to at least 19 crimes, with the police making a video of his confession. He killed, he said, because: 'I hate the Americans and what they have done to Iraq. I killed without fuss and there were no proper facilities at the hospital to perform autopsies.'

As well as murdering the wounded, Louay also tended members of the insurgency and helped militants escape their armed escorts. At the end of his filmed confession the doctor was asked whether he had betrayed his profession:

We [other doctors in the terrorist group] could do something to liberate the country. Later our network went astray but we had to keep working and we had to keep committing these crimes... I never considered how terribly brutal my crimes were, and I never thought I would be so easily captured. *I got on so well with all the people at the hospital. They seemed to like me.* [author's italics]

Dr Louay today

Capital punishment is a legal penalty in Iraq. It was commonly used by the government of Saddam Hussein, who was himself ultimately executed by hanging, thereby reinforcing the old maxim 'What goes around comes around'. To say that Iraq is not shy to use the rope would be something of an understatement. After a moratorium on executions imposed by the US administrator, L. Paul Bremer, in 2003, capital punishment was reinstated in Iraq on 8 August 2004. Executions resumed in September the following year after three men convicted of murder were hanged by the 'long drop' method, which can be a bit of a hit-and-miss business at the best of times, as was demonstrated when Chemical Ali plunged to his doom, losing his head into the bargain.

On 9 March 2006, Iraq's Supreme Judicial Council confirmed that authorities had executed the first insurgents by hanging. It was a punishment that Comical Ali escaped for the safety of the UAE, but as for Dr Louay Omar Mohammed al-Taei, his whereabouts is still unknown.

Paramedics Andrzej Nowocien and Karol Banas

Only someone with nothing to smile about
smiles at the rear of an elephant.
– OLD POLISH PROVERB

Every true-crime reader, every criminologist, physician, surgeon and avid aficionado of murder-most-foul knows of the 1828 case of killers William Burke and William Hare; their selling of 16 fresh cadavers to Dr Robert Knox for dissection and medical research at his Edinburgh anatomy lectures (see also the Introduction to this book). That, of course, is an historic case, though not to be dismissed just for that reason, but how about the dozens of Polish doctors, nurses and paramedics who truly brought nineteenth-century Burke and Hare medical homicide goings-on bang up-to-date? And I really *do* have to say this yet again – one couldn't make up this sickening story if one tried, so to Poland our medical road trip takes us next.

Uncontrolled madness

It was *not* a medically trained resident hospital whistle-blower who spilled the beans. It was, as often can be the case, local media which, after years of painstaking investigation, discovered one of the longest, most macabre cover-ups in world medical history.

Never mind any liberal handwringing and soul-searching, or any mitigation, repentance or forgiveness, if anyone deserves to be damned eternally it has to be Polish paramedics Andrzej Nowocien and Karol Banas. These two worked on Łódź Hospital's emergency ward and, between 2000 and 2001, murdered countless patients.

Whether or not they are damned for eternity, Nowocien and Banas were not executed for their crimes. No, or as they say in Poland, *Nie*, because Nowocien was sentenced to life in jail, while the very least the authorities could do for Banas was lock him up for 25 years. But why long sentences, and not a first-rate hanging, the fate of serial murderer Paweł Alojzy Tuchlin (of whom I have written in my 2024 book, *Talking with Psychopaths: Guilty But Insane*)? Well, in 2014 Poland ratified Protocol 13 to the European Convention on Human Rights (ECHR), which provides for the abolition of capital punishment. So how can I say this with a modicum of decency? These medical monsters, paramedics Andrzej Nowocien and Karol Banas, sold their victims' bodies to local undertakers – *just before* or *after* they were dead! At least Burke and Hare waited until *after* their prey were dead.

So, with a little Polish insight, let's imagine that your granny (*babunia*) has taken a slip down a few stairs on her way to the post office to collect her pension. Otherwise she's as sprightly-healthy, as sharp-witted, as can possibly be. And you love her, of course you do. So the ambulance rushes, blue lights flashing, to Granny's assisted-living home. Can readers picture this now? The paramedics are kind, courteous, a comforting presence with their warm, reassuring words such as: 'Trust us, love. You're in safe hands now … We're just going to give you a tiny injection to ease the pain.'

But they are murdering her, you see – executing her for their own profit. By the time the ambulance parks up your granny is stone-dead.

Yet that was not the end of it by a long chalk. Two other men were also jailed. Dr Janusz Kuliński was sentenced to six years' jail for knowingly failing to protect the lives of ten patients, while Dr Pawel Wasilewski was given a five-year sentence after being convicted of the same charge. All four were also charged with taking money from undertakers in exchange for information about new deaths, although it would be fair to say that the lesser charges might have been the least of Nowocien and Banas's worries. But that was still not the end of it by an *even longer* chalk.

An organised-crime network

To this very day, investigators are *still* trying to establish the roles played by dozens of doctors, nurses and paramedics in what trial judge Jaroslaw Papis called an 'organised-crime network' and a form of 'uncontrolled madness'. The court heard how allegedly more than 40 paramedics, doctors, nurses and undertakers conspired to ship seriously ill elderly patients straight to funeral parlours, rather than hospitals, as a way to make quick cash, in a grisly money-making scheme that investigators have said could have been going on for almost 20 years ... yes, *20 years* ... with only a handful of victims having been identified. There are hundreds of dead people still unaccounted for, like marbles that have rolled down a street and into some drainage abyss.

> I should be given a medal by the national health system
> for taking so many old people off of its hands.
>   – Andrzej Nowocien: boasting to cellmates

According to an article by Ed Holt in *The Lancet* (17 February 2007):

> The case was one of the longest in Polish legal history…
> The group in Łódź, central Poland, which reportedly
> got larger every year as more medical staff were roped
> in, cashed in on the fact that many families, in the
> face of death, are often incapable of making decisions
> about practicalities such as choosing the funeral home.
> Instead doctors and other medical staff working at Łódź
> Hospital's emergency ward would recommend to the
> victims' relatives a certain home with which under-
> the-table deals had already been arranged.

The article continues: 'Undertakers would pay up to GB£300 pounds for notification of a new corpse, nicknamed a "skin". And when they wanted to speed up the deaths the paramedics would inject them with a drug to kill them.' All of which gives this author a damned good reason not to fall ill in Poland. In fact, it would be a toss-up between Poland or the Philippines. The former would probably come out on top as it's a member of the European Union and NATO. The Philippines is not.

And here is how these Polish medical murderers worked their MO: ambulance drivers, with the full knowledge of, and nods of tacit cooperation from, dishonest physicians, injected ill patients with massive doses of the muscle relaxant pancuronium bromide (Pavulon) – which is used in lethal-injection executions in the US (and for which I coined the toe-tag label: 'Goodnight Juice') – to kill them, then waited as their patients lay dying on gurneys inside the ambulances.

During the trial, Nowocien, who was later described by the judge as 'an agent of darkness', said:

On one occasion we were to transport a severely ill patient from Łódź to a nearby hospital in Głowno. The driver was going off duty in half an hour so we went to the emergency department and while I waited for the new driver to get ready for his shift, I smoked some cigarettes. All this time the woman was lying for half an hour in a locked ambulance. When we finally set off, we figured there was little sense in travelling all the way to Głowno because the patient was about to die any minute anyway. So we headed straight for the undertakers instead, knowing the problem would solve itself on the way, so we passed on the woman's corpse direct to the funeral home.

The Polish Health Ministry did not directly comment on the sentencing, but state officials suggested that low pay for government-employed medical workers *might* have been the motivation for the macabre scheme. I take a somewhat different view. While it *is* correct to say that corruption in the Polish health sector is *perceived* to be rife, we have to remember that we are talking about only a very few rotten apples in a basket otherwise containing thousands of thoroughly good, compassionate, Hippocratic Oath-abiding fruit. These medically trained monsters – nicknamed the 'Skin Hunters' by the media – betrayed not only their vulnerable patients, but the entire Polish medical establishment, as did all of the killers previously described in this book. Nevertheless, as Ed Holt wrote in *The Lancet*:

> Surveys by groups such as the international corruption watchdog Transparency International repeatedly high-light high levels of perceived corruption in local health care. Anecdotal evidence from ordinary Poles has also suggested that many have either given, or been in, a situation where they have felt expected to give a bribe of some sort to a doctor or medical health worker in return for good treatment.

He adds: 'Wages for medical staff in Poland can be as low as UK £300 pounds per month – a wage locals say is barely enough to provide for one person, let alone someone with a family.'

★

I offer these cynical endnotes to this chapter:

1. I am pleased to confirm that Andrzej Nowocien and Karol Banas will *not* be enjoying a cushy life behind bars. And why not? Tragically, because those sick and elderly patients who trusted themselves to their care were worth more zloty dead than alive, which means that these medically trained scum are most unlikely to be treated gently in jail.

2. What of the others; the patently culpable doctors and nurses whose names and true identities remain anonymous? One can bet one's last zloty that, with a few back-handers, they are still practising medicine in some place or another, with their patients saying: 'My doctor and nurse are such caring persons, I trust them with my life.'

Dr Geza F. P. de Kaplany de Kaplanhaza

I've hurt my wife. I've hurt her bad. She may die.
– Dr Geza de Kaplany: telephone call to police,
10.18 P.M., 28 August 1962

Evidence doesn't lie, people do, so it would be remiss of me
not to mention in this book the Hungarian-born emigrant
to the USA, Dr F. P. Geza de de Kaplany, aka the 'Acid
Doctor'. At trial, the air was thick with psychobabble, with
him variously described as psychotic, schizophrenic and
suffering from 'multiple personality syndrome' – yet 'perfectly
sane'. Notoriously, such obscure medical terminology means
different things from different experts' mouths, depending
on which side of the court's benches one is sitting on,
which demonstrates that the side most skilled in confusing
psychobabble frequently wins. So how on earth, you may
ask, did de Kaplany get to become a physician/surgeon?

Let's pause for a moment and take stock of his most awful crime – murder most foul.

Hajna Piller

Hungarian Hajna Piller was 25; a former fashion model and showgirl at Bimbo's 365 in San Francisco. The reader can find out all about the club by looking it up on *Wikipedia*. This was a hot-to-trot venue indeed.

Hajna, the beauty-queen daughter of György Piller, the 1956 Olympic fencing champion who defected to the West with the rest of his team after the Games – which wereheld in Melbourne, Australia – in protest at Soviet Russia's brutal suppression of the 1956 Hungarian Uprising. Hajna went with her mother Ilona from Hungary to join her father in San Francisco the same year; he died in 1961. A strikingly beautiful girl who dressed in exotic and revealing outfits, Hajna was much sought after by wealthy men, but chose to marry smooth-talking, if unprepossessing, Geza de Kaplany, a 36-year-old Hungarian-born anaesthetist at San Jose's Doctor's Hospital. She had moved into his apartment, No. 30 at 1135 Ranchero Way, three weeks after the wedding, following a fortnight's honeymoon in Hawaii.

In the short time that they had known her, neighbours had found Hajna 'bright, friendly and talkative'. She liked to sunbathe by the apartment pool in a bikini with a towel over her face to protect her delicate skin from too much sun. By contrast, her husband seemed 'sullen and introverted'. He had already been spotted keeping an eye on his wife's pool-side card games. One resident had marked him down as an over-jealous husband, later telling investigators: 'The guy was spooky. A wimp. He was giving us the creeps.'

The sound of music

On 28 August 1962, Hajna got home at about 8 p.m. The couple were seen to greet each other, but not kiss, before going into their apartment and closing the door. Not long afterwards very loud music was heard coming out of Apartment 30. A few days earlier de Kaplany had purchased extra speakers for his hi-fi system and was now apparently trying them out.

Between 8.30 and 9 p.m. a neighbour called to invite the de Kaplanys around for cocktails. The doctor answered. Dressed only in Bermuda shorts, he appeared bewildered or confused. 'No, no, I'm very busy. Thank you,' was his abrupt answer to the invitation. Then he slammed the door. Two women schoolteachers shared the apartment directly beneath No. 30. They heard the sound of music, then a short time later they heard something else that sounded like moaning, which soon became a 'continuous monotone without a break', as they later told police.

At 10.11 p.m., the San Jose Police Department got a call. It was incomprehensible owing to the deafening music and screaming in the background. Two minutes later the same caller tried again, but this time the music had been turned down. 'Send the police,' came a male voice. 'I've hurt my wife. I've hurt her bad. She may die.'

At 10.18 p.m., police arrived at 1135 Ranchero Way, where they met several residents outside of the complex, all of whom could now hear the terrible screams coming from Apartment 30. Still in Bermuda shorts but now wearing surgical gloves, de Kaplany opened the door. 'I suppose you'd better come in,' he told the two cops. Then, indicating the bedroom door with a jerk of his hand, he said, 'She's in there.'

At this point I would ask readers to put themselves in the position of Robert Moir, the cop who was the first to enter the room, where the air was filled with choking acid fumes.

Your eyes and nostrils are burning. You see this once-beautiful girl on the floor between the twin beds. She's bound hand and foot with electrical flex and surgical tape. She is naked. She is screaming louder and louder. Her left breast is bleeding. Her face, arms and chest are covered with a toxic yellowish substance. Now imagine that Hajna was your own young daughter …

When the ambulance arrived, paramedics had some difficulty untying Hajna. They tried to apply baking soda to neutralise the nitric acid burns, only to burn their hands in the process. Finally, they rushed her to hospital. The seemingly detached de Kaplany sat motionless on a sofa.

Officer Moir now went back to examine the bedroom. The sheets and pillows on one bed were yellow with acid stains. There was a large hole burned in the carpet where Hajna had lain. There was also a surgical glove and compresses on the floor. If nitric acid can easily burn a large hole in a carpet right down to the flooring below, it is not difficult to imagine what it can do to human flesh and bone.

On the bureau in the bedroom was a note in a language that Officer Moir could not understand. There was a full bottle of whisky, also a leather attaché case containing an unused surgical glove. There were unopened bottles of sulphuric acid and hydrochloric acid, and a bottle of nitric acid that was two-thirds empty. When translated from Hungarian the note read:

<u>IF YOU WANT TO LIVE!</u>
<u>DO NOT SHOUT OUT</u>
<u>DO WHAT I TELL YOU</u>
<u>IF NOT YOU WILL DIE</u>

Arrest

On his way to the police station de Kaplany told the arresting officers: 'I know she was unfaithful for a fact. She only married me because of my station in life.' He denied having intended to kill Hajna. 'I just wanted to take her beauty away from her … I did it to frighten her … to put the fear into her against being an adulteress.'

Meanwhile in the County Hospital, Hajna was not expected to survive the night. She had third-degree acid burns over 40 per cent of her body, with her face, upper torso and genital area particularly affected. Her right nipple had been cut off, and she was blind in one eye. A priest gave her the Last Rites while a detective close to tears took what everyone thought at the time was a death-bed statement from the once-beautiful girl. She said:

Dr de Kaplany closed all the windows. He wanted to make love to me. He did make love to me. He tied my arms and legs. He cut me on the breast with a knife. He poured stuff on me several times. I was out of my mind with pain. He ejaculated over me. I need to die now. All my life is gone.

Die? – not just yet!

Hajna might have been spared a great deal of suffering had she died that night, but Hungarians are born of strong stock. She lingered on for more than a month, while in the county jail Dr de Kaplany sat 'aloof and impassive', contemptuously advising psychiatrists who came to examine him with a curt 'Go see my attorney!'

On 6 September, Hajna was transferred to St Francis Hospital in San Francisco, to be assessed for plastic surgery. Gifts and money for hospital expenses from the community, and from the patrons of Bimbo's 365 Club, were constantly arriving, as well as blood and skin for grafts, but despite continual doses of morphine, she was in great agony every time the nurses moved her. The skin on her face had tightened so much that she was unable to close her eyes. Doctors had to sew her eyelids shut.

On the night of Sunday, 30 September, 33 days after the acid attack, with her mother at her bedside, the terribly disfigured Hajna de Kaplany lost her brave struggle for life. Three days later the District Attorney's office dropped the charges of attempted murder, assault with a deadly weapon, assault with corrosive acid and mayhem against Geza de Kaplany, substituting the charge of murder in the first degree. He now faced the prospect of going to the green-walled gas chamber in San Quentin State Prison and I am sure that many readers will agree with me in saying 'If only had that been the case.'

Hitherto impassive and apparently emotionless behind his tinted spectacles, the fearful physician broke down and collapsed in his cell, muttering over and over again, 'Don't let them hurt me.' It is not clear who he thought was going to hurt him while he was in prison, although knowing the horrors of the gas chamber, one suspects he was thinking about his executioners.

Although Dr de Kaplany entered a plea of insanity at trial, which began on 9 January 1963, the defence had to prove 'by a preponderance of the evidence' that he was insane or had been at the time of the attack. Anyone who has read my book, *Talking with Psychopaths: Guilty but Insane*, will realise that this defence should have been a non-starter from the outset. The legal definition of insanity, according to Californian law, was that a person be: '… either incapable of appreciating the nature and consequences of an act or unable to distinguish between right and wrong'. Neither was true of de Kaplany.

The usual array of opposing psychiatric 'experts' was produced. But as the exact sequence of events leading up to the acid attack was established, the murder began to look less and less like a moment of insanity and more like a carefully premeditated act, with the District Attorney carefully telling the jury why this was evident by outlining the events as they had unfolded.

Prior to the attack, Hajna had left for San Francisco on the morning of Monday, 27 August to pick up her unemployment cheque, as usual. Dr de Kaplany had followed her. She spent the night and all the next day with her mother, and he went to see Jane Hajdu, a 58-year-old friend who spitefully told him that his wife was having an affair.

On the following morning this extremely vain man had a manicure at the St Francis Hotel, where he was a regular customer; the manicurist testified that he 'seemed normal'. Then he went to see a divorce lawyer in Berkeley named Scott Anderson, who advised him that it would take time to prove adultery and that they would need a private investigator to gather evidence. (The American catch-'em-with-their-pants-down reality TV show *Cheaters* had yet to come into being.) As de Kaplany left the lawyer's office he turned around and said, 'I cannot wait that long. I could not control myself for a long time,' and slammed the door behind him.

De Kaplany then bought three pint bottles of acid in Berkeley, as well as a roll of adhesive tape and some electric flex, before heading back to San Jose. At 4.30 p.m. he was at the hospital picking up some surgical gloves, and when the medical administrator, who had been trying to reach him all day, saw him, as he told the jury: 'He was definitely upset. Something seemed to be bothering him.'

At 6 p.m. the hospital called de Kaplany at home, asking if he could assist in surgery that evening. 'I have a case already scheduled,' was the anaesthetist's reply. There was no such case on the surgery roster at the doctor's hospital. The prosecution contended that this alleged case to which he had alluded was the acid attack on his wife, for which he had now carefully assembled all the necessary components.

Dr de Kaplany never took the stand at his trial, but his police interviews paint a grim picture of what happened that August night when Hajna got home. The couple argued, then they had a drink and went to bed. But de Kaplany, thinking of how, as he believed, she had been with her lover, found himself impotent. 'We tried to make love,' he told Detective Don Edwards, 'but I just, I just couldn't. I finally blew up.'

The medical bigot

There was never a single shred of evidence that the beautiful Hajna had been having an affair with anyone. In contrast, Geza de Kaplany had had four girlfriends in San Francisco apart from Hajna Piller – some apparently at the same time. All were called as witnesses.

Clara Gabriel, a nurse at the hospital where he worked, went out with him three or four times in June 1961. He then proposed marriage, which she refused because she found him over-possessive.

Geraldine Smith, a 21-year-old clerk at the hospital, dated de Kaplany on and off up to April 1962. She went with him to a ski lodge in Yosemite, but refused to share his bed. When she woke up the next morning, he had left, telling her to walk home (Yosemite to San Jose is about 180 miles).

Margaretha Herbst, a West German nurse who arrived in the USA in July 1961, also had a relationship with de Kaplany between August and December 1961. He took her to concerts and the opera. 'He made love, more or less to me,' she told the court (that 'more or less' seems somewhat equivocal to me). After temporarily breaking with Hajna in early 1962, when friends warned him of her alleged 'loose morals', de Kaplany saw Yvonne Sinonaglu, a 28-year-old divorcée, but she too rapidly lost interest in him.

★

In his summing up, the District Attorney, Louis Bergna, contended that de Kaplany's words 'I finally blew up' described a jealous rage, which was not a defence for crime

321

under Californian law. The doctor had therefore condemned himself out of his own mouth. The jury agreed. Yet despite this, when it came down to deciding on punishment, they concluded that although de Kaplany was legally sane, he *was* mentally ill – which it takes some intellectual convolutions to swallow. After 19 hours of deadlock, their recommendation was life imprisonment, not death in the gas chamber.

It will come as no surprise to readers that not everyone was happy with the jury's decision. The particularly horrific nature of Hajna's torture-murder by her husband was sickening enough. That he was a doctor was almost unimaginable, and had shocked San Jose; as, even more so, did the fact that the creepy 'Acid Doctor' had escaped the death penalty. One juror received threatening phone calls. Told of the sentence, Ilona Piller, the dead girl's mother, who had been too distressed and ill to testify at her son-in-law's trial, called it 'a terrible verdict; gas is too good for him.' I am among many who agree with her.

When the trial was over, de Kaplany came out of his shell and spoke in public for the first time at a press conference on 2 March 1963. 'I would like to save other lives for the life I have taken,' he piously told reporters. Asked by his jailers how he felt, he replied coolly, 'Well, I can relax now the tension is finally off.'

The trial was another case when a psychiatrist for the defence won the argument. Dr Lindsay E. Beaton testified that while de Kaplany was sane, he was mentally ill – a somewhat fine-line distinction, it has to be said. Dr Beaton averred that de Kaplany had an 'excessive devotion' to his mother, whom he 'idolised' and whom he had tried desperately and unsuccessfully to bring to the United States from Hungary to join him. In fact, it *appeared* his mother had taken little interest in him as a child, having left it to governesses and servants to bring him up. His father, a Central European aristocrat of the old school, had been stern and distant with all four of his sons. Young de Kaplany had lived through the Second World War in Hungary (which had allied itself with Nazi Germany), during which time his three brothers had all been killed within months of each other. He had also lived through the Soviet invasion of Hungary in 1956, following the Uprising, when many of his fellow countrymen had also been killed.

Dr de Kaplany claimed that he had had his first sexual experience at 16 with 'a bad, bad girl', with whom he found himself unable to perform. Then at 18, he did manage to have sex with a 'nice girl'. According to Dr Beaton, his impotence with Hajna, who friends had warned him was 'a bad girl', *may* have been related to this early experience. Note my italics here. It's all *appeared* and a *maybe*, with nothing concrete at all. Dr Beaton continued: 'Uprooted from his home, he had come to America, where in April 1961, he was treated for lymphosarcoma, or blood cancer, which he believed to be fatal.' De Kaplany's hospital records, however, actually showed that he had not been expected to die at all, although he claimed that he had been convinced he would. Notwithstanding this, this extreme narcissist had proposed to a string of women in the next year, finally marrying Hajna who was, he claimed, 'obviously temperamental, wholly unsuitable and a whore'.

Harrowing photographs

Perhaps one might also take into consideration what happened when Dr Milton Watson, resident surgeon at the County Hospital, took the stand, and the drama that erupted as he described the terrible injuries he had observed on Hajna's body. The Assistant DA, John Schatz, produced a horrific half life-size post-mortem photograph of the naked corpse to show the jury. When de Kaplany caught sight of the image, his frozen calm deserted him.

He shot to his feet and rounded the counsel table, staring at the photograph and shouting, 'No! No! What have you done to her?' Then he lunged towards the startled Schatz, who shrank back against the jury box. Deputy Sheriff Scott was the first to react; grabbing de Kaplany around the middle from behind, he lifted the tall but slightly built man up bodily and manhandled him back into his seat.

When the session finally resumed, the defendant spent the rest of the day with his face buried in his folded arms to avoid seeing any more of the harrowing photographs. That night in his cell he muttered incoherently to jailer DeVilbiss: 'I'm a doctor ... if I did this ... I must have done this ... then I'm guilty.' Later, the Hungarian, allegedly a deeply devout Roman Catholic, told his jailers, 'I have made my peace with God.' But there was a bizarre twist to come.

Pierre's baby

The most extraordinary phase of the trial occurred when defence psychiatrist Dr Russell Lee took the stand and said that de Kaplany had a 'multiple personality'. And yes, I can hear readers now saying, 'Oh, no! Not another bullshit defence!' But alas, yes. The shrink in the box claimed that in effect the murder had been carried out not by Geza de Kaplany, but by his alter ego, French journalist Pierre la Roche. He added that Pierre had popped into existence in 1956, and that de Kaplany had invested him with all the macho characteristics he felt he lacked himself. He even claimed that Pierre had fathered a child by a German woman who had subsequently returned to Europe. To everyone's astonishment, the prosecution traced the woman and produced her as a surprise rebuttal witness. Ruth Krueger testified that she had a son, Andreas, by then 20 months old, in Germany, and that the defendant was indeed the father. Tellingly, she added that she had known him not as Pierre la Roche, but only as de Kaplany.

One could make this up if one tried

Having shot himself in both feet, Dr Russell Lee must have wished that he could become the Invisible Man as he stood down from the witness box. He was, however, merely one among so many shrinks who have believed, and still believe, in this multiple personality defence over the decades. The American serial killer Kenneth Bianchi, who I interviewed at the Washington State Penitentiary in Walla Walla, WA, had many of America's most prominent psychiatrists believing that he had several multiples who suddenly appeared pre-trial, never to reappear. In my book, *Talking with Psychopaths: Guilty but Insane*, Thomas Dee Huskey, aka the 'Zoo Man', had (allegedly) five multiples and must have thrown most of Tennessee's law enforcement out of whack when he concocted these alter egos and the cops found themselves reading the Miranda Warning to each of them. Since his incarceration, very much like Bianchi, not one of these 'alters' has been seen or heard of again.

The same applies here to de Kaplany. Not a single person on earth had ever heard of a French journalist named Pierre la Roche. Not the defendant's parents, nor any of his many girlfriends, and certainly not anyone at the hospitals where this murderous doctor worked.

Today, it is just possible that Dr Geza de Kaplany is alive and free. He was released on parole in 1975, having served 12 years, the average for a life tariff in the Golden State. Deported from the US (he had been due to become an American citizen on the very day of the murder), he went to Taiwan, where he worked in a missionary hospital. If still alive, he is one year short of his hundredth birthday. His wife was 25 when he so brutally murdered her.

Some Hospital Bedtime Narratives

We have almost arrived at the end of our road trip into cases of medical people who have committed some of the most godawful murders in history, and it all comes down to breach of trust in its most extreme form, so I will not labour the point here.

As for any punishments meted out? I will let the reader decide. I could have and I wanted to include many other wicked murderous doctors, nurses and medically trained people in this book – alas, word count dictates otherwise but the question of why? will always remain within our minds.

We remember how William Wills described the commonest motives earlier on in this book:

- the desire of avenging some real or fanciful wrong;
- of getting rid of a rival or obnoxious connection;
- of escaping from the pressure of pecuniary or other obligation;

- of obtaining plunder or other coveted objects;
- of preserving reputation, or of gratifying some other selfish or malignant passion.

All of the above criteria are based upon 'need'; the noun describing circumstances in which something is necessary: necessity being a thing that is wanted or required. To most psychologists, 'need' is a psychological attribute that stimulates an organism to work towards a goal, giving an aim and direction to behaviour. Maslow's 'Hierarchy of Needs', the most widely known academic model of needs, was initially proposed by psychologist Abraham Maslow in his 1943 paper, 'A Theory of Human Motivation', published in the journal, *Psychological Review*. Of course, the need may be a lawful social need (e.g. to eat or catch a bus) but a need may be antisocial (to steal another's property or, in the cases outlined in this book, the need to take a person's life).

'Motive' is something that causes us to act or behave in order to reach a goal or desired endpoint. A motive is *why* you do something, and it can be lawful (e.g. to work hard to support a family or find a better job) but it can also be an unlawful and antisocial (e.g. financial gain or to rid oneself of someone's presence). But 'need' and 'motive' are almost inextricably entwined: as Wills says, 'it is almost impossible to distinguish between the two.'

In the context of the murderers featured in this book, all of them needed to kill so as to fulfil a certain end; with those who did so for financial gain the need stares us straight in the face. Other needs are more complex.

Committing homicide for financial gain is tangible enough.

For example, the Polish paramedics killed for financial gain. Doctors Adams, Pritchard, Cream, Petiot, Cavaness – to a lesser extent Shipman – needed money and they killed to fulfil this need. As far as I can determine, nurse 'Jolly Jane' Toppan fell into this category too, but Toppan also killed to meet the other needs listed above, which makes her stand out above the others as truly evil.

Doctors Ruxton and de Kaplany fall into another category: that of the desire to avenge some real or fanciful wrong, to preserve some conceived reputation, or to gratify some other selfish passion. Dr Louay Omar Mohammed al-Taei, for one, surely falls under 'satisfying a selfish or malignant passion'.

Care-home manager, nurse Rachel Baker, came undone because she had the need to satisfy a drug addiction. Instead of seeking help in a rehab clinic she selfishly took the lives of the vulnerable in her care. Nurses Ivo Poppe and Stephan Letter both committed murder to 'gratify a selfish and malignant passion'. Gwendolyn Graham and Cathy May Wood enjoyed a mutual selfish, malignant passion in the form of a wicked lesbian love pact.

So where does a nurse like Beverley Allitt come into all of this? It is claimed that she suffers from Munchausen syndrome by proxy (MSP) and has wheedled her way into a cushy secure mental hospital. But one must ask this question: does this mental illness rise to the level of her not knowing the difference between right and wrong or being unable to understand the wicked nature of her acts of murder?

And here are a few more medical killers that *almost* made it into this book and who might whet your appetite for further study ...

Dr Hawley Harvey Crippen

The astute true crime afficionado that you truly are will no doubt be asking why I have left out mild-mannered homeopath Dr Crippen (1862–1910). To be honest with you, I did make a start on a chapter dedicated to him because by the strict moral standards of the day the case was a notable, grim cause célèbre for several reasons: it was salacious to the nth degree and Dr Crippen was hanged for the poisoning and dismemberment of his wife, Cora Henrietta, while having a sort of 'redtop' *News of the World* affair with his typist, Ethel Le Neve. Oh, and yes, he was the first criminal in all of world history to be captured with the aid of wireless telegraphy. But here is the rub: Hawley probably didn't kill Cora, although how her corpse (or *a* corpse) ended up buried in the cellar of his leased house, 39 Hilldrop Crescent in Holloway, North London, is anyone's guess. So, with that established, I have left his story for another day.

Dr Jeffrey Robert MacDonald

I thought long and hard about American 'Green Beret' army doctor, Jeffrey MacDonald, whose wife and children were murdered in horrific fashion on the cold night of Tuesday, 17 February 1970. This was a blood-fest equalling the cowardly Charles Manson by-proxy murders. As usual, there was a spirited defence, but it was the prosecutor who had the last word to the jury: 'The physical evidence simply *cries out* an explanation,' he argued. 'The fact that 21 thrusts through the pyjama top can make 48 holes that line up with 21 holes in the victim's chest is a singular significant fact which proves to me beyond a reasonable doubt that Jeffrey MacDonald killed his wife, Colette. And it is a very short leap from that to say that he killed the two children too.'

Judge Dupree sentenced MacDonald to three consecutive terms of life imprisonment, the harshest sentence he was empowered to apply. Under federal law the death sentence could not be imposed. The case remains one of the most litigated in American criminal history. At the time of writing MacDonald is aged 80 and is incarcerated at the Federal Correctional Institution in Cumberland, Maryland.

Nurse Charles Edmund Cullen

A mentally unstable American serial killer out of the 'Garden State' New Jersey, murdered dozens, possibly hundreds of patients in various medical centres, by administering lethal overdoses of intravenous medication such as insulin and the heart medication digoxin or epinephrine, during a 16-year career. He was finally arrested on 15 December 2003. His *Wikipedia* entry puts him in the premier league of medical murderers past, present and those to come (which there surely will be). During his trial, he proved disruptive, though not violent, and received at the end of it 24 life sentences.

Miyuki Ishikawa

As far as nurses go, this Japanese midwife, real-estate agent and serial killer went right over the top during the Allied occupation of Japan following the end of the Second World War in 1945. *Wikipedia* gives us some insight into how she and several accomplices are believed to have murdered dozens of infants in a crime spree known as the 'Kotobuki

San'in Incident', and I can tell you this much: if the reader thinks that the USA has a high homicide rate, try the online encyclopaedia's entry 'List of major crimes in Japan'. It will blow your mind. At the time of writing, Miyuki is 90 years old and toothlessly eating her way through some ramen, takoyaki, udon or Japanese street food dishes, because she was sentenced to a mere four years' imprisonment!

Anders Hansson

Known as the Malmö Östra Hospital serial murders, this Swedish case concerned 18-year-old Hansson who, between October 1978 and January 1979, fatally poisoned some 27 elderly patients with the corrosive cleaning agents Gevisol and Ivisol during his shifts as an orderly. *Wikipedia* tells us that he also attempted to kill a further 15 patients, adding that in August 1979, 'Hansson was sentenced to closed psychiatric treatment, where he remained until 1994.' Where he is presently I can't tell you.

Edson Isidoro Guimarães

Imaginatively dubbed by Brazilian media 'the Nurse of Death', Guimarães is suspected of murdering circa 131 patients in total. In February 2000, the nursing assistant at Salgado Filho Hospital in Rio de Janeiro confessed to five kills, of which he was convicted of four, and the case is of interest as far as motive is concerned. He told reporters: '… the oxygen mask was taken away, yes. There were five patients this happened to … I chose the patients I saw suffering generally, patients with AIDS, patients who were almost terminal. I am at peace because the patients were in a coma and had no way of recovering.'

This is reminiscent of Dr Bodkin Adams' 'easing the passing' of patients while cashing in on the deceased's estates – a kind of euthanasia mitigation, if you will. According to Rio's secretary for public security, Guimarães was thought to have been paid $US60 a time to inform local funeral homes of a patient's death so that they in turn could inform the deceased's relatives, but in doing so to earn money, he lost all control, in much the same way as the Polish 'Skin Hunters' of Łódź referred to earlier. This motive fits neatly with St Paul's famous text (1 Timothy 6:10): 'For the love of money is the root of all evil'. (KJV). Born in 1957, Guimarães was sentenced to 76 years in jail.

Genene Anne Jones

Using injections of digoxin, heparin and later, succinyl-choline to induce medical crises in her patients and causing numerous deaths, Jones fits the serial-killer category in that while employed as a licensed vocational nurse in the paediatric intensive care unit at the Bexar County Hospital (now University Hospital of San Antonio), Texas, during the 1970s and 1980s, she was responsible for the deaths of 60 infants and children in her care. In 1985, she was sentenced to 99 years in prison for killing 15-month-old Chelsea McClellan with succinylcholine, a skeletal muscle relaxant used during surgery or while on a breathing machine. In effect it is a paralytic agent and administration may lead to respiratory arrest and death.

In 1986, Nurse Jones was sentenced to a concurrent term of 60 years in prison for the attempted murder of Rolando Santos with heparin, an anticoagulant used to decrease the clotting ability of the blood and help prevent harmful clots from forming in blood vessels (i.e. a blood thinner). She will not be eligible for parole until around 2037, when she will be 87.

Niels Högel

Niels Högel was born on 30 December 1976 in the coastal town of Wilhelmshaven, on Germany's North Sea coast, into a respectable middle-class family. His father and grandmother were nurses, and he followed suit, qualifying in the role in 1997. In 1999 he went to work at the Oldenburg Clinic, not far south of Wilhelmshaven, in its cardiac surgery intensive care unit. By 2001 an unexpected increase in resuscitations and deaths on the ward was noted, the majority of which, some of his colleagues observed, happened while Krankenpfleger (male nurse) Högel was on duty. He was transferred to the anaesthesiology ward. While he was there, it was noted that he was often present when there was a medical emergency, and after a number of patients were found in life-threatening conditions, the head clinician confronted him.

Armed with a good reference, Högel transferred to Delmenhorst Clinic, also not far from his birthplace, where a comparable spike in emergencies and deaths was observed. It was only in June 2005, when a colleague saw Högel administering an unprescribed drug to a patient, that all became clear – he had been administering various unprescribed medications to cardiac and other patients in order to bring about a cardiac emergency; he would then hurry forward to resuscitate the patient. He did not always succeed in resuscitating them, but allegedly he hoped at least to win the admiration of his colleagues and superiors. Indeed, he was reportedly nicknamed 'Resuscitation Rambo' by some colleagues.

Högel was arrested in June 2005. His first trial convicted him of one attempted murder, but this was increased to three murders and two attempted murders in 2015. A three-year investigation followed as victims' family members came forward. Högel twice received a life sentence, in 2015 and 2019, having at the latter been convicted of 100 murders. As of 2020, it is believed that he had murdered as many as 300 people.

Orville Lynn Majors

Diabolical acts and a parallel of evil at its most wicked.

Presiding judge Ernest Yelton: sentencing Majors to 360 years imprisonment:

And back to the USA, where licensed practical nurse and serial killer Orville Lynn Majors murdered up to 30 patients at the Vermillion County Hospital, in Clinton, Indiana, between 1993 and 1995. Witnesses testified that Majors 'hated elderly people' and that they were 'whiners and should be gassed'. He was serving his time at Indiana State Prison, Michigan City, when he died of heart failure, aged 56, on 24 September 2017.

Richard Angelo

I wanted to create a situation where I could cause the patient to have some respiratory distress or some problem and through my intervention or suggested intervention or whatever come out looking like I knew what I was doing. I had no confidence in myself.

   – Richard Angelo, when charged with murder

Between September and October 1987, 26-year-old Angelo murdered circa 25 male and female patients at the Good Samaritan Hospital, Islip, Long Island, New York. On the face of it, he had a good background of: '… doing good things for people as an Eagle Scout and volunteer fireman' (source *Murderpedia*). He also had on out-of-control desire to be recognised as a hero.

Possessed of what is literally a fatal flaw, this type of individual is an attention-seeker, while the word 'histrionic' can also be applied to nurses like Beverley Allitt. The word means 'dramatic' or 'theatrical'. For people with histrionic personality disorder, their self-esteem depends on the approval of others and does *not* come from a true feeling of self-worth. Simply put, they are 'plastic' and 'fake', with an overwhelming desire to be noticed, and they often behave dramatically or inappropriately to win attention. So back to Richard Angelo …

Pathologically unable to achieve the level of praise he felt he rightly deserved in life, Angelo decided that he would inject Pavulon (pancuronium bromide) or Anectine (suxamethonium chloride, abbreviated to 'sux') into patients, while telling them that he was administering something that would make them feel better. Well, if you can't trust the nurse by your bedside then who can you trust? However, for many patients his plans fell short mof expectations, and in 37 'Code-Blue' emergencies only 12 patients lived, with those who survived describing feeling numb and their breathing becoming constricted, as did their ability to communicate with doctors and nurses. They were suffocating and drowning in lung fluid.

If any reader is considering being euthanised, then *do not read any further*, because in Belgium and the Netherlands, pancuronium bromide is recommended as a muscular relaxant in the protocol of euthanasia. After administering sodium thiopental to induce coma, pancuronium is 'delivered' in order to stop breathing. It is also used as one component of a lethal injection in applying the death penalty. Please do not take my word for it, though. Check this out online, because this form of lethal injection can be more painful than a bullet to the back of the head or the 'long drop' method of hanging. And to confirm this: pancuronium has *no* effect on levels of consciousness. Let's say it in medical contradictive jargon: if the anaesthetic used is insufficient the individual *may* be awake but unable to cry out or move, the state experienced by those who survived Angelo's lethal injections. Think about that for a moment, because this sleepy death, as practised and advertised by euthanasia proponents, might not be all that it is cracked up to be, to wit: countless examples of death row inmates being strapped down onto a gurney and given 'the Goodnight Juice', with the procedures sometimes lasting up to 20 minutes or more, and the condemned person moaning and groaning as the 'execution practitioners' struggle to find a suitable vein. Blowbacks can also occur, with the fluids being sprayed around the death chamber. If a suitable vein cannot be located, the needle is inserted into the toes. In short, pancuronium bromide has no effect, I repeat, *no effect* on consciousness. And with that, back to Nurse Angelo.

Working the aptly named 'graveyard shift' placed Angelo in a nearly perfect position to work on his feelings of inadequacy – until he came undone. On 11 October 1987, he fell under suspicion after one of his intended victims, Gerolamo Kucich, managed to use the call button for assistance after receiving an almost lethal injection from the 'trusted' nurse. One of the staff who responded to the call for help took a urine sample and had it analysed, the test proving positive for both Pavulon *and* Anectine, neither of which had been prescribed to Kucich. Angelo was soon charged with two counts of 'depraved indifference murder'; in effect, second-degree murder. There followed one count of second-degree manslaughter, one count of criminally negligent homicide and six counts of assault with respect to five of the patients. He was sentenced to 61-years-to-life and will not become eligible for parole until 2049, when he will be 87.

The BS defence

It was the feeble wannabe fireman and saviour of humanity Angelo's bullshit defence that intrigued me because his lawyers fought tooth and nail to prove that their murderous pseudo-nurse of a client suffered from dissociative identity disorder. In layman's terms, this means that he was allegedly able to dissociate himself completely from the crimes he'd committed and was thus unable to recognise the risk of what he had done to the patients. In other words, his attorneys maintained that Angelo had been subject to dissociative fugue, a temporary state in which a person suffers memory loss (amnesia).

So, are we really to believe that Angelo had a multiple personality which he could move in and out of, unaware of the actions of the other persona?

You see, dear reader, this multiple personality disorder (MPD) comes straight from the Dr Jekyll and Mr Hyde playbook, so we have Robert Louis Stevenson's novella partly to blame for it. But it is typical of all US defence attorneys to be able to cook up any cock-and-bull mitigation to get a client off the hook. (See, for instance, Kenneth Alessio Bianchi in my *Talking with Serial Killers*, Thomas Dee Huskey, aka the 'Zoo Man', in *Talking with Psychopaths: Guilty but Insane*, and Dr Geza de Kaplany in the previous chapter of this book.) Nevertheless, the upshot was that while the defence fought to prove the MPD theory by introducing polygraph tests, which Angelo had passed during questioning about his murdered patients, the judge would have none of it, leaving the defendant to face 61-years-to-life.

Ending on a Happy Note

As always, I like to draw a book to a close on a positive, even happy, note. It's also my opportunity to say 'Thank you, dear reader' for joining me throughout our medical murderers' journey from the golden Victorian days to more-or-less the present. But here's the thing …

The physician has sworn the Hippocratic Oath, the nurse pledges to abide by the Nightingale principles, so all of the killers featured here have broken a sacred trust, that of a dedication to the care and saving of lives and not, for whatever perverse motive, take it upon themselves to act as medically trained executioners. In this regard I think we might say that they *are* the lowest of the low, but one thing is certain: there *will be* more of them to come.

'First do no harm' is a fine principle by which anyone

might live their life. For medical professionals, it is an essential, abiding and unbreakable rule. When rogue medics betray it, they are guilty not only of murder, but of murder under trust, which, as I wrote earlier, is the most grievous betrayal of all. There is no escape from that judgement.

So, back to where we started. Ah, yes, if I recall we were in the Philippines, where this book found its genesis with me wearing flip-flops on a stove-hot sugar-sand beach in El Nido, Palawan. But – groan! – I have a headache coming in my direction, or is it dengue fever, or malaria? Maybe I should call a doctor … What do you think?

Happy days – and no nightmares, please.